All We Need Is
a Paradigm

Also available, the companion volume:

*The Space of Love and Garbage: And Other Essays
from The Harvard Review of Philosophy,*
edited by S. Phineas Upham

All We Need Is a Paradigm

Essays on Science, Economics, and Logic
from *The Harvard Review of Philosophy*

EDITED BY

S. PHINEAS UPHAM

OPEN COURT
Chicago and La Salle, Illinois

To order books from Open Court, call toll-free 1-800-815-2280, or visit our website at www.opencourtbooks.com.

Open Court Publishing Company is a division of Carus Publishing Company.

Library of Congress Cataloging-in-Publication Data

All we need is a paradigm : essays on science, economics, and logic from the Harvard review of philosophy / edited by S. Phineas Upham.
    p. cm.
   Includes bibliographical references and index.
   ISBN-13: 978-0-8126-9635-6 (trade paper : alk. paper)
   1. Philosophy. I. Upham, S. Phineas. II. Harvard review of philosophy.
   B29.A2465 2008
   190—dc22

                                 2009000488

Contents

Foreword

I know of no more rational and attractive place to begin and to continue to survey the reaches of philosophical possibility than that provided in the pages of *The Harvard Review of Philosophy*. This is amply verified by the quality and range of the essays in *All We Need Is a Paradigm* and its companion volume, *The Space of Love and Garbage*, by the high quality of the contributors to these volumes, and by their quite unmatched (in any comparable journal I am aware of) range of subjects and modes of thinking.

Professional journals are the life's blood of every field of instruction and investigation throughout the modern university. National and international reputations of scholars can be begun and established by publication in them; collections of journal articles are assigned in virtually every university lecture hall and seminar room; graduate students and assistant professors characteristically make the cases for their initial positions and their advancement for tenured positions on the basis of their texts' selection for publication in journals whose articles are subject to blind review. In the field of philosophy, although this has undergone some change in recent years, the publication of books rather than articles by prominent figures in the field remains distinctly rarer than in the other humanities and in humanistically inclined registers of social inquiry, and a book by a philosopher is itself characteristically a collection of articles separately published over a period of years by its author, sometimes revised for their conjunction and perhaps for their reading beyond the profession.

The particularity of the value of the fact of students at the origin of *The Harvard Review of Philosophy*'s existence must be a function of its value simultaneously for students and for the profession of philosophy. For those directly involved in its publication and the imagination of that fact by their fellows, at Harvard and beyond, the heightened attention to issues and words destined to be made public and at stages before a final version is arrived at makes real and immediate for them the world of a community of scholarship as little else can. For *The Harvard Review of Philosophy*, the fact that potential recruits to the profession are involved in the work of the profession before they have become credentialed professionals is an irreplaceable reminder that institutions, indeed the institutionalization of the profession of philosophy itself, the field of study and instruction dedicated to self-reflection, will tend to become complacent and to resist change when change may be called for.

I think here especially of resistance to pedagogical change, of what is regarded as essential to philosophical learning and training. This is in at least three obvious ways a more fateful matter in the study of philosophy than in any other field.

First, at least in the United States, the study of philosophy, unlike the other humanities and the sciences, is only exceptionally offered in high schools, so it is mostly first encountered systematically in university courses, where time for intellectual experimentation rapidly diminishes.

Second, there is no general agreement among philosophers on the best way to begin study of the subject. Like every other feature of the field, any particular beginning is open to criticism. A case may well be made that history or epistemology or logic or ethics should come first, or that one should postpone things until a schedule can accommodate more than one of these regions in the same semester.

Third, whichever path is entered upon is apt to shape the future course of your philosophical expectations. Professional philosophers inevitably take pains to define what they expect of philosophy—to declare and exhibit what mode or modes of thinking count for them as philosophically pertinent and fruitful—and these expectations are inevitably somewhat at variance with a student's own expectations, so often formed, to the extent they have reached articulate form, by rumor, by one-sided enthusiasms or disappointments expressed by more experienced students, perhaps by a puzzling yet fascinating book (from a strange culture or an ancient time) that may or may not pass as current philosophy.

We might summarize these registers of perplexity by saying that there is no substitute for acquiring philosophical experience in charting and evaluating your own course of philosophical education. Here is an initial paradox in studying philosophy: You already have to possess philosophical experience in order to acquire it. An initial relief from the paradox is the discovery that we all have more such experience than, we have, left to ourselves, recognized.

The service *The Harvard Review of Philosophy* has provided over the years simultaneously to the continuity of the profession of philosophy and to those in search of introductions to its riches is something for which its community of teachers and its students owe permanent debts of gratitude. I am honored to congratulate those who have devoted themselves to so superbly valuable a project.

STANLEY CAVELL

Preface

This book contains fourteen philosophical essays exploring topics such as physics, mathematics, economics, and music. At the *Harvard Review of Philosophy* we stress the value of philosophy's rigor for exploring the widest range of fields and issues. Indeed, perhaps one of its chief strengths is that it is useful as a versatile methodology for analysis, that it can be used in conjunction with other disciplines rather than only in isolation from them. We believe philosophy can be as enriching to the lawyer, the physicist, the craftsman, and the musician as to the professional philosopher.

In particular, the authors in this collection employ philosophy to better understand important topics in the hard and social sciences. There is a burgeoning and productive study at the intersections of philosophy and science of evolving scientific paradigms and of the assumptions underlying the 'laws of nature'. Many of the authors in this collection find philosophy particularly helpful in understanding the principles that underlie the experimental and theoretical ideas in these other fields and in unfolding and resolving the paradoxes that confound traditional approaches.

Three major themes come up again and again in the essays and often lead to fruitful philosophical insight—the nature of language, the nature of causality, and the nature of human cognition. Many authors point to the problem Wittgenstein critiqued as the confounding vagaries of language itself—"deep disquietudes, their roots are as deep in us as the forms of our language." Secondly, causality is not surprisingly a concern for physicists and others involved in the physical sciences given their need to predict outcomes, but it is surprising to see how applicable philosophical insights from Kant, Hume, and Leibnitz are to such problems in the hard sciences that might seem unrelated to philosophical inquiry. An exploration of human cognition also plays a significant part in these essays—asking questions about whether events in the world are real or perceived, whether human action is rational or irrational, whether arithmetic is logical, analytical or even 'true'.

Israel Kirzner in his essay "Human Nature and the Character of Economic Science" traces the conception of the wealth-seeking *Homo economicus* of Adam Smith to the purposeful rationality of Ludwig von Mises's *Homo agens*. Kirzner examines how an exploration of the "laws of the human mind" leads to the epistemic uniqueness of economic science and how it has contributed to our understanding of human nature—man as not only an aggregator of wealth but with more complex desires, more broadly defined goals, and fears. For Mises, man acts purposefully to improve his situation with worthwhile but previously unconsidered ends and with always evolving means so that "in any real and living exchange every actor is always an entrepreneur." For Kirzner human rationality is not an expression of optimal constraint maximization but essentially entails alertness to new opportunities.

In "Frege's Theorem: An Introduction" Richard Heck examines the epistemic status of our understanding of arithmetic—is arithmetic an outcome of reason and are its principles analytically true, or do they depend on human intuition and cognition? Frege tries to resolve this tension by showing that arithmetic truths can be drawn directly from premises that are fundamental truths of pure logic without extraneous assumptions. Since existing systems of logic were insufficient to this task, Frege tried to develop a system he calls *Begriffsschrift* which is a full second-order logic which accommodates quantification over 'concepts'. This system of logic restricted inferential steps to syntactic criteria revealing all assumptions being used in all proofs. Frege transforms the epistemological problems of arithmetic with his system and mathematical argumentation making proofs possible. Frege's system contributes to axiomizing arithmetic as Euclid axiomized geometry. His formalization brings the resources of mathematical logic to bear now on philosophical problems as well and from this flows questions of what can be solved or proven from what assumptions. The analytic philosophy of Russell and Wittgenstein draws deeply on Frege's *Begriffsschrift*. Heck also challenges the certainty of Hume's principle in logic upon which Frege depends, suggesting ways in which it could be challenged and showing its internal contradictions.

"What Is the Problem with Measurement?" Simon Saunders asks in his essay on the paradoxes within quantum mechanics. The problem, both physical and philosophical in nature, centers on the finding that in quantum mechanics two states of the atomic world can exist until the moment of the discrete change in the action when 'the quantum jump' and 'the collapse of the wavepacket' are observed and they then are collapsed into one outcome. Physicists and philosophers have grappled with this problem in various ways. Saunders describes Bohr's powerful Copenhagen Interpretation where "an objective phenomenon is only defined relative to an observation" and "any observation of atomic phenomena will involve an interaction with the agency of observation . . . with its inherent 'irrationality'." The origins, implications, and resolutions of Bohr's 'Quantum Postulate' have not only a philosophy background but as Sanders points out in this essay, they all depend on philosophical arguments "of a metaphysical order that we have not seen since Decartes."

In an unusual and very amusing philosophical tribute, Warren Goldfarb of Harvard University writes a poem for his long time colleague Van Quine on his retirement from the Harvard faculty. The poem, "The Modern Neo-Positivist," is in the style of the Gilbert and Sullivan operas Quine enjoyed so much and offers a tongue-in-cheek description of his friend and the school of thought he identified with, Neo-Positivism. This early twentieth-century philosophical movement—in some ways an anti-philosophical movement— originated in the discussion groups of the Vienna Circle and was inspired by Russell and Wittgenstein. Quine was perhaps one of its last great members. The goal of this school, to quote another important contributor, Rudolf Carnap, was "the elimination of metaphysics through the logical analysis of language." The idea was that many philosophical problems originated from bad metaphysics and if this could be corrected then people would be able to speak in verifiable scientific statements or beautiful poetry and not mix the two like "mad beasts." Of course the clever irony of Goldfarb's poem is that he describes a school that was adamant about the division between poetry and science and uses poetry to describe science.

In this volume of philosophical essays, our authors productively tackle important questions about the world in ways one would not expect. They show how valuable the rigor and insight of philosophical analysis and thought are in a broad array of fields, including, perhaps especially, economics, physics, and logic.

S. Phineas Upham

1

Human Nature and the Character of Economic Science: The Historical Background of the Misesian Perspective

ISRAEL M. KIRZNER

Israel Kirzner, who has written widely in the area of Austrian Economics, is Professor Emeritus of Economics at New York University. His published works include The Economic Point of View *and* Competition and Entrepreneurship. *His most recent book is* Ludwig von Mises: The Man and His Economics.

It has long been recognized that economics depends, for the derivation of its theoretical propositions, upon its understanding of human nature. This chapter pursues this insight in order to understand Ludwig von Mises's position on the epistemological character of the propositions that make up economic theory. Our thesis will be that, in the course of the history of economic analysis from the classical economists to Mises, the manner in which these propositions depend upon our understanding of human nature came itself to be understood in a more profound way—with consequently more sensitive appreciation for the epistemological uniqueness of economic science.

Mises's assertions concerning the a priori character of economic science are fairly well known. These assertions were, at the time they were first made in the 1930s, considered rather strange, even by economists otherwise sympathetic to Mises's economics.[1] Our objective in this paper is not to defend Mises in any systematic way against his critics. Our purpose, rather, is to acquire insight into his position by reference to its historical background. In developing our thesis we shall discover that Mises's views on the a prioristic character of what he called the "science of human action"[2] depend critically upon the refinements that he introduced into our understanding of the manner in which the theorems of economic science derive from "human nature."

Classical Economics and Homo Oeconomicus[3]

The notion of 'economic man' played a central role in classical economics from Adam Smith to David Ricardo to John Stuart Mill. Although this notion underwent some modification during the classical period, it was at all times closely associated with the idea of wealth, which, for all the classical economists, constituted a central focal point for defining the field of political economy (as economics was then known).

The earlier classical economists in fact defined their discipline as simply the study of the phenomena of wealth; they did not define their discipline in terms of 'economic man'. Rather, because they believed that wealth phenomena are universally characterized by the relentlessness and the uncompromising self-interest with which they are pursued, they saw such pursuit, driven by systematic materialistic interest, as enabling them to derive determinate regularities prevalent in the phenomena they had chosen for study.

Mill explored the epistemological character of economics more deeply than earlier classical economists had done. In an essay published in 1836 (but apparently written several years earlier), he analyzed the idea of "laws of the production of . . . wealth" and pointed out that some of these laws are physical laws. What belongs in political economy are only those of the laws of the production of wealth that "are laws of the human mind." Political economy, Mill went on, does not treat the whole of man's nature: "it is concerned with him solely as a being who desires to possess wealth. . . . It makes entire abstraction of every other human passion or motive; except...aversion to labor, and desire of the present enjoyment of costly indulgences."[4] In other words, while Mill retained the central focus upon wealth in his conception of the scope of political economy, he did not see the discipline as the study of the phenomena of wealth itself. Instead, Mill conceived of political economy as the study of the operation of human wealth-seeking activities. Because such wealth-seeking activities were seen as significantly actuated by selfish, materialistic desire, political economy was now, in effect, the science of 'economic man' (classically defined). Because Mill recognized that other motives may often be significant, too, he saw political economy as a hypothetical science. In other words the conclusions at which economic theory arrives (by employing the assumption of 'economic man') are true only insofar as that assumption is indeed valid.

As Marion Bowley showed in *Nassau Senior and Classical Political Economy*, Nassau Senior sharply disagreed with Mill regarding the hypothetical character of political economy. Senior attempted to establish political economy on firmer ground, arguing (in the 1840s) that the science does not depend on the hypothesis that "wealth and costly enjoyments are the only objects of human desire"—but only on the weaker claim that "wealth and costly enjoyments" are "universal and constant objects of desire."[5] The validity of economic theory is then positive, not hypothetical, although Senior of course recognized that the theory holds only "in the absence of disturbing causes." Moreover, Senior defined wealth more broadly than the earlier classical economists had done, including in it also immaterial goods, including services.[6]

Human Nature and the Character of Classical Economics

Whether (as with the earlier classical economists) the selfish, materialistic character of economic man is a device employed to achieve determinate analytical results believed to be manifested in the real world, or (as with Mill) the assumed character of economic man defines the discipline itself (or, with Senior, 'wealth' is made broader, to include services), the classicals shared one perspective. This perspective is their picture of human nature, expressed in the portrait of 'economic man', which shapes the conclusions of classical political economy. Economic knowledge, for classicals, meant knowledge of the implications of selfish, wealth-seeking behavior.

The major thinkers at the close of the classical era, Mill, Senior, and John E. Cairnes, did debate the epistemological status of the propositions so derived. These debates (like so many that would roil economics during the subsequent half-century), focused on the roles of induction and deduction in arriving at these propositions, the empirical basis for the assumptions made about the character of 'economic man', or the nature and role of supplementary premises required to apply pure theoretical insights to concrete situations.[7] What is significant for our present purposes, however, is not these disagreements but rather the shared perspective that pervades the methodology of these writers. As Mises has argued, there is a sense in which, despite superficial rhetoric to the contrary, all of them can be seen as pointing, at least, to the possibility of a purely a priori science of human action. Their focus was no longer on things, but on human nature. And, for Mises, as we shall see, the essential element in human nature permits us to derive new knowledge, independent of empirical observation. On the other hand, however, we must also emphasize that for all of these thinkers the foundation of economic understanding did depend on the validity of a particular empirical observation, namely, the wealth-seeking behavior of human beings;[8] none of these writers endorsed, or could have endorsed, Mises's view of economics as a purely a priori science.

What is responsible for this inability of classicals to accept the Misesian view of economics as a pure logic of human action is of course the non-Misesian view of human nature that, in spite of their differences, they shared. The behavior of 'economic man' follows very specific patterns. It is true that the classical economists believed these patterns to be widely and typically observed; however, they would not have disputed the possibility, at least, that some patterns of behavior would not fit the mold of *Homo oeconomicus*. The observed behavior of familiar human beings suggested the suitability of working with the model of 'economic man'. But we can easily imagine a society of human beings whose behavior would not fit that model. Most importantly, the deductive logic used by the economic theorist was in no way itself characteristic of *Homo oeconomicus*. Although the economic theorist uses his own logic to understand the behavior patterns of wealth-seeking human beings (who are certainly presumed to use their logic in choosing their courses of action), what defines *Homo oeconomicus* is not his use of logic, but rather the particular purposes for which he deploys that logic.

The human nature (or rather the view of human nature) that provided the key to classical economics decisively diverted classical attention from the sense in which, as Mises was to argue, their own work might be said to point towards a purely a priori science of human action.

Lionel Robbins and the Character of Neoclassical Economics[9]

The term 'neoclassical economics' suffers from certain well-known ambiguities. For present purposes we use it to refer very broadly to the core of microeconomic theory as it developed from the marginalist revolution of the 1870s to its modern incarnation in contemporary textbooks. A crucial element in this microeconomics was identified and emphasized by Lionel (later Lord) Robbins in his extremely influential 1932 book, *An Essay on the Nature and Significance of Economic Science*.[10] There is much to suggest that, in crystallizing this element, Robbins was not merely putting his finger on a central feature of the economics that he knew in his own time, but was also significantly shaping the character of microeconomics as it would develop during the remainder of the century.

Robbins identified the perspective of the economist as that which focuses on the allocative aspect of human behavior. Because man desires many goals, and because he possesses only limited resources with which to achieve these goals, it is necessary for him to economize, that is, to apportion his scarce means among his multiple ends in such a way as to reflect faithfully his own ranking of the importance of these ends. Economics, for Robbins, "is the science which studies human behavior as a relationship between ends and scarce means which have alternative uses."[11]

Robbins went out of his way to emphasize not simply the novelty of his definition of economics, but the extent to which the very character of that definition differs from previous conceptions of the subject. As he pointed out, his definition did not (as earlier definitions had done) "attempt to pick out certain kinds of behavior, but focuses attention on a particular aspect of behavior, the form imposed by the influence of scarcity."[12] Earlier definitions had held that it was possible to identify certain acts and activities as being "economic." Robbins, however, saw this adjective not as describing specific kinds of activity, but as identifying a particular point of view from which actions (and their social consequences) could be examined.

Robbins saw the propositions of economics as derived from the recognition by the discipline of the economizing aspect of human behavior. The circumstance that human beings do allocate, economize, and strive to achieve efficiency shapes their actions in ways that can be systematically understood. What is responsible for economic understanding is not (as classical economics maintained) the circumstance that we know that human beings are selfish or materialistic wealth-seekers. What is responsible for economic understanding is, instead, our recognition of the influence of the human propensity to economize—a propensity that does not depend on the particular objects of human preference that empirical observation reveals. The validity of the theorems of economics no longer depends, as they did for classical economics, upon such empirical observation.

Robbins did not, however, conclude on the basis of understanding the foundations of economic knowledge in this way, that this knowledge is known to us a priori. It is true that much of Robbins's 1932 book downplays the role of empirical observation in the achievement of economic knowledge.[13] But Robbins drew attention to the distinction between the chains of deductive reasoning that make up economic theorizing and the premises that afford the basis for those chains of reasoning.[14] These premises include the "main postulates of the theory of value," which consist of the observed facts of a) scarcity, b) the multiplicity of factors of production, and c) the ignorance of the future under which economic agents suffer.[15] He drew further attention to the empirical character of these premises—as "elements in common experience"—as well as to that of the other results of "realistic investigations" for which he finds a place in economics. Robbins notes that the "validity of a particular theory" may depend safely upon the elements of common experience, but that "its applicability to a given situation depends upon . . . the forces operating in that situation"[16]—the determination of which may call for systematic investigation. There is no reason to doubt that Robbins would have accepted James Buchanan's distinction between the "pure logic of choice," which he described as "general but empty," and the "abstract science of economic behavior", which he described as "non-general but operational."[17] Robbins was explicit in his insistence that economics is not empty: "The concern of the economist is the interpretation of reality."[18]

Nonetheless we can perhaps yet understand how Mises (who, as Buchanan noted,[19] appears to reject Buchanan's distinction in favor of a thesis defending the scientific character of a general science of human action) cited Robbins as one of those who take the subject of economics to be human action (and who must, one gathers from Mises's discussion, therefore see economic science as an a priori science). The economic analysis of which Robbins was writing did, after all, consist in the deductive chains of reasoning that fill the theory textbooks. The premises or postulates that make up the basis upon which these chains of reasoning are constructed are unquestionably in the background. It is true that Robbins wrote that progress in economics has, at crucial stages in its history, consisted in "the discovery of the premises themselves." It is true that he believed that the "perception and selection of the basis of economic analysis is as much economics as the analysis itself."[20] But all this might still permit Mises to read Robbins as suggesting that the new knowledge that economic theorizing provides has been produced entirely by the human mind. Or so one might believe on reading Mises's references to Robbins (and, one might add, on reading Robbins's own frequent references to other aspects of Mises's work).

The lingering doubts one has on the validity of such a reading by Mises (of the implications of Robbins's insights for the epistemological character of economics) reinforce one's sense of the distance beyond Robbins that had been (or which would be) traversed by Mises himself. And, we shall suggest, this difference is responsible for Mises's own strongly held convictions concerning the a priori character of economics, seen as the science of human action.

Mises and the Character of Economics as the Science of Human Action[21]

At about the same time that Robbins was expounding the foundations of the neoclassical microeconomics that would dominate for the rest of the century, Mises was articulating his own conception of economics as the purely a priori science of human action.[22] It is something of a paradox that, although in the preface to his 1932 book Robbins acknowledged his "especial indebtedness to the works of Professor Ludwig von Mises," the influence of Robbins's book has been to set neoclassical economics on a path decisively different from that to which Mises's own work was pointing.[23] For both Mises and Robbins, the source of economic theorizing lies in our understanding of the individual human decision. (This is an insight, one gathers, that Robbins gained from Mises's works.) But the notion of human decision making for Robbins—the notion that, as we have seen, focuses on allocative efficiency—is not what Mises had in mind when he identified economics as the science of human action.[24]

For Robbins (and for modern neoclassical microeconomics), the idea of the decision presumes the prior awareness by the decision maker of both the means at his disposal and his preference ranking among relevant (already identified) ends. Decision making itself then consists in selecting that course of action that will faithfully express, at the level of the scarce means, the postulated preference ranking among ends. It is for this reason that the decision is seen, in modern microeconomic theory, as a mathematical exercise in constrained maximization. (Microeconomic theory then proceeds to explore the possibilities of the simultaneous fulfillment, in a market society, of the individual decisions so made by the market participants.) But for Mises matters were quite different.

For Mises the notion of human action itself includes the agent's determination of the facts of the ends-means framework relevant to his action. What is central to the notion of action is not any allocative pattern in which it may be expressed, but in the purposefulness of the agent. 'Purposefulness' (which for Mises is a word used virtually synonymously with 'rationality') is what inspires the agent to notice opportunities for improving his situation—with opportunities revealing themselves in the form of ends seen for the first time as worthwhile striving towards, and/or of means now discovered to be available. Human action then comprises both the discovery of hitherto unnoticed opportunities and the steps taken to exploit them: "In any real and living economy every actor is always an entrepreneur."[25]

For Mises the rationality of human action does not refer primarily to the mathematical logic that can ensure successful computation of the solution to constrained maximization problems. It refers also, and more fundamentally, to the alertness of the agent to the potential discovery of opportunities for beneficial action. The science of economics becomes the science of human action because the theorems of economics must depend not only upon the calculations of decision makers operating within given frameworks of ends and means, but, more crucially, upon their alert discoveries of opportunities for gain, with such opportunities presenting ends-means frameworks that had not been "given" at all. A science of human action, à la Mises, is not content

to articulate the conditions that must be satisfied in order to permit all max-
imizing decisions in a society to be carried out as planned. It focuses, in particular, on the dynamic processes generated by entrepreneurial discoveries of
situations where the decisions of market participants do not dovetail. It is this
perspective of Misesian economics which is responsible for the circumstance
that, whereas the dominant neoclassical microeconomics has virtually no role
whatever for the entrepreneurial element in markets,[26] Mises's own economics, the science of human action, places entrepreneurship at the very heart of
the theory which forms its core.

Even so sympathetic a colleague and follower of Mises as Friedrich
A. Hayek failed to recognize this element in Mises's system. Thus, in a
famous 1937 paper (to which he would later in his career repeatedly refer
as representative of an important turning point in the development of his
own economic understanding), Hayek pointed out that economics seen as
a pure logic of choice is simply not sufficient for the derivation of the
important conclusions of economic science. For the latter it is necessary
to rely upon (in addition to the logic of choice) our empirical observations concerning the way in which knowledge (of relevant economic opportunities) is communicated through the price system to decision makers.
Hayek was, in this paper, delicately distancing himself from those Misesian assertions that saw economic theory as a purely a priori body of
knowledge. The important conclusions of economic theory depend, Hayek
argued, upon more than our understanding of the logic with which men
choose (within given ends-means frameworks); they depend significantly
upon patterns of learning upon which a priori logical analysis is unable
to make pronouncements.

As this writer has elsewhere argued,[27] however, Hayek was proceeding
from a Robbinsian, rather than a Misesian, point of departure. By the logic
of choice, Hayek clearly understood choice within a given framework of perceived ends and means. From this perspective, the knowledge upon which
such a given framework became given and the patterns of learning such knowledge are by hypothesis outside the logic of choice. They form part of economic understanding only to the extent that such understanding embraces
also the economist's empirical observation of the ways in which knowledge
is acquired. For this reason Hayek was, given his Robbinsian point of departure, entirely justified in distancing himself from Mises's pure a priorist stance.
But, given our interpretation of Mises's conception of economics as the science of human action, Hayek's critique of the a priorist position can surely
be deflected. In fact, Hayek's very objection may help us understand more
clearly the sense in which Mises could claim economics to be an a priori science. What is involved here is recognition of the progressive abstractness in

the view of human nature as it relates to economic analysis, which is (in contrast to Robbins) present in Mises.

As we saw, the classical economists derived their economic regularities only by assuming very specific objectives on the part of economic man. It was, we found, difficult to ignore the empirical component in the knowledge that economists were, in this way, able to produce. Again, in assessing the neoclassical approach crystallized in Lionel Robbins's conception of economic science, we found it difficult to ignore the empirical elements that Robbins saw as the basis for the deductive chains of economic reasoning. These empirical elements were distinct from those chains of reasoning, yet they played a definite role in arriving at the conclusions of economic theory. The pure logic employed in those chains of reasoning was itself not sufficient to generate those conclusions. Hayek's identification of the patterns of learning upon which market equilibration must depend reinforces the conclusion that, for Robbinsian economics, a priori reasoning is simply not sufficient. Mises's perspective on economics does, however, permit us to see matters rather differently.

For Mises, we have seen, the "rationality" and purposefulness that inspire human action explain not only the allocative patterns that action will generate (once the relevant ends-means frameworks have been determined), but also the very perception of relevant ends-means frameworks. Such perception, built into the bedrock concept of human action, permits us to recognize, on purely a priori grounds, the tendency that alert human agents possess, to notice available opportunities. The tendencies, which economic theorizing takes for granted, for relevant knowledge to become acquired by relevant agents, need not depend, at least in the most general sense, on observed patterns of learning revealed in empirical investigations. Such tendencies are already implicit in the very idea of human action. Thus the theorems articulated by economic science can be seen to be already implicit in our understanding of the character of human action. The theorist, himself a human being, understands this character directly. In this sense Mises held economic theory itself to be independent of empirical input—although he was of course well aware of the importance of such input for the application of economic reasoning.

For classical economics it would be necessary for the economist seeking to understand human behavior to go beyond the essentials of his own introspective experience in order to postulate the selfish, materialistic, wealth-seeking behavior upon which he relies for his analysis. He could not predict such behavior merely on the basis of the rationality that he, the theorist, and the examined economic agent, share. He must, for his analysis, supplement his own direct insight into rational behavior by empirical information concerning the examined agents' objectives and style of activity. But for Mises the idea of action (including, as it does, the potential of arriving at entirely new ends-means frameworks as relevant for action) is broad enough to permit the theorist to reach conclusions simply on the basis of the rationality, the purposefulness, by which he, like the examined agents, is inspired. Mises saw in Robbins's formulations insights sufficiently close to his own as to suggest his a prioristic perspective. Hayek saw in Robbins's formulations (and especially in his own application of those formulations to patterns of market learning) the limitations that those formulations imply for the possibility of purely a prioristic theorizing. Because Mises offered a view of economics that went, in its abstractness, beyond Robbins, he was able to identify a sense in which the theorist's knowledge is indeed, at the purest level, independent of empirical observations.

Human Nature and the Character of Economic Science

In insisting on the purely a priori character of economic theory, Mises did not believe that he was offering any revolutionary epistemological doctrine. He believed that, whether or not they quite realized it, the great economists, at least from Mill, Senior, and Cairnes onwards, were in fact pointing to this very insight. He saw the evolution of the economists' view of market participant decision-making, from the wealth-seeking behavior of classical *Homo oeconomicus*, to the efficiency-seeking Robbinsian economizer, to the purposeful rationality of his own *Homo agens*—as a process of steady epistemological refinement. The contribution of the pure economic theorist, he saw, does not itself depend (and never has really depended) upon information for which he must go beyond his own direct introspective understanding of human behavior.

We referred earlier to Buchanan's distinction between (a) the "general but empty" character of Mises's science of human action, and (b) the "non-general but operational" abstract science of human behavior. Mises himself might perhaps not have objected strongly to the validity of this distinction. But he would have insisted on the epistemological autonomy within any "abstract science of human behavior" of the general, a priori science of human action. Only by insisting on such separability and autonomy, he believed, can the unique contributions of economic theory be recognized for what they are.

This writer once asked Mises how we know that human beings "other than ourselves" are in fact rational and purposeful. His answer was both surprising and revealing. He replied: "By observation." I take this to mean that, in insisting on the a priori character of economic theory, he was referring strictly to the chains of reasoning of which economic theorizing consists. He was not challenging the sense in which the relevance (and certainly the applicability to specific situations) of such theorizing must rely on empirical observation. But clearly, also, he viewed the observation that there exist other purposeful human beings in this world, as a background observation, not at all as part of the new knowledge and understanding that economics itself can provide. It is because such observations are so emphatically background observations that Mises felt able to insist (for reasons that go beyond the scope of this paper) on the epistemological autonomy of the pure science of human action that, for Mises, makes up the identifiable core of economic theory.

2

The Hardest Logic Puzzle Ever

GEORGE S. BOOLOS

George S. Boolos was Professor of Philosophy at MIT up until his death in 1996. He is the author of The Logic of Provability; Logic, Logic, and Logic, *and with Richard Jeffrey and John Burgess,* Computability and Logic.

Some years ago, the logician and puzzle-master Raymond Smullyan devised a logical puzzle that has no challengers I know of for the title of Hardest Logical Puzzle Ever. I'll set out the puzzle here, give the solution, and then briefly discuss one of its more interesting aspects.

The puzzle: Three gods A, B, and C are called, in some order, True, False, and Random. True always speaks truly, False always speaks falsely, but whether Random speaks truly or falsely is a completely *random* matter. Your task is to determine the identities of A, B, and C by asking three yes-no questions; each question must be put to exactly one god. The gods understand English, but will answer all questions in their own language, in which the words for 'yes' and 'no' are 'da' and 'ja', in some order. *You do not know which word means which.*[1]

Before I present the somewhat lengthy solution, let me give answers to certain questions about the puzzle that occasionally arise:

- **It could be that some god gets asked more than one question (and hence that some god is not asked any question at all).**

- **What the second question is, and to which god it is put, may depend on the answer to the first question. (And of course similarly for the third question.)**

- **Whether Random speaks truly or not should be thought of as depending on the flip of a coin hidden in his brain: if the coin comes down heads, he speaks truly; if tails, falsely.**

- **Random will answer 'da' or 'ja' when asked any yes-no question.**

The Solution: Before solving The Hardest Logic Puzzle Ever, we will set out and solve three related, but much easier, puzzles. We shall then combine the ideas of their solutions to solve the Hardest Puzzle. The last two puzzles are of a type that may be quite familiar to the reader, but the first one is not well known (in fact the author made it up while thinking about the Hardest Puzzle).

Puzzle 1: Noting their locations, I place two aces and a jack face down on a table, in a row; you do not see which card is placed where. Your problem is to point to one of the three cards and then ask me a single yes-no question, from the answer to which you can, with certainty, identify one of the three cards as an ace. If you have pointed to one of the aces, I will answer your question truthfully. However, if you have pointed to the jack, I will answer your question 'yes' or 'no', completely at random.

Puzzle 2: Suppose that, somehow, you have learned that you are speaking not to Random but to True or False—you don't know which—and that whichever god you're talking to has condescended to answer you in English. For some reason, you need to know whether Dushanbe is in Kirghizia or not. What one yes-no question can you ask the god from the answer to which you can determine whether or not Dushanbe is in Kirghizia?

Puzzle 3: You are now quite definitely talking to True, but he refuses to answer you in English and will only say 'da' or 'ja'. What one yes-no question can you ask True to determine whether or not Dushanbe is in Kirghizia?

Here's one solution to Puzzle 1: Point to the middle card and ask, 'Is the left card an ace?' If I answer yes, choose the left card; if I answer no, choose the right card. *Whether the middle card is an ace or not*, you are certain to find an ace by choosing the left card if you hear me say yes and choosing the right card if you hear no. The reason is that if the middle card is an ace, my answer is truthful, and so the left card is an ace if I say yes, and the right card is an ace if I say no. But if the middle card is the Jack, then *both* of the other cards are aces, and so again the left card is an ace if I say yes (so is the right card but that is now irrelevant), and the right card is an ace if I say no (as is the left card, again irrelevantly).

To solve puzzles 2 and 3, we shall use *iff*.

Logicians have introduced the useful abbreviation 'iff', short for 'if, and only if'. The way 'iff' works in logic is this: when you insert 'iff' between two statements that are either both true or both false, you get a statement that is true; but if you insert it between one true and one false statement, you get a false statement. Thus, for example, 'The moon is made of Gorgonzola iff Rome is in Russia' is true, because 'The moon is made of Gorgonzola' and 'Rome is in Russia' are both false. But, 'The moon is made of Gorgonzola iff Rome is in Italy' and 'The moon lacks air iff Rome is in Russia' are false. However, 'The moon lacks air iff Rome is in Italy' is true. ('Iff' has nothing to do with causes, explanations, or laws of nature.)

To solve puzzle 2, ask the god not the simple question, 'Is Dushanbe in Kirghizia?' but the more complex question, 'Are you True iff Dushanbe is in Kirghizia?' Then (in the absence of any geographical information) there are four possibilities:

1. **The god is True and Dushanbe is in Kirghizia: then you get the answer yes.**

2. **The god is True and Dushanbe is not in Kirghizia: this time you get no.**

3. **The god is False and Dushanbe is in Kirghizia: you get the answer yes, because only one statement is true, so the correct answer is no, and the god, who is False, falsely says 'yes'.**

4. **The god is False and Dushanbe is not in Kirghizia: in this final case you get the answer no, because both statements are false, the correct answer is yes, and the god False falsely says 'no'.**

So you get a yes answer to that complex question if Dushanbe is in Kirghizia and a no answer if it is not, *no matter to which of True and False you are speaking*. By noting the answer to the complex question, you can find out whether Dushanbe is in Kirghizia or not.

The point to notice is that if you ask either True or False, 'Are you True iff X?' and receive your answer in English, then you get the answer yes if X is true and no if X is false, regardless of which of the two you are speaking to.

The solution to puzzle 3 is quite similar: Ask True not, 'Is Dushanbe in Kirghizia?' but, 'Does da mean yes iff Dushanbe is in Kirghizia?' There are again four possibilities:

1. **Da means yes and Dushanbe is in Kirghizia: then True says 'da'.**

2. **Da means yes and Dushanbe is not in Kirghizia: then True says 'ja' (meaning no).**

3. **Da means no and Dushanbe is in Kirghizia: then True says 'da' (meaning no).**

4. **Da means no and Dushanbe is not in Kirghizia: then both statements are false, the statement 'Da means yes iff Dushanbe is in Kirghizia' is true, the correct answer (in English) to our question is yes, and therefore True says 'ja'.**

Thus you get the answer da if Dushanbe is in Kirghizia and the answer ja if not, regardless of which of da and ja means yes and which means no.

The point this time is that if you ask True, 'Does da mean yes iff Y?' then you get the answer da if Y is true and you get the answer ja if Y is false, regardless of which means which.

Combining the two points, we see that if you ask one of True and False (who we again suppose only answer da and ja), the very complex question, 'Does da mean yes iff, you are True iff X?' then *you will get the answer da if X is true and get the answer ja if X is false*, regardless of whether you are addressing the god True or the god False, and regardless of the meanings of da and ja.

We can now solve The Hardest Logic Puzzle Ever.

Your first move is to find a god who you can be certain is not Random, and hence is either True or False.

To do so, turn to A and ask Question 1: *Does da mean yes iff, you are True iff B is Random?* If A is True or False and you get the answer da, then as we have seen, B is Random, and therefore C is either True or False; but if A is True or False and you get the answer ja, then B is not Random, therefore B is either True or False.

But what if A is Random?

If A is Random, then neither B nor C is Random!

So if A is Random and you get the answer da, C is not Random (neither is B, but that's irrelevant), and therefore C is either True or False; and if A is Random and you get the answer ja, B is not random (neither is C, irrelevantly), and therefore B is either True or False.

Thus, *no matter whether A is True, False, or Random*, if you get the answer da to Question 1, C is either True or False, and if you get the answer ja, B is either True or False!

Now turn to whichever of B and C you have just discovered is either True or False—let us suppose that it is B (if it is C, just interchange the names B and C in what follows)—and ask Question 2: *Does da mean yes iff Rome is in Italy?* True will answer da, and False will answer ja. Thus, with two questions, you have either identified B as True or identified B as False.

For our third and last question, turn again to B, whom you have now either identified as True or identified as False, and ask Question 3: *Does da mean yes iff A is Random?*

Suppose B is True. Then if you get the answer da, then A is Random, and therefore A is Random, B is True, C is False, and you are done; but if you get the answer ja, then A is not Random, so A is False, B is true, C is Random, and you are again done.

Suppose B is False. Then if you get the answer da, then since B speaks falsely, A is not Random, and therefore A is True, B is False, C is Random, and you are done; but if we get ja, then A is Random, and thus B is False, and C is True, and you are again done. FINIS.

Well, I wasn't speaking falsely or at random when I said that the puzzle was hard, was I?

A brief remark about the significance of the Hardest Logic Puzzle Ever:

There is a law of logic called 'the law of excluded middle', according to which either X is true or not-X is true, for any statement X at all. ('The law of non-contradiction' asserts that statements X and not-X aren't both true.) Mathematicians and philosophers have occasionally attacked the idea that excluded middle is a logically valid law. We can't hope to settle the debate here, but can observe that our solution to puzzle 1 made essential use of excluded middle, exactly when we said 'Whether the middle card is an ace or not. . . .' It is clear from The Hardest Logic Puzzle Ever, and even more plainly from puzzle 1, that our ability to reason about alternative possibilities, even in everyday life, would be almost completely paralyzed were we to be denied the use of the law of excluded middle.

By the way, Dushanbe is in Tajikistan, not Kirghizia.[2]

3

Saying and Showing and the Continuity of Wittgenstein's Thought

MARIE McGINN

Marie McGinn is Professor of Philosophy at the University of East Anglia. Her Most recent work is Elucidating the Tractatus: Wittgenstein's Early Philosophy of Logic and Language.

1

Wittgenstein's rejection of the idea that philosophy results in philosophical doctrine is, from the very outset, a central element in his thought. In the Preface of the *Tractatus*, he stresses that the work is "not a textbook" (*TLP*, p. 3). He describes the aim of the book as one of "draw[ing] a limit to thought" or "to the expression of thoughts" (*TLP*, p. 3). In *TLP* 4.112, he remarks that "a philosophical work consists essentially of elucidations," and that it "does not result in 'philosophical propositions'." And in the penultimate remark of the work, after characterizing his propositions as "elucidations," he glosses what he means by this as follows:

> anyone who understands me eventually recognizes them as nonsensical, when he has used them—as steps—to climb up beyond them. (He must, so to speak, throw away the ladder after he has climbed up it.) (*TLP* 6.54)

It seems clear from this that however we understand the philosophical activity of "elucidation," nothing substantial—nothing that could be viewed as a philosophical answer to a philosophical question—should survive at the end of it. What remains unclear is exactly what the activity of elucidation amounts to or what exactly its purpose is. The word suggests that something is illuminated or clarified, but are we to understand this process of clarification as leading to a form of philosophical understanding or insight? If so, does that mean that there is a kind of philosophical understanding that cannot be expressed in the form of a philosophical doctrine about what is the case? The idea may strike us immediately as problematic. It seems to threaten to turn philosophy into something mystical or irrational.

James Conant and Cora Diamond have argued very persuasively that any attempt to preserve the idea that Wittgenstein intends the philosophical activity in which he is engaged to lead to a distinctive sort of insight or understanding—one whose "unsayability . . . precludes its being said, [but] which we can nevertheless grasp" (Diamond 1991, p. 69)—fails to do justice to the radical nature of his thought. If we take seriously Wittgenstein's claim that he eschews philosophical doctrine, then the only end of the philosophical activity in which he is engaged must, they argue, be the realization that there are no philosophical insights—expressible or otherwise—to be had:

> The aim is to undo our attraction to various grammatically well-formed strings of words that resonate with the aura of sense. The silence [Wittgenstein] wishes to leave us in at the end is one in which nothing has been said and there is nothing to say (of the sort we had imagined there to be). . . . The silence we are left with is not a pregnant silence that comes with a conscious posture of guarding the sanctity of the ineffable. (Conant 1991a, p. 344)

Diamond's and Conant's "resolute reading" of Wittgenstein's *Tractatus* certainly succeeds in making sense of Wittgenstein's closing image of his intended achievement: "anyone who understands me eventually recognizes [my propositions] as nonsensical, when he has used them—as steps—to climb up beyond them. (He must, so to speak, throw away the ladder after he has climbed up it" (*TLP* 6.54). On their reading, nothing is left standing at the end of the work: all the sentences that appear to express philosophical ideas, including the remarks that make up what they call "the body" of the *Tractatus*, have been revealed as nonsensical. The idea is that we begin by taking Wittgenstein's words at face value, but when we try to give them a sense we see them fall apart and melt away; at the end of the work we realize that there is nothing that we were trying but failing to say. As Conant puts it, Wittgenstein uses "one piece of nonsense . . . [to] show that another less self-evidently nonsensical piece of nonsense is nonsense" (Conant 1991a, p. 345); "the illusion of sense is exploded from within" (Conant 2002, p. 424). The attack on the "ineffability" or "metaphysical" reading of the *Tractatus* that has grown out of this attempt to take Wittgenstein at his word in *TLP* 6.54 seems to me completely persuasive. I do not, therefore, want to dispute Diamond's and Conant's claim that we must find a way of reading the text on which it is entirely free of metaphysical or theoretical claims about the relation between language and the world, even ones that are deemed to be ineffable. However, I do want to question whether this takes us all the way to the idea that the only work of the text is its undermining of itself. It seems to me that something is going on in the text that cannot accurately be characterized as the systematic unraveling of philosophical utterances (including those that make up the work). It is not only that this idea strikes me as inherently paradoxical, but it seems to me that there is something positive—something we might want to characterize as an 'insight'—achieved by the remarks of the *Tractatus,* which is in danger of being lost in Diamond's and Conant's preoccupation with the distinction between sense and nonsense. What I want to do in this paper is to defend a slightly less resolute reading of Wittgenstein's early work, which follows Diamond and Conant in avoiding committing him to philosophical doctrines (including ineffable ones), but which sees him as doing more than showing that philosophical utterances (including his own) fail to express a determinate thought. The interpretation will also preserve Diamond's and Conant's claim that there is a profound continuity between the early and the late philosophy.

2

It is reasonable to connect Wittgenstein's characterization of his remarks as 'elucidations' (*TLP* 6.54) with his view of the problems with which his text deals, namely, the problems of philosophy. He expresses his view of these problems in the Preface to the *Tractatus* as follows:

> The book deals with the problems of philosophy and shows, I believe, that the reason why these problems are posed is that the logic of our language is misunderstood. (*TLP*, p.3)

He makes the same point at *TLP* 4.003, when he says that "most of the propositions and questions of philosophers arise from our failure to understand the logic of our language." This conviction remains, of course, central to the later philosophy. It is for this reason that the questions of philosophy do not call for discoveries or for the construction of theories. Rather they call for a kind of investigation the result of which is not that these problems are answered, but that they are seen to disappear completely.

However, the idea that the questions of philosophy are not real questions, but are based on some kind of misunderstanding, might itself give rise to a question. Why, if he is so convinced the problems are illusory, does Wittgenstein concern himself with them? I think that this is an important question. And it is clear from Wittgenstein's remarks that his view that philosophical problems are nonsensical—that is, are incapable of receiving an answer—is not to be equated with the claim that they are trivial or uninteresting or plain silly. It is clear right from the beginning that Wittgenstein sees the problems of philosophy as touching on something 'deep'. Thus:

> And it is not surprising that the *deepest* problems are in fact *not* problems at all. (*TLP* 4.003)

He expresses the same thought in the *Philosophical Investigations* as follows:

> The problems arising through a misinterpretation of our forms of language have the character of *depth*. They are deep disquietudes, their roots are as deep in us as the forms of our language and their significance is as great as the importance of language. (*PI* 111)

If the interpretation of Wittgenstein's remarks is to fit with what he himself says in the text, about the nature of philosophy and about the nature of philosophical problems, then it must reveal not only an absence of doctrine and the unintelligibility of philosophical questions, but also the way in which the latter touch on something 'deep'. What we want is an understanding which allows Wittgenstein's remarks to achieve something positive, something which is connected with the 'depth' of the problems with which the work deals, and yet which stops short of treating these remarks as putting forward a substantial philosophical theory. This might, I believe, be taken to characterize the central interpretative issue for the whole of Wittgenstein's philosophy.

The resolute reading of the *Tractatus*, as we've just seen, places the emphasis on Wittgenstein's self-conscious use of nonsense to expose illusions of thought. The clarification that Wittgenstein achieves is to be understood entirely in terms of the exposure of the philosopher's failure to mean anything at all by the words he utters. By contrast, I want to focus on the distinctions which form the background to Wittgenstein's critique of traditional philosophy. This allows for a more positive, less paradoxical, interpretation of the *Tractatus*, while preserving Diamond's and Conant's sense of a fundamental connection between the early and the later work. On the interpretation that follows, the central purpose of the *Tractatus* is aptly characterized by a remark which Wittgenstein uses to describe the philosophical aims of the *Philosophical Investigations*: "We want to establish an order in our knowledge of the use of language: an order with a particular end in view; one out of many possible orders; not *the* order" (*PI* 132). This description of Wittgenstein's philosophical purpose brings out the way in which his elucidations are directed, not only at exposing failures of sense, but at bringing a certain order to something—"our knowledge of the use of language"—of which we as readers of the work are already in possession. The suggestion of this more positive characterization of Wittgenstein's philosophical aims is that he is engaged in a form of reflection which is intended to clarify, or bring a certain order to, our ordinary mastery of language; that is, to reveal, and to reveal the significance of, distinctions in use which we, as masters of language, already have a practical grasp.

If, as Wittgenstein believes, the problems of philosophy arise through a misunderstanding of the workings of our language, then all that we need to expose them as pseudo-problems is already in our possession, in the form of a practical mastery of the use of the sentences of our language. Recognizing these problems for what they are—unintelligible—does not require us to discover anything, but depends upon our seeing what is involved in our mastery of language in a new light, that is, on our being brought to see "a certain order in our knowledge of the use of language." Uncovering this order is not a matter of our coming to know something we did not know before and which Wittgenstein must inform us of, but of our grasping in reflection distinctions or differences that we already grasp or manifest in our practice of using expressions. On this view, the positive work of Wittgenstein's remarks does not concern itself with relations between language and something outside it, but with distinctions and relations between expressions that are internal to language itself. The value of the order that Wittgenstein brings to our reflections on our practical mastery of language is not, however, to be understood in terms of its corresponding with 'the facts', but in terms of its freeing us from the confusions that lie at the root of philosophical puzzlement. The peace that Wittgenstein's elucidations are intended to bring does not depend upon the discovery of doctrines, but nor is it merely a matter of our discovering that we have been prone to illusions of thought. Rather it is connected with a recognition of a certain order in our knowledge of the use of language, on which we see that the philosophical problem does not arise. What we come to see is that the appearance of the problem depended upon a false sense of analogy, a failure to see, or to see the significance of, logical distinctions, i.e. distinctions in use. It is, however, precisely their connection with this order that gives the philosophical problems their 'character of depth'.

3

The *Tractatus* is concerned to clarify or reveal a large number of logical distinctions: between names and propositions, between material functions and the so-called truth-functions (which he calls operations), between genuine concepts and formal concepts, between the propositions of logic and genuine propositions, and so on. However, the central distinction in the order that Wittgenstein's elucidations are concerned to bring to our knowledge of the use of language is, I want to argue, the distinction between saying and showing. This distinction, which I want to make central to Wittgenstein's philosophy, both early and late, is one which Conant believes "requires completely relinquishing." Conant sees interpretations that make this distinction central to Wittgenstein's philosophy as committed to some form of ineffability thesis that depends upon what he calls the "substantial conception of nonsense." The substantial conception of nonsense distinguishes between two different kinds of nonsense: mere nonsense, which is simply unintelligible and expresses no thought; and substantial nonsense, which tries and (inevitably) fails to express a logically incoherent thought, that is, a thought which somehow conflicts with the logical structure of our language. Insofar as the proponent of the saying/showing distinction appears to accept the idea that there is something a speaker may try but fail to say with words which in themselves express no determinate thought, Conant believes he is committed to the idea that there is a thought which we can grasp but cannot express, that is, to the idea of substantial nonsense. The distinction between saying and showing seems to Conant to amount to nothing more than the dubious idea that there are thoughts—for instance thoughts about the logical structure of language, or about the relation between language and the world—which language itself prevents us from expressing. A speaker who attempts to put these unsayable thoughts into words inevitably finds himself violating the bounds of sense: the logical structure of language, or the nature of the relation between language and the world, itself precludes the possibility of describing it in language without violations of logical syntax.

I find the idea of substantial nonsense, or of ineffable thoughts, very difficult to make sense of, and in defending the centrality of the distinction between saying and showing for Wittgenstein's philosophy, I do not mean to commit myself to it. Thus, I do not want to accept Conant's claim that the standard conception of the saying/showing distinction "figure[s] in the work as [a] dialectical way station . . . [a] rung on the ladder that the reader is invited to ascend and—once having ascended—called upon to throw away" (Conant 2002, p. 377). Rather, I want to argue that the standard interpretation of the distinction is not one that Wittgenstein ever articulates, but is, from beginning to end, a complete misreading of his remarks. The idea that the distinction between saying and showing is central to the order that Wittgenstein attempts to bring to our knowledge of the use of language rests on the claim that there is an alternative way to understand what the distinction amounts to. Very roughly, I want to understand the distinction as itself a logical distinction that is internal to language. What can be shown but cannot be said is everything that is essential to a sign's being used, on a specific occasion, to express a determinate sense, that is, with what makes it possible for a sign which is used to express a thought to express the thought it does. What can only be shown and not said has nothing to do with thoughts (for example, with truths about the relation between language and something outside it) that cannot be expressed without violations of logical syntax. Rather, what shows itself in the application of language is everything that is essential to the system within which alone the thoughts we express can be expressed; the system of language within which thoughts are expressed is revealed only in its use, in the application that we make of it, i.e. in our use of sentences with sense. It is this essential connection between what is shown and what essentially reveals itself only in the use or application of language that makes it impossible to say what shows itself. Thus, the idea of the saying/showing distinction is not that there are unsayable thoughts—for example, thoughts about the relation between language and the world—that lie beyond the limits of language, but that the limits of language—everything that is essential to our using language with sense—are revealed only in its application. What is shown only in the actual use of words with sense is something of which we have an essentially practical mastery, something which cannot—by its nature—be expressed in the form of a proposition. However, what is here expressed—misleadingly—in the form of a claim is something that Wittgenstein—by means of a series of comparisons—gets us to see by bringing a certain order to our knowledge of the use of language.

4

Thus, from the opening of the *Tractatus*, Wittgenstein's fundamental elucidatory purpose is to bring a certain order to our knowledge of the use of language. The order is intended to get us to see that the distinction between the accidental or the merely possible (what we describe in language) and the essential or the a priori (the opposite of which cannot be imagined) is essentially a logical one, one that is essentially connected with the distinction between saying and showing. We should not, on this understanding of the work, see the opening remarks as a series of metaphysical assertions about the nature of a language-independent reality—or even as a series of meta-physical assertions whose sense is later to be put in doubt—but as a material picture of our language, which Wittgenstein uses purely as a means of clarifying a series of distinctions. Thus, facts, states of affairs and objects serve merely as material correlates of linguistic distinctions between propositions, elementary propositions and names, respectively. It is not Wittgenstein's aim in these remarks to say something about the constitution of the world conceived independently of language, but to use the material correlates of linguistic distinctions to help us to see the significance of these distinctions more clearly. If we approach the distinctions between the accidental (contingent, a posteriori) and the essential (necessary, a priori), or between propositions and elementary propositions, or between propositions and names, directly through language, then we are inclined to miss their significance. The superficial similarity between ordinary, contingent propositions and the propositions of logic, between propositions containing logical constants and those without, between propositions and sub-propositional expressions, and so on, prevents us from clearly perceiving a series of essential, or logical, distinctions that it is Wittgenstein's intention to make clear. What we can see much more clearly in the concrete myth of facts, states of affairs and objects is that facts (propositions) are essentially complex, that objects (names) are essentially the simple constituents of states of affairs (elementary propositions), that the objects (names) exist in any possible state of affairs (elementary proposition), that we grasp an object (name) only insofar as we grasp its possibilities for occurring in states of affairs (elementary propositions), and so on. Wittgenstein uses the material image of language to lead us into looking at language as a logically articulated whole; we can make distinctions within this whole, but none of these distinctions can be grasped independently of the others or of the totality within which they are discerned. From the very beginning, Wittgenstein is working in a way that is intended to acknowledge that our reflections are carried out from a position in the midst of language; we can reflect on our knowledge of the use of language and draw distinctions "for a particular purpose," but we cannot approach it piecemeal, from a position outside it; we cannot construct a route into it, but must reflect on it as something already, in a sense, complete and displaying an order that we must be careful not to blur or elide. What we are doing is, from the beginning, quite distinct from explanation.

It is within this general approach that Wittgenstein works to clarify the logical distinction between the accidental (what is the case) and the essential (the opposite of which cannot be imagined). What we can see much more clearly in the concrete myth of the world as the totality of facts is, first of all, the need for a distinction between the accidental and the essential, and secondly, that the essential is not just another fact about the world, but rather belongs to a distinct logical category: the insubstantial limit of possibility. The essential, the necessary, the a priori, which comes in with the idea of the possible, is not something alongside the possible, or something that could exist independently of the possible. The essential is connected with the possible, not in the sense of being part of it, but in the sense of being its insubstantial limit. It is not something that can be discerned *in* the world, and neither is it a boundary that we can draw round the world, but it is something that the world—or language—makes manifest in the limit of what is possible, in the limits of description.

Wittgenstein characterizes the distinctions I have just introduced in terms of the contrast between content (objects), structure (the arrangement of objects in states of affairs) and form (the limit of the possible arrangement of objects in states of affairs). He then goes on to use these distinctions in remarks which serve to elucidate, or provide a way of seeing, the manner in which a picture represents or models what it pictures. In particular, he applies these distinctions to pictures in a way that allows us to see the contrast between what is accidental in a picture—what could be otherwise and it still be a picture of a state of affairs—and what is essential to it—what could not be otherwise without it ceasing to be a picture—in a new way. We are brought to see that a picture must have something in common—an implicit horizon of possibilities for combining its elements in intelligible structures—with what it depicts. Wittgenstein calls what a picture has in common with what it depicts its 'pictorial form'. It is vital that we do not understand this idea of what a picture and what it depicts have in common as a contingent or external relation between two independent realities. The idea that the picture and what it depicts share something in common is essentially the idea of an internal relation between the picture and what is pictured. This internal relation expresses itself in the fact that what is the case if the picture is correct is precisely what the picture pictures: the correctness of the picture is not something that we can point to independently of the picture. Our grip on what is possible is not independent of our grip on what can be pictured.

Wittgenstein now goes on to draw our attention to the way in which this aspect of a picture—its pictorial form—cannot be a subject of depiction. A picture depicts a particular state of affairs in virtue of the way its pictorial elements are combined in a determinate structure. We can see plainly that the picture's depiction of this possible state of affairs is completely independent of whether the state of affairs exists or not. Thus, we see that a picture depicts its subject correctly or incorrectly, depending on whether or not things are arranged in the way it depicts. Pictorial form, however, is what a picture has in common with what it depicts; it is that in virtue of which the articulation of the picture's elements into a determinate structure constitutes a representation of a possible state of affairs. Again, it is important to see that this is not an *explanation* of a picture's ability to represent, but merely a reflection on the boundary between pictures and nonsense, that is, between pictures and what may look like a picture, but which actually pictures nothing. We can now see clearly that these two aspects of a picture—what it depicts correctly or incorrectly and what is essential to it *qua* picture of a possible state of affairs—are inimical to one another. If we could depict what is essential to a picture, what it has in common with what it depicts, then this would have to be something that it depicts either correctly or incorrectly, and which it and what it depicts could therefore lack. Thus, "[a] picture cannot . . . place itself outside its representational form," for whatever a picture represents from a position outside is something that can be the case or not be the case, and which the picture could therefore represent as being otherwise. This, I'm suggesting, is not to be seen as a theory of representation—that is, as an account which explains what a picture's ability to represent consists in—but as a process of drawing distinctions, or marking differences, which, in some sense, we already grasp.

5

The importance of the above points begins to emerge fully when we begin to see an analogy between pictures and propositions. Wittgenstein uses our sense of an analogy here as a means to make something clear about propositions: propositions are complex; propositions describe possible states of affairs; a proposition agrees or fails to agree with reality; a proposition represents in virtue of its form (the form of a proposition is logical form); we cannot tell from a proposition alone whether it is true or false; there are no propositions that are true a priori. The upshot of the comparison between pictures and propositions is that we come to see logical form—the form in virtue of which a proposition describes a possible state of affairs—as the limit of possible depiction, that is, the limit of depiction of states of affairs. Again, no explanation of language's ability to depict states of affairs is being put forward, and no boundary is being drawn: the limit shows itself in the use of language and is not something that can exist independently of it. Thus, by reflecting on the comparison between propositions and pictures, we come to recognize the way in which logical form—the form in virtue of which a proposition expresses its sense—is essentially revealed in the application of language, and cannot be described by means of it.

The distinction between what can be described in language and what the application of language shows is further developed in Wittgenstein's observations on the role of variables and on the status of the propositions of logic. Wittgenstein introduces the idea of a variable via the distinction between a sign and a symbol. A sign is simply the physical aspect of a symbol; the inscription or mark or sound; it is "what can be perceived of a symbol" (*TLP* 3.32). The symbol, on the other hand, is "the sign taken together with its logico-syntactical employment" (*TLP* 3.327). "In order to recognize a symbol by its sign we must observe how it is used with a sense" (*TLP* 3.326). The distinction between a sign and a symbol focuses attention on the connection between the sense of a sign and its use: it is in use that the sense of a sign (the essence of a symbol) is revealed or determined. Thus it is use that represents everything that is essential to a sign. What Wittgenstein is gradually getting us to see is that logical form—everything essential to the sense of a sign—cannot, as we've already seen, be described *in* language, but it makes itself manifest in the way that expressions are used with a sense. In the same way, we grasp what is essential to the sense of a sign, not theoretically in the form of a piece of propositional knowledge, but *practically* in our mastery of how to use a sign with a sense.

Formal concepts—the concept of a name, an object, a function, a proposition, and so forth—are expressions which purport to describe the logico-syntactic category of an expression, that is, to describe what is essential to the sense of a sign. We can see that these concepts are not genuine concepts, since the propositions containing them are not genuine pictures, that is to say, they do not describe a state of affairs which may either exist or fail to exist. In the case of a proposition of the form 'A is an object' it is either a tautology or what it expresses is unimaginable (a contradiction). But this, Wittgenstein wants us to see, is equivalent to recognizing that these words express no thought at all, that they lack a sense. As he remarks of such propositions in the *Philosophical Investigations*, "we say 'I can't imagine the opposite'. Why not: 'I can't imagine the thing itself'?" (*PI* 251). What we now see is that what we try to say by means of propositions containing formal concepts "instead is shown in the very sign" (*TLP* 4.126), or more accurately, in its use with a sense. The proper description of the use of a sign is not, Wittgenstein now goes on, by means of a pseudo-concept, but by means of a variable whose values are all the expressions which belong to a particular logico-syntactic category: "So the expression for a formal concept is a propositional variable in which this distinctive feature [viz. the use] alone is constant" (*TLP* 4.126). What Wittgenstein now draws our attention to is that a variable is only introduced via the signs that are its values, and never independently: "A formal concept is given immediately any object falling under it is given. It is not possible, therefore, to introduce as primitive ideas objects belonging to a formal concept *and* the formal concept itself" (*TLP* 4.12721). The variable gets its significance *via* the symbols it replaces and has no independent meaning. Thus, a proposition in which all the signs have been replaced by variables says nothing, it merely puts a particular form on show. The form itself—what is shown by the variable—cannot be grasped via the variable alone, but only by a practical mastery of the logico-syntactical use of the symbols the variable replaces.

We see exactly the same points emerge in connection with the propositions of logic. Thus, Wittgenstein shows, in just the same way, that the propositions of logic are not strictly speaking propositions (symbols) at all. They do not picture states of affairs; they lack a sense that could be either true or false. In this case, Wittgenstein uses the formal device of the truth-functions to display the tautologous nature of the propositions of logic. But the important point here is not the identification of the propositions of logic by means of a purely formal feature, but the recognition that what these propositions put on show— namely, the logical relations between propositions that are constructed by means of the truth-functions—is something that is properly shown only in the actual use of language. As in the case of variables, we cannot grasp the significance of a proposition of logic directly, but only via a practical mastery of the logical relations between genuine propositions that is displayed in our inferential practice. The propositions of logic tell us nothing; our ability to recognize them as logical propositions depends entirely upon our prior, practical mastery of the internal relations between propositions that the so-called propositions of logic articulate. Thus, the propositions of logic do not constitute a system of a priori truths and they cannot provide an independent route to mastery of what is a priori in language: the a priori is everything that the use of language shows and it is necessarily mastered purely practically. Thus, the idea that the propositions of logic say nothing—are tautologies—is connected with the idea that they simply articulate or put on show the logical or inferential connections between genuine propositions of our language, which are manifest in its use, and a practical grasp of which is essential to our understanding of language. In understanding language we necessarily already grasp all that the propositions of logic articulate, but this grasp is practical not theoretical. Insofar as logic is everything that is essential to the sense of the sentences of our language, it must be grasped in a practical way *before* the question of the truth or falsity of any proposition with a sense can arise.

6

The order that Wittgenstein brings to our knowledge of the use of language is thus one that turns on the distinction between what is shown in the actual use of expressions and what is said in language; between what is grasped essentially practically and theoretical knowledge of truths. It is in seeing this order that we come to see that the philosopher's attempt to state what kinds of things exist, to treat logic as a system of truths in need of justification, to explain how language connects with the world, and so on are based on a mis-understanding. Philosophical question are the "deepest questions" precisely insofar as, in their nature, they tóuch—in a confused and misleading way—in a way that makes us feel the need for some form of account or explica-tion—on what shows itself in the use of language. This is both what differentiates them from scientific questions and what renders them unintel-ligible, or unanswerable. Thus, as far as the question of justifying logic is concerned, we now see that logic does not consist of a system of truths for which the question of justification might arise. Rather, the whole of logic is coeval with the phenomenon of language and the logician is merely postu-lating a notation in which inferential relations between propositions, of which everyone who understands language already has a practical grasp, are put perspicuously on display. Once we have language in use, we already have the whole of logic. We can see now that it makes no sense to ask whether the so-called laws of logic are true, or whether the world will conspire to make them usable: to think of the world is already to think according to the laws of logic. This is not to ground logic in something absolute outside language—it is not in any sense to *justify* logic—but is rather to recognize the status that logic has for language. There is no conceiving of the world as something to which the logic of our language might or might not apply. The idea that "logic per-vades the world: the limits of the world are also its limits" (*TLP* 5.61) is not, therefore, a metaphysical claim about the necessary correlation of two sys-tems—the world on one side and language on the other—but part of the order that we now perceive in our knowledge of the use of language. There is no proof that language necessarily fits the world conceived independently of lan-guage: the world is mirrored in language; logical form is the form of reality.

What the reader of the *Tractatus* is gradually brought to see is that the use of language to state truths about the world rests on, or presupposes, a prac-tical mastery of the use of expressions with sense, that is, of everything that is essential to the sense of a sign, which, in the *Tractatus* is equivalent to its logical form. Nothing can be made the basis of my practical grasp of logical form: the practical grasp of what is essential to the sense of a sign is neces-sarily prior to the use of variables to describe it. What I come to see is that I cannot get outside logic and give it any foundation: I essentially already inhabit—that is, use—logic; my life with language means that I am already in the midst of logic. All this, I've tried to show, is an expression of a partic-ular way of looking at the distinction between the essential (the a priori) and the accidental (the a posteriori). What is a priori is what shows itself in the use of language, and what shows itself has to do, not with something that we *know* (i.e. not with something that is *true*), but with something that we *do*. What is shown is something that is grasped and lived rather than known. It follows from this that what is shown cannot be given any foundation. All explanation, description, justification, and so forth takes place within the limits of what shows itself in the application of language. Ultimately all we can say is: this is what we do.

<h1 style="text-align:center">7</h1>

The distinction between saying and showing which Wittgenstein introduces in the *Tractatus* remains, I believe, central to his thought and is clearly at work throughout the later philosophy. Thus, in *On Certainty*, a collection of remarks which Wittgenstein wrote in the last year and a half of his life, the distinction between the a priori, or what is shown in the use of language, and the a posteriori, or what is said in language, is fundamental to his diagnosis of philosophical scepticism and its dogmatic alternative. The critique of Moore's commonsense rejection of sceptical doubt is to be seen as an attempt to show that Moore—like the philosopher who sets out to justify logic—treats a question which concerns the sense (use) of our words as if it were a question concerning a matter of fact. He tries to get us to see that we cannot understand Moore's claim to know that 'This is a hand' as an empirical claim with true/false poles. Moore's words are shown rather to have the status of what Wittgenstein now calls a "grammatical remark": they are in themselves empty (they say nothing about the world), but, like the propositions of logic in the *Tractatus*, they bear a distinctive relation to our practice of using language. These so-called propositions have a peculiar role insofar as they are an attempt to articulate something that is presupposed in our ordinary use of language, something which manifests itself in that use, which is essential to the sense of our words, and which, as masters of language, we already have a practical grasp. The shift that takes place through Wittgenstein's critique of Moore is one that mirrors the shift in our understanding of the status of the propositions of logic in the *Tractatus*. The shift is from a question of truth—'Does Moore know that this is a hand?'—to a question of sense: 'Does it make sense to doubt that this is a hand?' What we're brought to see is that it is not a question of whether Moore knows something for certain, but of the way in which certainty in the use of expressions belongs to the essence of the language game.

It is not, therefore, simply a matter of Moore's (or our) being under an illusion that his words succeed in expressing a determinate thought, but of the way in which the precise nature of Moore's failure to mean anything by his words show us that the illusory dispute between Moore and the sceptic touches on something 'deep'. The sort of certainty Moore tries, but necessarily fails, to express with the claim "I know that this is a hand," is not a kind of certainty for which we can imagine an opposite, but represents a limit of our use of words. The role of this certainty in our language game means that we cannot place it against a background of other attitudes; it is essential to our mastery of our language and therefore prior to our assertion of anything as true or false. When we see it in this light, we begin to recognize that the certainty Moore tries to articulate in words cannot be expressed in propositions with true/false poles. What we have here is something that serves as a foundation of our thought in a quite different way from something which I assume to be the case, but which may turn out to be false, and which I might replace with a different assumption. I've tried to show how, in the *Tractatus*, Wittgenstein tries to get us to recognize that, insofar as the so-called propositions of logic touch on what is essential to the sense of our words, our mastery of what they articulate is essentially practical and prior to the formulation of the laws of logic in (pseudo-)propositions. In the same way, he tries to get us to see that the certainty which Moore attempts to express in the form of a claim to know something, is essentially a form of practical certainty that we necessarily acquire in grasping what is essential to the sense of expressions, namely their use. The certainty that Moore has that "This is a hand" is a practical certainty regarding the use (the sense) of words and is quite distinct from the epistemic certainty that arises in connection with the acquisition and justification of beliefs about the world.

It is important to see that, on this view of Wittgenstein's philosophical purpose, nothing that he says provides, or is intended to provide, either a justification of the certainty that belongs to the essence of the language game or a refutation of the scepticism of the idealist. We are rather brought to see that the realist and the idealist each attempt to answer a question that is unintelligible: the question whether we are justified in believing that our language applies to the world. To speak or think about the world is already to apply or use language, already to inhabit the language game in which language is functioning as a going concern. The practical certainty in our use of language which is the essence of our life with language, like our practical mastery of logic, has a role in our understanding of language that cannot be expressed *in* language, for it determines the sense of expressions and is not expressible as an employment of them. Insofar as our certainty belongs to the essence of (is presupposed by) the language game, the idea of justifying it by appeal either to a rule or to what is the case is unintelligible. On the one hand, this certainty in how our language is used is essentially prior to the formulation of a rule whose use has not yet been determined by application; on the other, there can be no question of justifying our certainty by appeal to the facts, for description of the facts already presupposes the certainty that is a condition of the sense of the description. Only what could conceivably be otherwise can be justified by an appeal to what happens to be the case; in the current case, however, we cannot imagine the opposite. By the same stroke, nothing about what is the case follows from our practical certainty in using language. All we can say is: this is what we do.

8

I hope we can now see why Wittgenstein calls his remarks "elucidations" and why he thinks of his philosophy as a form of activity which does not result in answers to philosophical questions. Wittgenstein's philosophical purpose *vis-à-vis* traditional philosophical problems depends upon his bringing us to recognize the way in which we inhabit language, the way in which we are already in the midst of it and cannot get outside it or give it a foundation in truths. We do not learn anything new from the philosophical journey Wittgenstein takes us on, but we have been brought to a realization of what constitutes the essential background to our ability to describe the world (truly or falsely) in language. It is by bringing us to recognize the distinction between the determination of sense and the employment of sense—and its connection with the distinction between practical and theoretical knowledge, or between saying and showing—that Wittgenstein diagnoses the "misunderstanding of the logic of our language" that lies at the root of philosophical problems. The philosopher's error is to suppose that what determines sense—everything essential to language—can be described in a series of true propositions, when it is in fact what shows itself in the use of language, in the limits of what can be said. Wittgenstein brings the philosopher in us peace, by showing that what he had wanted to assert, unintelligibly, as a piece of information is essentially a matter of the grammar of our language, that is, a question of sense rather than truth. What the philosopher tries to say is, we come to see, something which shows itself only in our actual use of words.

REFERENCES

J. Conant, J. 1991a. Throwing Away the Top of the Ladder. *The Yale Review* 79, pp. 328–364.

————. 1991b. The Search for Logically Alien Thought: Descartes, Kant, Frege, and the *Tractatus*. *Philosophical Topics* 20, pp. 115–180.

————. 2002. The Method of the *Tractatus*. In E. Reck, ed., *From Frege to Wittgenstein: Perspectives on Early Analytic Philosophy* (Oxford: Oxford University Press).

Diamond, C. 1991. Ethics, Imagination, and the Method of Wittgenstein's *Tractatus*'. In R. Heinrich and H. Vetter, eds., *Bilder der Philosophie* (Wiener Reihe, 5), pp. 55–90.

————. 1995. Throwing Away the Ladder: How to Read the *Tractatus*'. In *The Realistic Spirit* (Cambridge, Massachusetts: MIT Press), pp. 179–204.

McGinn, M. 1999. Between Metaphysics and Nonsense: Elucidation in Wittgenstein's *Tractatus*. *The Philosophical Quarterly* 49, pp. 491–513.

————. (forthcoming) What Kind of Senselessness is This? A Reply to Conant on Wittgenstein's Critique of Moore. In J. Conant and A. Kern, eds., *Scepticism and Context* (Stanford: Stanford University Press).

Wittgenstein, Ludwig. 1961. *Tractatus Logico-Philosophicus*. Trans. D.F. Pears and B.F. McGuinness. London: Routledge. Referred to in this chapter as *TLP*.

————. 1963. *Philosophical Investigations*, ed. G.E.M. Anscombe and R. Rhees, trans. G.E.M. Anscombe (Oxford: Blackwell, 1963). Referred to in this chapter as *PI*.

4

Text of Texts

L U C I A N O   B E R I O

Luciano Berio was one of the leading composers and musical thinkers of the late twentieth century. He conducted the Cleveland Orchestra, Israel Philharmonic, New York Philharmonic, the Royal Dutch Concertgebouw, and many others. He founded the Studio di Fonologia Musicale at RAI and the Tempo Reale, an institute for music research and production in Florence, and won numerous awards for his compositions. He passed away in Rome in 2003.

It is understandable that a composer should offer a certain resistance to speaking about Music as Text, since he, if anyone, is aware that a text written to be verbalized has little in common with a piece of music written to be performed. A musical Text is not only a written score or what a performer plays or what an audience hears. A musical score is a means of providing a professional musician with the information necessary for the piece's performance, and does not necessarily imply a listener or specific modes of listening, though the composer is of course fully aware that he cannot separate the music he writes from its acoustical realization. A verbal Text, on the other hand, is available to everyone and open to every kind of interpretation, and implies, within a given linguistic community, a writer and a reader, a speaker and a listener.

   A person speaking always implies, in broad general terms at least, the possibility that what is being said can also be formulated in writing (though of course not every written text obeys the rules of oral grammar). The musical score is an instrument of specialized non-linguistic knowledge, in which an exorbitant number of perceptual experiences and expressive and intellectual choices converge. The composer, as manager of these convergences, becomes himself a musical Text, he is programmed as a Text, but, at the same time, he cannot describe himself objectively as a Text. If this were possible, we would have neither Text nor composer.

If I have been unable to resist the temptation to write about Music as Text, the reason is because I feel relatively free. I do not have a musical theory of the Text to offer but only a few general convictions which, while presupposing on the one hand the specific experience of musical performance, invite us on the other not to ignore the experience of the literary Text. It nonetheless remains true that, like the literary text, the musical Text too, whatever kind it belongs to, is made up of Texts that mutually condition each other. In fact, in the case of musical creativity also, intertextual conditioning can become such a potent force that, the more the "speakers" are (or feel they are) "being spoken," the more they lose the courage to speak, the more they take refuge in silence.

"Text of Texts as Song of Songs." This allegorical title implies the possibility of an obvious hermeneutical inversion—Songs of Song or Texts of Text—but it also evokes the intrinsic otherness of Songs (and Texts) and the immanent pluralism of Texts (and Songs). Furthermore, my title is intended to suggest the idea that in music, as in literature, it is possible to imagine an alternative between the Text's supremacy over the Reader and the primacy of the Reader over the text: the Reader, in other words, becomes his own Text. As Harold Bloom has remarked: "You are or you become what you read," and "What you are is the only thing you can read." But music implies performance, and the choice between these two options can become terribly complicated, given the fact—let me repeat what I have already affirmed—that performing and interpreting a musical Text is not the same thing as reading and interpreting a literary Text.

A literary Text is customarily the object of repeated scrutiny and contemplation. It is preserved and protected by cultural canons and contexts, because it translates into words values significant to the members of a cultural community. In and around a Text cultural investments of great scope and duration are given concrete realization; between individuals and textual objects continual and repeated contacts take place.

There are texts made to be spoken, 'performed' in other words, such as theatrical works, liturgical texts, official speeches, and so on; but since we value the ability to read and write, we expect the individual to establish a personal contact with these Texts through reading. In western cultures (apart from expressions of the folk and oral tradition) there are no verbal texts that exist only to be listened to: they always imply reading. This is not true of music. Perhaps it would be undemocratic to require universal musical literacy, but if this were to occur, the "victims" of this enforced literacy would enjoy as a result the privilege of establishing a multifaceted and possibly more creative relationship with the musical Text, to say nothing of a more responsibly free one.

Music as Text is a matter strictly for musicians. We, as musicians, live constantly with Texts, but we don't talk about them much because our Texts are usually ideas, or, precisely, a score with which we hand over to performers, convinced that it can speak for itself. Its performance may suspend or give a structure to the passing of time. It will give the listener a provisional coherent "being-in-time," which, incidentally, is the only human experience to which we can attribute a universal value.

It is of course possible for a musician to approach a score as if it were a poem to be read, making it an object of pleasure through prolonged private contemplation. But, whereas a Haydn string quartet represents a highly "discursive," that is to say, grammatical and syntactical, kind of music, which can be read and re-read easily and pleasurably by musicians, an orchestral score by Debussy, Webern, Stravinsky or Boulez can demand considerable effort and experience if it is to be "heard" accurately through silent reading.

It can happen for composers to feel themselves prisoners of Texts. They may get the overwhelming sensation that they are being "spoken" by Texts, and, as I previously remarked, they may lose the courage to "speak." As a consequence, they withdraw into themselves, displaying a kind of resentment with regard to an evolutionary and stratified idea of the Text. Their musical rebellion tends to manifest itself in pseudo-mystical meditations on silence, as well as in flight into sound events which pursue a monodimensional idea of music as acoustical experience comfortably and passively ensconced within us, in time. A non-musically-active presence is formless. Listeners can only coexist with it, their inner being has no way of dancing with it. It cannot be directed or "choreographed," nor can it be touched by experience, history, the unexpected, knowledge or the emotions. If we were to imagine ourselves interpreting this passive time, the time-that-is-not, we would not find much to interpret or discover, because this passive acoustical material has nothing to do with one basic properties of the Text, the property of always meaning something more (if not indeed something else) than it intended to say.

When James Joyce declared that his *Ulysses* would keep scholars busy at least for a hundred years, his Mephistophelian nature was showing. He knew that scholars would not be able to resist the temptation to identify references, once they knew the references were there. But Joyce also knew that getting in touch with evaded and disguised truths was an important aspect of the poetic and narrative conception of *Ulysses*. We are aware that interpretations of a literary Text involve not only the production of other Texts but also a hierarchy among the values we attribute to the various interpretations of the Texts themselves. I myself tend to admire analytical listeners and performers, but I realize that there is a delicate, even precarious balance (to be defended, however, at all costs) between the recognition of conventions, stylistic reminiscences, references and codes on the one hand and independence of them on the other. The ability to remember can become a poison, unless it is counterbalanced by the desire to forget and communicate, even in the absence of interlocutors and without conscious reference to specific codes of listening. The Text needs forgetfulness.

Listeners, performers, even composers must know the experience of consciously infusing new life into a work inasmuch as it is an object of knowledge. They must undergo a kind of alchemical transformation in which the recognition and awareness of conceptual links—the fruits, in other words, of their relationships with Texts—are spontaneously transformed into a "being" which transcends and sublimates technical realities. We are profoundly conscious of this whenever we write or perform music, whenever we ask ourselves—however unconsciously—the eternal questions regarding the Text's profound relationship with ourselves, our own being as Texts, our constant need to be emancipated from a given notion of the Text, and our evolving and proliferating relationship with a Text which—without thereby wishing to deify it—seems to be everywhere and nowhere at the same time and which seems to exist even when no one is talking about it.

5

Frege's Theorem: An Introduction

RICHARD G. HECK, JR.

Richard Heck, who received his Ph.D. from MIT, is Professor of Philosophy at Brown University. His fields of interest include the philosophy of language and logic, as well as the work of Gottlob Frege. Some of his recent publications include "Non-conceptual Content and the 'Space of Reasons'," Philosophical Review, *and "Are There Different Kinds of Content,"* in Contemporary Debates in the Philosophy of Mind.

1. Opening

What is the epistemological status of our knowledge of the truths of arithmetic? Are they analytic, the products of pure reason, as Leibniz held? Or are they high-level empirical truths that we know only *a posteriori*, as some empiricists, particularly Mill, have held? Or was Kant right to say that, although our knowledge that '5 + 7 = 12' depends essentially upon intuition, it is nonetheless *a priori*? It was with this problem that Gottlob Frege was chiefly concerned throughout his philosophical career. His goal was to establish a version of Leibniz's view (and so to demonstrate the independence of arithmetical from geometrical reasoning), to show that the truths of arithmetic follow logically from premises which are themselves truths of logic. It is this view that we now call *Logicism*.

Frege's approach to this problem had a number of strands, but it is simplest to divide it into two: a negative part and a positive part. The negative part consists of criticisms of the views of Mill and Kant, and others who share them. These criticisms, although they are found in a variety of places, mostly occur in the first three chapters of *Die Grundlagen der Arithmetik*.[1] The positive part consists of an attempt to show (not just that but) *how* arithmetical truths can be established by pure reason, by actually giving proofs of them from premises which are (or are supposed to be) truths of pure logic. There is thus a purely mathematical aspect of Frege's project: it is this on which I intend to focus here.

Frege was not the first to attempt to show how arithmetical truths can be proven from more fundamental assumptions. His approach, however, was more rigorous and encompassing, by far, than anything that had come before. Leibniz, for example, had attempted to prove such arithmetical truths as '2 + 2 = 4'. His proofs, however, like those of Euclid before him, rest upon assumptions that he does not make explicit: for example, Leibniz make free appeal to the associative law of addition, which says that $(a + b) + c = a + (b + c)$, that is, allows himself freely to 're-arrange' parentheses. But it is essential to *any* attempt to determine the epistemological status of the laws of arithmetic that we be able precisely to determine upon what assumptions the proofs of such laws depend. That is to say, it is essential that the proofs be presented in such a way that, once the premises on which they are to depend have been stated, no *additional* assumptions can sneak in unnoticed. Frege's idea was to give the proofs within a 'formal system' of logic, in which the permissible inferential steps are explicitly specified, by purely syntactic criteria, so that it becomes no more complicated to determine what assumptions are employed in the proofs than it is, say, to check calculations by long division.

Existing systems of logic, deriving from the work of George Boole (and, ultimately, from Aristotle), were, however, inadequate for this task, for two reasons: first, the systems were ill-suited to the presentation of *proofs*; and, secondly, they were inadequate even to represent the sentences which were contained in those proofs. In particular, it is impossible, in Boole's system, to express sentences containing multiple expressions of generality, such as 'Every horse's head is an animal's head' or, more to the point, 'Every number has a successor'. In a *sense*, these sentences can be represented within Boole's logic, but not in such a way that one can see, on the basis of that representation, why the former follows from, but does not imply, 'Every horse is an animal'—and so, not in such a way that proofs even of such simple facts can be carried out within it.

It was for this reason that Frege was forced to develop a new system of formal logic, which he first presented in *Begriffsschrift*.[2] His system is, as he frequently points out, adequate for the representation of sentences like those mentioned above; its rules of inference, though limited in number, allow us to carry out the sorts of proofs that could not be formalized in Boole's system. And once a system adequate to the representation of actual mathematical argumentation has been developed, the question of the epistemological status of arithmetic is transformed. It would be too strong to say that it *reduces* to the question from what assumptions the laws of arithmetic can in fact be proven—for, once such assumptions have been identified, we will be left with the question what the epistemological status of those assumptions is. But nonetheless, the philosophical question takes on a purely mathematical aspect, and mathematical techniques can be brought to bear on it.

It would, I think, be impossible to over-emphasize the importance of the contribution implicit in Frege's approach here. Frege's idea that, through formal logic, the resources of mathematics can be brought to bear upon philosophical problems, pervades contemporary analytic philosophy, having come down to us through the work of Russell, Wittgenstein, Carnap, and others. But its influence is not limited to philosophy. Mathematical logic, as we now have it, is obsessed with the question what can or can not be proven from particular assumptions, and it is only against the background of Frege's system of formal logic—or, at least, a system of formal logic that meets the conditions his was the first to meet—that this question can even be stated in a way that makes it mathematically tractable.

It is in that sense, then, that Frege's approach was more rigorous than existing ones. There is also a sense in which it was more general. When Leibniz attempts to prove the laws of arithmetic, he focuses on such claims as that '2 + 2 = 4'. Frege, however, is interested in more fundamental arithmetical truths, and for good reason. If it is to be shown that *all* truths of arithmetic are provable from logical laws, then, since there are infinitely many of these, this can not be established by literally proving all of them. Rather, some basic arithmetical truths need to be identified, from which all others plausibly follow, and then these *basic* truths need to be proven. That is to say, arithmetic needs to be *axiomatized*, just as Euclid had axiomatized geometry, and then proofs need to be given of the axioms. Frege was not the first to publish such axioms: that honor is typically accorded to Giuseppe Peano, though the historical record makes it clear that Richard Dedekind was actually the first to formulate them.[3] Nonetheless, Frege does state axioms for arithmetic (which are interestingly different from Dedekind's) and his proofs are directed, in the first instance, at these. He also proves, as Dedekind does, that the axioms are sufficient to characterize the abstract, mathematical structure of the natural numbers (up to isomorphism, as it is said, this being a standard test of the sufficiency of an axiomatization).[4]

Of course, one cannot, in the strictest sense, prove the axioms of arithmetic within a system of pure logic: none of the expressions in the language
in which the system is formulated even purport to refer to numbers, so the
axioms of arithmetic cannot even be written down in such a system. What
are required are definitions of the basic notions of arithmetic in terms of logical notions; proofs of the axioms of arithmetic will then become proofs of
their definitional translations into the formal, logical system. The mathematical project is thus, in contemporary terminology, to "interpret" arithmetic in
a system of formal logic: to interpret one theory—call it the target theory—
in another—call it the base theory—is to show that definitions can be given
of the primitive vocabulary of the target theory (in this case, arithmetic) in
terms of the primitives of the base theory (in this case, some formal theory
of logic), so that definitional transcriptions of the axioms of the target theory
become theorems of the base theory.[5] At the very least, such a result shows
that the target theory is *consistent*, if the base theory is: for, if there were a
proof of a contradiction to be had within the target theory, that proof could
be replicated within the base theory, by proving the needed axioms of the target theory within the base theory, and then appending the derivation of a contradiction, in the target theory, to them. Hence, if there is no proof of a
contradiction to be had within the base theory, there will be none to be had
within the target theory, either.

Such interpretability results were well-known to geometers working in
Frege's time—and, indeed, Frege was a geometer by training. Such techniques
were among the most frequent used to establish the consistency of various
sorts of non-Euclidean geometries—geometries which reject the parallel postulate. Proofs of the consistency of such geometries usually amounted to
proofs that they could be interpreted within other sorts of theories, whose
consistency was not in doubt (for example, within Euclidean geometry itself).

It is worth emphasizing, however, that interpreting arithmetic within a
system of formal logic will not necessarily help us to discover the epistemological status of arithmetic—*even if* we are agreed that the 'system of formal
logic' really is a system of *logic*, or in other words, that all of its theorems are
analytic truths. The problem can be illustrated as follows. It was Frege's view
that, not just arithmetic, but also analysis (that is, the theory of real numbers),
is analytic. If so, given a definition of ordered pairs, the theory of Euclidean
geometry can be interpreted in analysis, by means of Cartesian co-ordinates.
Does it then follow that, on Frege's view, Euclidean geometry must be analytic? That would be unfortunate, for Frege explicitly agreed with Kant that
the laws of Euclidean geometry are synthetic *a priori*. But, in fact, there is
no inconsistency in Frege's view here. What the interpretability result establishes is just that what *look like* the axioms of Euclidean geometry can be

proven within analysis. The question is whether what *looks like* the parallel postulate really does mean what the parallel postulate means. That is, the question just begs to be asked whether the 'definitions' of fundamental geometrical notions in fact capture the meanings of those notions, as we ordinarily understand them—for example, whether 'a point is an ordered triple of real numbers' is a good definition of the word 'point', as it is used in geometry. If it is not, it has not been shown that the truths of Euclidean geometry can be proven in analysis: not if we identify "truths of Euclidean geometry" by what they *mean* and not just by their orthographic or syntactic structure.

A corresponding question will arise in connection with Frege's definitions of fundamental arithmetical notions. It will, that is to say, be open to a Kantian to question whether the definitions Frege gives do in fact capture the meanings of arithmetical notions as we ordinarily understand them. If they do not, then Frege will not have shown that the truths of arithmetic can be proven within logic, but only that sentences *syntactically* indistinguishable from the truths of arithmetic can be so proven. And that is not sufficient. So another large part of Frege's project has to be, and is, to argue that the fundamental notions of arithmetic are *logical* notions, that his definitions of them in logical terms are good definitions, in this sense.

Let me summarize the discussion to this point. Frege's philosophical project, to show that the laws of arithmetic are analytic, that they can be known on the basis of reason alone, has a mathematical aspect. The primary goal is to define the fundamental arithmetical notions in terms of notions of pure logic, and then, within a formal system of logic, to prove axioms for arithmetic. That is how Frege will identify "the basic laws of arithmetic," the fundamental assumptions on which arithmetical reasoning is founded. As important as this part of the project is, however, it does not answer the epistemological question on its own, for two sorts of questions remain open. First, there is space for the question whether Frege's definitions of the basic arithmetical notions really do capture their meaning—and so whether we have really succeeded in proving the axioms of *arithmetic* and so in identifying its basic laws. And second, even if that question is answered affirmatively, we will have to ask what the epistemological status of the basic laws is: only if they are themselves truths of logic, analytic truths, will the proof show that the axioms of arithmetic are analytic truths. As we shall see, both questions have been prominent in the literature generated by Frege's project.

2. Frege's System of Formal Logic

The formal logical system Frege develops in *Begriffsschrift* is, in essence, what we now know as full, impredicative second-order logic: it allows for quantification over 'concepts'—the extra-linguistic references of predicates—and relations, as well as over objects. The system as it is presented in *Begriff-sschrift* does not, however, meet the demands of rigor Frege imposes. In particular, one of its most important rules of inference is never explicitly stated, the rule in question being a rule of substitution. One might think that Frege's omission here is inconsequential: isn't it just obvious that, if one has a proof of some formula, then the result of substituting various other expressions for the variables that occur in that theorem should also be a theorem? Maybe so, but the claim that substitution is a valid form of inference is, in the context of second-order logic, an extremely powerful one.

In Frege's system, the rule of substitution plays the role played in more modern formulations by the so-called axioms of comprehension: the comprehension axioms characterize the concepts and relations over which the variables of the theory are supposed to range; that is, each of them asserts that a particular concept or relation *exists*. In full second-order logic, one has such a comprehension axiom for every formula of the theory, and the comprehension axioms then jointly assert that every formula $A(x)$ defines a concept, namely, that true of the objects of which the formula is true; that every formula $B(x, y)$ defines a two-place relation; and so forth. And without comprehension axioms, second-order logic is very weak. Indeed, even if we allow ourselves so-called predicative comprehension axioms—that is, even if we assume that formulae which do not *themselves* contain second-order quantifiers (which do not quantify over all concepts and relations) define concepts and relations—the resulting logic is still weak, in a well-defined technical sense.

Many philosophers have worried that appeal to impredicative axioms of comprehension introduces a kind of circularity into the characterization of the concepts and relations over which the variables of the theory range. The worry, as it appears in Russell, for example, is that it must be circular to characterize the concepts the theory talks about by quantifying over the concepts the theory talks about. Although Frege never discussed this problem, his response, I think, would have been to say that he does not propose to *say* what concepts lie within the domain of the theory by means of the comprehension axioms: the domain is to contain *all* concepts, and the question how any one of them might be *defined* should not be allowed to determine whether it *exists*; the comprehension axioms simply *assert* that every formula defines a concept.[6] But let me not pursue the matter further here.

Frege's failure to state a rule of substitution in *Begriffsschrift* is, thus, an important omission. But it is one he remedies in his later presentation of his formal theory in *Grundgesetze der Arithmetik*. In fact, his presentation of the system there is as rigorous as any before Gödel mathematized syntax in the early 1930s.

The axioms of arithmetic cannot, however, be proven within full second-order logic alone. It can easily be shown that even the claim that there are two distinct objects is not a theorem of second-order logic; but arithmetic posits the existence, not just of two, but of infinitely many natural numbers. It is *this* claim that is the central obstacle to any Logicist development of arithmetic. Indeed, it is hard to see that there is any more difficult problem facing one who would answer the epistemological question with which we are concerned than to explain the genesis of our knowledge that there are infinitely many numbers, whatever sort of answer she might ultimately want to give.

3. Three Lessons and a Problem

As said above, Frege argues, in the first three chapters of *Die Grundlagen*, that Kantian and empiricist philosophies of arithmetic will not do. He comes away with three lessons on which he proposes to base his own view, and with one very large problem. The first lesson is that the natural numbers are to be characterized, as Leibniz suggested, by defining "zero" and "increase by one." This is clear enough, and we shall see below how Frege intends to define these notions. The second lesson is harder to understand: Frege puts the point by saying that "the content of a statement of number is an assertion about a concept" (*Gl*§55). What he means is that that to which number is ascribed is not, strictly speaking, *objects*. Suppose I were to say, pointing to a pile of playing cards, "How many?" You might answer by counting the cards and telling me that there are 104. But then again, you might answer 2. It all depends upon how you take my question, which contains an ambiguity that can be resolved by asking: How many *what*? How many cards? Or how many complete decks? But then, it would seem, the number 104 is ascribed not to the pile of cards, their aggregate (or "fusion"), that somewhat scattered object whose parts are all and only the parts of the cards: for the number 2 can as justly be ascribed to that aggregate (for the decks have the same parts the cards do). One might conclude from this that ascriptions of number are subjective, that they essentially depend upon our way of *regarding* the aggregate to which number is assigned. But there is an alternative: to say, with Frege, that number is ascribed to a *concept*, in this case, either to *card on the table* or to *complete deck of cards on the table*.

That having been said, it is overwhelmingly natural to suppose that numbers are a kind of higher-order property, that they are *properties* of concepts.[7] For example, 0 would be the property a concept has if nothing falls under it (so the concept *disco album in my collection* has the property zero, since I do not own any disco albums). A concept will have the property 1 if there is an object that falls under it, and every object that does fall under it is identi-

cal with that one (so the concept *object identical with George Clinton* would
have the property 1, since George Clinton falls under it, and every object that
does is identical with him). And a concept will have the property *n+1* if there
is an object, *x*, that falls under it and the concept *object that falls under the
original concept, other than x*, has the property *n*. Thus, the concept *object
that is identical with either George Clinton or James Brown* will have the
property 1 + 1 (i.e., 2), for there is an object falling under it, namely, the Godfather of Soul, such that the concept *object that is identical with either George
Clinton or James Brown, other than the Godfather of Soul*, has the property
1, for this is just the same concept as *object identical with George Clinton*,
described in other words.

Frege discusses this sort of proposal in §§55–61 of *Die Grundlagen*. It is
not entirely clear why he rejects it, but it seems plausible that his reason, ultimately, is that such an account will not enable us to prove the axioms of arithmetic—not, that is, without some further assumptions. Suppose that there
were exactly two objects in the world, call them George and James. Then there
will be a concept that has the property 0; there will be others that have the
property 1; and there will be one that has the property 1 + 1. But there will
be no concept that has the property 1 + 1 + 1: for there to be such a concept,
there would have to be one under which three objects fell and, by hypothesis, there are only two objects in existence. Nor would any concept have the
property 1 + 1 + 1 + 1, for the same reason. Just how one wants to describe
the situation here is a delicate question: one can either say that there is no
number 1 + 1 + 1 or one can say that 1 + 1 + 1 and 1 + 1 + 1 + 1 turn out, in
this case, to be the same. Either way, though, there will be only finitely many
numbers, and the laws of arithmetic cannot be proven. (For example, depending upon how we choose to describe the situation, either 2 + 2 will not exist
at all, or it will be the same as 2 + 1.)

Of course, there are not just two objects in existence: but a similar problem will arise if there are only finitely many. The situation can be remedied
if we simply assume, as an axiom, that there are infinitely many objects: this
is the course Russell and Whitehead take in *Principia Mathematica*. Frege
would not have had any interest in this sort of 'solution', though. As I have
said, the really hard problem facing the epistemologist of arithmetic is to
account for our knowledge that there are infinitely many numbers. It is hard
to see how assuming that we know that there are infinitely many *other* sorts
of things is supposed to help. Proving the laws of arithmetic from such an
assumption simply leaves us with the question of its epistemological status,
and that is no advance, since the epistemological status of just this assumption was the hard problem with which we started. Moreover, if the objects we
assume to exist are supposed to be *physical* objects like George Clinton, it

seems unlikely that the claim that there are infinitely many of these is one *logic* could establish: indeed, one might well wonder whether it is even *true*.

The third lesson, then, is supposed to be that, despite the fact that an ascription of number makes an assertion about a concept, numbers themselves are *not* properties of concepts: they are *objects*. To put the point grammatically, number-words are not *predicates of predicates*, but *proper names*. (It should, all along, have seemed strange to speak of zero as being a property of a concept, to say such things as that the concept *disco album in my collection* has the *property* zero!) One might wonder how these two doctrines can be jointly held: the answer is that we need only insist that the most fundamental sort of expression that names a number is one of the form 'the number belonging to the concept F', and that this is a proper name. Ascriptions of number, such as 'There are 102 cards on the table', then get re-cast as identity-statements, for instance: the number belonging to the *concept card on the table* is identical with 102. This does, as it were, *contain* an assertion about a concept, but the number 102 does not appear as a *property* of a concept.

This, however, leaves Frege with a problem. He has denied that arithmetic is either synthetic *a priori* or *a posteriori*, partly on the ground that numbers are not given to us either in perception or in intuition. How then *are* they given to us? What, so to speak, is the mode of our cognitive access to the objects of arithmetic? Frege's way of answering this question is subtly to change it, writing:

> Only in the context of a proposition does a word mean something. It will therefore suffice to explain the sense of a proposition in which a number-word occurs. . . . In our present case, we have to define the sense of the proposition "the number which belongs to the concept F is the same as that which belongs to the concept G"; that is to say, we must reproduce the content of this proposition in other terms, avoiding the use of the expression 'the number which belongs to the concept F'. (Gl§62)

It is here that Frege makes 'the linguistic turn'. It is not, of course, that no philosopher before him had ever been concerned with language; Locke, for example, was obsessed with it and argued, repeatedly, that various sorts of philosophical problems were the results of illusions fostered by misunderstandings of language. (Perhaps Locke was the first logical positivist.) What is original about Frege's approach is that the epistemological problem with which he begins is transformed into a problem *in the philosophy of language*, not so that it can be discarded, but so that it can be *solved*.

The answer to the epistemological question that is implicit in Frege's treatment of it is that our cognitive access to numbers may be explained in terms of our capacity to *refer* to them, in terms of a capacity to denote them by means of expressions we understand. Of course, if the capacity to refer to an object by means of a proper name itself depended upon our having, or at least being able to have, perceptions or intuitions of it (or of other objects of its kind), no actual benefit would accrue from reconceiving the problem in this way. But it is precisely to deny that the explanation must proceed in such terms that Frege invokes the 'context principle', the claim that the meaning of an expression can be explained by explaining the meanings of complete propositions in which it occurs. The goal, in this case, will be to give the definition of 'the number belonging to the concept F is the same as that belonging to the concept G' in terms of concepts which themselves belong *to pure logic*. If that should be possible, it will follow that there is, so to speak, a purely logical route to an understanding of expressions which refer to numbers, that is, to a capacity to refer to them—and so to a capacity for cognitive access to them.

Frege notes, quoting from Hume, that a criterion for sameness of number is ready to hand. Suppose, for example, that I want to establish that the number of plates is the same as the number of glasses. One way, of course, would be to count them, to assign numbers to the concepts *plate on the table* and *glass on the table* and then to see whether these numbers are the same. But there is another way: I can pair off the plates and the glasses, say, by putting one and only one glass on each plate, and then see whether each plate ends up with a glass on it and whether there are any glasses left over. That is to say, I can attempt to establish a 'one-one correlation' between the plates and the glasses: if there is a one-one correlation to be had, the number of plates is the same as the number of glasses; otherwise not.

Indeed, as Frege is fond of pointing out, the process of counting itself relies upon the establishment of one-one correlations.[8] To count the plates *just is* to establish a one-one correlation between the plates and an initial segment of the natural numbers, beginning with 1; the last number used is then assigned to the concept *plate on the table* as its number. Why, indeed, does the fact that the same number is assigned by this process to the concepts *plate on the table* and *glass on the table* show that the number of plates is the same as the number of glasses? Because, says Frege, if there is a one-one correlation between the plates and the numbers from 1 to n, and another between the glasses and the numbers from 1 to m, then there will be a one-one correlation between the plates and the glasses if, and only if, n is m.

The notion of one-one correlation can itself be explained in logical terms (assuming, that is, that we accept Frege's claim that the general theory of concepts and relations, as developed in second-order logic, does indeed count as logic). For a relation R to be a one-one correlation between the Fs and the Gs is for the following two conditions to hold:

1. The relation is one-one, that is, no object bears R to more than one object, and no object is borne R by more than one object

2. Every F bears R to some G and every G is borne R by some F

In contemporary symbolism:

$$\forall x \forall y \forall z \forall w[Rxy \ \& \ Rzw \rightarrow (x = z \equiv y = w)] \ \&$$

$$\forall x[Fx \rightarrow \exists y(Rxy \ \& \ Gy)] \ \& \ \forall y[Gy \rightarrow \exists x(Rxy \ \& \ Fx)]$$

And we can now say that *there is* a one-one correspondence between the Fs and the Gs if *there is* a relation R that satisfies these conditions. Say that the Fs and Gs are 'equinumerous' if so. The definition on which Frege settles is then:

the number of Fs is the same as the number of Gs if, and only if, the Fs and the Gs are equinumerous.

This has come to be called *Hume's Principle*, since, as I have said, Frege introduces it with a quotation from Hume (*not* because anyone thinks Hume really had this in mind).

4. The Caesar Problem and Frege's 'Solution'

The status of this explanation of 'the number of Fs' is one of the major open problems with which Frege's philosophy of arithmetic leaves us. It is worth emphasizing, however, that the problem is more general than whether it provides us with a *purely logical* route to an apprehension of numbers. Frege's idea is that a capacity for reference to abstract objects can, in general, be explained in these sorts of terms. Thus, he thinks, our capacity to refer to *directions* can be explained in terms of our understanding of names of directions, these in turn explained by means of a principle analogous to Hume's Principle, namely:

the direction of the line a is the same as the direction of the line b if, and only if, a is parallel to b.

This does not promise a *purely logical* route to an apprehension of directions, on Frege's view, since lines are given to us only in intuition. But that does not matter: the *directions* of lines are *not* given in intuition (or so he claims), and so there is a corresponding problem about how they are given to us, a problem to which he offers a corresponding solution (see G*l* §§64–65). This sort of answer to the question how we are to explain our capacity to refer to abstract objects thus generalizes in a natural way, and the exploration of its strengths and weaknesses has occupied a number of philosophers in recent years.[9]

Oddly enough, however, Frege ultimately rejects the claim that Hume's Principle *does* suffice to explain names of numbers. The stated reason is that the definition "will not decide for us whether [Julius Cæsar] is the same as the [number of Roman emperors]—if I may be forgiven an example which looks nonsensical."[10] Hume's Principle tells us what statements of the form "the number of *F*s is the same as the number of *G*s" mean; but it utterly fails to tell us what statements of the form "*q* is the number of *G*s" mean, except when "*q*" is of the form "the number of *G*s" (see G*l* §66). It is far from obvious, though, why this is supposed to be a problem. I myself have come to the conclusion that it is not one problem, but many. First of all, as Frege notes, we do not seem to be in any doubt about Caesar: whatever numbers might be, he's not one of them; *a fortiori* he's not the number of Roman emperors. And it's hard to see what the basis of this knowledge could be, if it was not somehow contained in our understanding of names of numbers. (It isn't an *empirical* fact that Caesar isn't a number!) But if it is, then the offered explanation of names of numbers must, at least, be incomplete, since it does not capture *this element* of our understanding of them.

The second worry can be seen as arising out of this one. When I said above that Caesar is not a number, I used *the concept of number*: if we understood the concept of number, it would be easy to answer the question whether some object, call it *a*, is the number of *F*s. For either *a* is a number or it is not. If it is not, it certainly isn't the number of *F*s; and, if it is, then it's the number of *G*s, for some *G*, so Hume's Principle will tell us if it is the number of *F*s. Moreover, it seems clear that what Frege needs to explain is not just our capacity to refer to individual numbers, but our understanding of the concept of number itself. Given Hume's Principle, the natural way to try to do so is to say that something is a number if there is a concept whose number it is. But if we spell that out, we find that what we have said is that *a* is a number if, and only if, there is a concept *F* such that *a* is the number of *F*s. And as said, Hume's Principle simply fails to explain what "*a* is the number of *F*s" is supposed to mean: so, unless there is some other way to define the concept of number, we will be without any understanding even of *what it means* to say that Cæsar is not a number.

All of this having been said, I think we can now begin to see what the problem with Hume's Principle—considered as a definition or explanation of names of numbers—is supposed to be. The object, recall, was to explain our cognitive access to numbers by explaining our capacity to refer to them;

and to do that by defining, or explaining, names of numbers in purely logical terms. But now consider Hume's Principle again:

the number of Fs is the same as the number of Gs if, and only if, the Fs and the Gs are equinumerous,

and focus especially on its left-hand side. This *looks like* an identity-statement: but what reason have we to think it really is one? Why think that "the number of Fs," as it occurs here, is a *proper name* at all? That is, that the sentence has the *semantic*, as opposed simply to *orthographic*, structure of an identity-statement? Why not say instead that "the number of Fs is the same as the number of Gs" is just an incredibly misleading way of *writing* "the Fs and the Gs are equinumerous?" If, in fact, the sentence *did* have the semantic structure of an identity-statement, it would have to be legitimate to replace "the number of Fs" with names of other kinds, for example, "Caesar," and so to consider such sentences as "Caesar is the number of Gs." Or again, it must be permissible to replace "the number of Fs" with a variable and so to consider such "open" sentences as "x is the number of Gs," and to ask whether they are true or false when the variable takes various objects, such as Caesar, as its value. But what the above observations show is that Hume's Principle, on its own, simply does not explain what sentences like this are supposed to mean. And that calls into doubt whether it really does explain *identity-statements* containing *names of numbers*.

This problem is of particular importance within Frege's philosophy. I mentioned earlier that one of his central goals is to explain the genesis of our knowledge that there are infinitely many numbers, that one of his central reasons for insisting that numbers are objects is that only then can this claim be proven. Frege's strategy for proving it is to argue thus: let 0 be the number belonging to the concept *object which is not the same as itself*; it is clear enough that 0 is indeed that number. Let 1 be the number belonging to the concept *object identical with 0*; 2, the number belonging to the concept *object identical with either 0 or 1*; and so forth. Again, it is clear enough that 1 and 2 are indeed these numbers; and only if we treat numbers as objects can we speak of such concepts as these. But, when we formalize Frege's argument within second-order logic, the expression 'the number belonging to the concept F' will be cashed as: the number of x such that x is an F. And thus, the definitions of 0, 1, and 2 become:

0 is the number of x such that $x \neq x$

1 is the number of x such that $x = 0$

2 is the number of x such that $x = 0$ or $x = 1$

And so forth. And when we replace '0' with its definition in the second line, we get:

1 is the number of x such that: $x =$ the number of y such that $y \neq y$

So Frege's definition of 1 contains an open sentence of the form "x is the number of Fs"—precisely the sort of sentence Hume's Principle is impotent to explain.

It is a nice question—a question which has been the focus of much research in recent years—whether there is a way around this problem. For present purposes, however, let me just record it. For, whatever its ultimate resolution, Frege himself declared it insoluble and so abandoned the attempt to use Hume's Principle as an explanation of names of numbers. In its place, he installs an *explicit* definition of names of numbers:

the number belonging to the concept F is: the extension of the concept *concept equinumerous with the concept F*.

Extensions here can be thought of as sets: the number of Fs is thus the set of all concepts which are equinumerous with the concept F. So 0 will turn out to be the set of all concepts under which nothing falls; 1, the set of all "singly instantiated" concepts; 2, the set of all "doubly instantiated" concepts; and so on and so forth.

This move, however, turned out to be disastrous. In order to give this definition within his formal system of logic, Frege requires some axioms that tell us what we need to know about the extensions of concepts. And, if Logicism is to be established, the axioms need, at least plausibly, to be logical truths. There is an eminently natural axiom to hand. Talk of the "extensions" of concepts is governed by a principle of extensionality, that the concepts F and G will have the same extension only if every F is a G and every G is an F—if, that is to say, the Fs just are the Gs. And surely, one might say, every concept must *have* an extension. So the necessary axiom can be taken to be the following:

the extension of the concept F is the same as the extension of the concept G iff every F is a G and every G is an F.

Taken as a *definition* or *explanation* of names of extensions, this principle would suffer from problems similar to those afflicting Hume's Principle. Frege therefore does not so take it, but regards it as an axiom, saying in *Die Grundlagen*, simply that he "assume[s] it known what the extension of a concept is" (*Gl* §68 note).

Unfortunately, however, this axiom, which in *Grundgesetze* becomes Frege's Axiom V, suffers from far greater problems of its own: in the context of full second-order logic, it is *inconsistent* since, as Russell showed, paradox arises when we consider the concept *object that does not fall under any concept whose extension it is* and ask whether *its* extension falls under it. If it does, it doesn't; and if it doesn't, it does. Whoops.

5. Frege's Theorem

In 1980, the story would have ended here. Frege does show that, given Axiom V and the definition of numbers as extensions of certain concepts, the axioms of arithmetic can all be proven. But this fact is uninteresting, since *anything* can be proven in an inconsistent theory. The axioms of arithmetic can be proven, but then so can their negations! A closer look at the *structure* of Frege's proofs reveals something interesting, however. Although Frege abandons Hume's Principle as a definition of names of numbers, he does not abandon it entirely—he continues to assign it a central role within his philosophy (see *Gl* §107). Frege is not entirely explicit about why, but the reason seems, to me anyway, to be that he did not regard Hume's Principle as *wrong*, but as incomplete. The concept of number really is, according to Frege, intimately bound up with the notion of one-one correlation; but one cannot use this observation to *define* names of numbers *via* Hume's Principle. Still, any acceptable definition must be compatible with Hume's Principle, must yield it as a relatively immediate consequence. Completing the definition then takes the form of providing an explicit definition from which Hume's Principle can be recovered. And, indeed, the very first thing Frege proves, once his explicit definition has been given, is that Hume's Principle follows from it.

It was Charles Parsons who first observed, in his paper "Frege's Theory of Number,"[11] that, once Frege has proven Hume's Principle, the explicit definition quietly drops out of sight—and, with it, all further references to extensions. That is to say, the proof proceeds in two quite separate stages: first, there is a proof of Hume's Principle from Axiom V and the definition of names of numbers in terms of extensions; and then, there is a proof of the axioms of arithmetic from Hume's Principle within pure second-order logic. The observation did not cause much of a stir, however, for no special interest would attach to it unless Hume's Principle were, unlike Axiom V, *consistent* with second-order logic, and Parsons did not so much as raise the question whether it is.

Almost twenty years later, Crispin Wright re-discovered what Parsons had observed and showed in detail how the axioms of arithmetic can be derived from Hume's Principle in second-order logic.[12] He also showed that an attempt

to replicate Russell's paradox within the new system fails—and he conjectured that the new theory was in fact consistent. Once formulated, the conjecture was quickly proved.[13] Call the second-order theory whose sole
'non-logical' axiom is Hume's Principle *Frege Arithmetic*. Then it can be
shown that Frege Arithmetic is consistent, if second-order arithmetic is; that
is, if Frege Arithmetic is inconsistent, so is second-order arithmetic. But if
second-order arithmetic were ever shown to be inconsistent, that would pre-
cipitate a crisis in the foundations of mathematics that would make the discovery of Russell's paradox look trivial by comparison. So Frege Arithmetic
is (almost certainly) consistent. And *second-order arithmetic can be interpreted within it*: given appropriate definitions, one really can prove the axioms
of arithmetic from Hume's Principle, in second-order logic. Let me say that
again: *All truths of arithmetic* follow logically from the principle—seemingly
obvious, once one understands it—that the number of Fs is the same as the
number of Gs if and only if the Fs are in one-one correspondence with the
Gs. It is this surprising and beautiful theorem that is now called Frege's Theorem. And study of the detailed, formal proof Frege gives of the axioms of
arithmetic in *Grundgesetze* has shown that, charitably read, it does indeed
amount to a proof of Frege's Theorem.[14]

How is Frege's Theorem proven? It would be inappropriate to give a complete proof of it here, but it is worth giving the reader some sense of how the
proof goes. Let us write "$\#x{:}Fx$" to mean "the number of x such that x is an
F;" let "$Eq_x(Fx,Gx)$" abbreviate the formula which defines "the Fs are equinumerous with the Gs." Then Hume's Principle can be written:

$\#x{:}Fx = \#x{:}Gx$ iff $Eq_x(Fx,Gx)$

Frege then defines zero as the number of the concept *non-self-identical*:

$0 =_{df} \#x{:}x \neq x$

We also need to define 'increase by one'. What Frege actually defines is
a *relation* between numbers which we may call the relation of predecession:
intuitively, a number m is one less than a number n if, so to speak, a concept
has the number m whenever it is one object short of being a concept which
has the number n. That is, m (immediately) precedes n just in case there is a
concept F and an object y such that: the number of Fs is n; y is an F; and the
number of Fs, other than y, is m. (Compare the definition of '$n{+}1$' considered in section 3.) Formally, Frege defines:

$Pmn \equiv_{df} \exists F \exists y[n = \#x{:}Fx \ \& \ Fy \ \& \ m = \#x{:}(Fx \ \& \ x \neq y)]$

Now, among the axioms of arithmetic will be the following three claims: that zero has no predecessor; that no number has more than one predecessor; and that no number has more than one successor. All of these are now easily proven.

Consider the first, for example. Suppose that zero did have a predecessor, that is, that, for some m, we had $Pm0$. Then, by definition, there would be a concept F and an object y such that:

$$0 = \#x{:}Fx \ \& \ Fy \ \& \ m = \#x{:}(Fx \ \& \ x \neq y)$$

That is to say, 0 is the number of Fs, y is an F, and m is the number of Fs, other than y. *A fortiori*, there is a concept F, whose number is 0, under which *some* object falls. But that is impossible. For 0 is the number of the concept *non-self-identical* and so, if 0 is the number of Fs, the number of Fs is the same as the number of non-self-identical things; and so, by Hume's Principle, there must be a way of correlating the non-self-identical things one-to-one with the Fs. But that there can not be, if something, say y, is an F: which non-self-identical thing is y supposed be correlated with? So nothing precedes zero. The proofs of the other two axioms mentioned are a little harder, but not much.

There are two more axioms that need to be proven; these axioms make crucial reference to the notion of a *natural* (or *finite*) number, and that has not yet been defined. One of the two axioms is the principle of mathematical induction. Induction is a method for proving that all natural numbers have some particular property: the method is to show (i) that 0 has the property, and then to show (ii) that, if a given number n has it, then, its successor, $n{+}1$ must also have it. Why, intuitively, does the method work? Well, suppose that both (i) and (ii) hold. Then, certainly, 0 has the property. And so, by (ii), $0{+}1$, i.e, 1, must also have it; hence, by (ii) again, $1{+}1$, i.e., 2 has it; so 3 has it; and so on. So, all natural numbers have it, because *all natural numbers can be "reached" from 0 by adding one.*

Frege's definition of natural number in effect transforms the italicized clause into a definition. Here is something we know about the concept *natural number*: (i′) 0 falls under it; and, (ii′) whenever an object falls under it, so does the successor of that object (if it has one). Now, there are lots of concepts which satisfy conditions (i′) and (ii′): for example, the concept *is self-identical* satisfies them, since *every* object falls under it. But not every concept satisfies the conditions: the concept *is identical with zero* does not, since 1 is the successor of 0 and does not fall under the concept, whence it fails to satisfy (ii′). So some concepts satisfy (i′) and (ii′) and some do not: call a concept *inductive* if it does. What can we say about the inductive concepts? Well, if a concept is inductive, surely every natural number must fall under it: 0 will, by (i′); so 1 will, by (ii′); and so on. Or, to put the point differently, if there is an inductive concept under which a does *not* fall, a is not a natural number. Conversely, if a is not a natural number, then there is an inductive concept under which it does not fall: namely, the concept *natural number* itself. So a is not a natural number if, and only if, there is an inductive concept under which it does not fall. Or, negating both sides of this claim:

> a is a natural number if, and only if, it falls under *every* inductive concept.

And that, now, can be taken as a *definition*. Note that it will just *fall out* of the definition that proof by induction if valid: for if the hypotheses of the induction, (i) and (ii), are satisfied, then the property in question is inductive; so every natural number will have it.

One might worry that there is some kind of circularity in the last paragraph. It is important to realize, however, that any circularity there might be here does not lie in Frege's definition. We can say what an inductive concept is without appealing to the concept of *natural number*. Formally, we have:

$$\text{Nat}(a) \equiv_{df} \forall F[F0 \,\&\, \forall x \forall y(Fx \,\&\, Pxy \rightarrow Fy) \rightarrow Fa]$$

Whatever circularity there might be lies, rather, in the argument used to motivate the definition, that is, *in the argument given for the claim that it properly defines the concept "natural number"*—and that sort of objection, as I said earlier, is in order here, since Frege does need for his definitions to capture the meanings of the primitive arithmetical notions. This sort of objection was originally pressed by Henri Poincaré, but has in recent years been developed by Charles Parsons.[15] Let me not discuss it further, however, except to say that it is bound up with the concerns about impredicativity mentioned earlier in connection with the comprehension axioms for second-order logic.

The only axiom for arithmetic that we have not discussed is the most important: that every natural number has a successor. The axioms so far established do not, on their own, imply that there are infinitely many numbers; in fact, they are consistent with there being only *one* number, namely, zero. In their presence, however, the claim that every number has a successor implies that there are infinitely many numbers: for then, 0 will have a successor, call it 1, from which it must be distinct; if 0 were 1, then 0 would precede itself, so 0 would have a predecessor, which it does not. But then 1 has a successor, call it 2; and 2 must be distinct from 0 (if not, 0 would again have a predecessor, namely, 1) and from 1 (otherwise 1 would precede itself and 0 would also precede it, contradicting the fact that no number has more than one predecessor). And then 2 will have a successor, call it 3, which will be distinct from 0, 1, and 2; and so on.

How, then, are we to prove that every number does have a successor? Frege's argument is far too complex for me to explain it in detail here, but the basic idea behind it has been mentioned above. Basically, we are to take the successor of 0 that is, 1, to be $\#x\!:\!x = 0$; the successor of 1, that is, 2, to be $\#x\!:\!(x = 0 \lor x = 1)$; and so forth. So, in general, the successor of a number n will be the number of x such that x is either 0 or 1 or . . . or n. The argument can be made rigorous, and it can be shown to work.

6. Closing: The Philosophical Significance of Frege's Theorem

So, Frege's Theorem shows that the axioms of arithmetic can be proven, in second-order logic, from Hume's Principle. What are we to make of this fact, philosophically? Does it show that Logicism is true? Not, presumably, if Logicism is the claim that the truths of arithmetic are truths of *logic*, for there is no good reason to suppose that Hume's Principle is itself a truth of logic. Indeed, given how the notion of logical truth tends to be understood in contemporary philosophy, so that a truth of logic is something true in all interpretations, Hume's Principle has just been proven *not* to be a truth of logic, since it is not true in any interpretation whose domain is finite.

Still, though, one might think that Hume's Principle is, even if not a truth of *logic*, at least of a similar epistemological status. Wright suggests, for example, that it can, and should, be understood, as embodying an *explanation* of names of numbers—or, to put the point less technically, that we can come to know that it is true simply by reflecting upon what number-words *mean*. If, in that sense, it is *analytic of* the concept of number, then the axioms of arithmetic turn out to follow from a Principle which is analytic, in an extended sense, and that would seem enough to satisfy Frege's epistemological ambitions. And if that is not Logicism, surely it is rightful heir to the name.

This view has been the subject of a great deal of discussion over the last ten years or so. The problems it faces may be divided into two groups: the Caesar problem and the "bad company" objection. Enough has already been said about the former above: the Caesar objection, as was said, purports to show that Hume's Principle *cannot* be taken as an explanation of names of numbers. But let me not discuss it further here.

The "bad company" objection is so-called because it has the following form. Even though Hume's Principle is not *itself* inconsistent, it is of a form which can give rise to inconsistency. For example, Axiom V is, as was said earlier, inconsistent, and the two principles are both of the form:

the blah of *F* is the same as the blah of *G* iff the *F*s so-and-so the *G*s

where "so-and-so" stands for some relation between concepts which is, in technical parlance, an equivalence relation (that is, which has the formal properties necessary to guarantee that the definition will not contradict the laws of identity). Now, one might well say, what's the problem? To quote Michael Jackson, "One bad apple don't spoil the whole bunch of girls." But still, if there are problems that affect claims formally similar to a given one, then, even if they do not themselves affect the given claim, it is natural to suspect that those problems will, upon closer examination, be seen to be manifestations of deeper problems that *do* affect the given one.

One way to develop this objection is as follows. The claim that Hume's Principle is *true* is one that commits us, minimally, to its consistency; it is hard to see how we can claim to *know* it to be true unless we are also prepared to claim that we *know* it to be consistent. Not that we do not know this: we do, as surely as we know much else we claim to know in mathematics. But the proof that it is consistent is one that can be formalized only within an exceptionally strong mathematical theory, one (by Gödel's theorem) essentially stronger than Frege Arithmetic (or second-order arithmetic) itself. And it seems to be asking us to swallow a lot to suppose that we can come to know anything like *that* simply by reflecting upon the concept of number.

This objection, however, is difficult to evaluate. For one thing, anyone attracted to the claim that arithmetic is analytic is already asking us to swallow a lot. The argument would seem to show, at best, that Wright ought to claim not just that we know Hume's Principle to be true, but that we know it to be consistent, which is more. And what's a little more? Moreover, there are worries about the form of argument that was deployed in the last paragraph: it appears to be of a sort that drives many kinds of skeptical arguments. Compare: if I know that there is a computer on my desk, then I must also know that there is an external world. Is it supposed to follow that my claim to know that there is a computer on my desk, as it were, depends upon my knowing *antecedently* that there is an external world? If so, we're in trouble, because it is hard to see how, if I suspend belief in all my particular items of knowledge about the world—i.e., subject that knowledge to Cartesian doubt—I could ever recover my senses. And it is a now-familiar move in epistemology to deny that, just because some claim *A* implies some other claim *B*, a claim to know *A* must be *supported by* a claim to know *B*: we may well know that *B* because we know that *A*, and not conversely. But then a similar move would appear to be available in this case: to grant that, if we know that Hume's Principle is true, we know it is consistent, but to deny that our claim to know that it is true need rest upon independent knowledge of its consistency.

However good this response might be, though, there are other worries. If the view is supposed to be that *every* consistent principle of the general form mentioned above is "analytic," it is refutable. Principles of that form are a dime a dozen. And some of the consistent ones are inconsistent *with each other*. Thus, for example, it is possible to write down such principles that, though consistent, imply that there are only finitely many objects. Since Hume's Principle implies that there are infinitely many objects, it is inconsistent with these ones. Worse, choose any proposition you like: it is possible to write down a principle of the form mentioned above that implies it; and, by the same token, it is possible to write down another that implies its negation.[16] So not all such consistent principles can even be *true*, let alone analytically true. What is needed, then, is some way of distinguishing the 'good' principles from the 'bad' ones. But this problem has only begun to be studied, and it is not yet clear whether success is to be had. Even if it is, the question will remain whether there is any ground on which to claim that the good ones are all analytic.[17]

It is worth saying, however, that one should not over-emphasize the importance of this question. Let it be granted that Hume's Principle is not analytic. It might nonetheless be that it has a role to play in a story about the genesis, or foundation, of our knowledge of the truths of arithmetic. The Principle does, after all, have powerful intuitive appeal, and the claim that it is, in some deep sense, integral to our understanding of the concept of number that concepts have the same number if, and only if, they are equinumerous could be true, even if it is *not* true that Hume's Principle is analytic, in any sense that will rescue Frege.

6

What Is the Problem of Measurement?

SIMON SAUNDERS

Simon Saunders was Assistant Professor of Philosophy at Harvard University from 1990 to 1995, and Associate Professor from 1995 to 1996. He is now Reader in Philosophy of Physics at Oxford University, and a Fellow of Linacre College, Oxford. He has published widely on the foundations of quantum mechanics and relativity theory, but he also has interests in logic, philosophy of science, and the history of philosophy.

Quantum mechanics, together with special relativity, are the basis of most of what we know of the very small, the very light, and the very fast. In these areas our knowledge is extensive; it would be hard to say how good these theories are (arithmetic, one might say, is good mathematics). For all that, there is a problem, a strange and amorphous difficulty: the *problem of measurement*. This problem has become much more interesting, and much more pressing, in recent years. Hitherto the difficulty has been so peculiar, and so formless, that physicists have on the whole thought it a matter of philosophy. But it has become increasingly clear that the problem is not *purely* philosophical; that on the contrary, it also has a *physical* dimension (some would say that it is *entirely* a physical problem). The measurement problem is finally coming of age.

What is the problem of measurement? As a first stab, we can say this: there is a difficulty in accounting for the fact that measurements have any outcomes at all. In Heisenberg's words: "it is the 'factual' character of an event describable in terms of the concepts of daily life which is not without further comment contained in the mathematical formalism of quantum theory, and which appears in the Copenhagen interpretation by the introduction of the observer."[1] The interpretation to which Heisenberg refers is usually credited to Niels Bohr, one of the founders of quantum mechanics. It was the orthodoxy for several decades since. But consensus on this matter has crumbled, and it no longer commands much agreement today.

First some remarks on the basic ideas of quantum theory. A fundamental concept of the standard formalism is the *state*, in many ways the analog of the classical concept of state, where one has an exhaustive specification of all the properties of a physical system at a given time. Classically, the state of a system changes in time according to dynamical equations of motion that are fully deterministic. In quantum mechanics there are also equations of motion for the state, called the 'unitary' equations of motion, which are *also* fully deterministic. Just like their classical counterparts, they too respect the familiar space-time symmetries. The important difference is that in quantum mechanics the equation of motion of the state is invariably *linear*. This means that given two quite different states, each a solution of the equations of motion (so each a physical possibility), the sum of the two states (with arbitrary coefficients) is also a solution (is also a physical possibility). From a mathematical point of view, this feature of quantum mechanics is at the heart of the measurement problem: it is called 'the superposition principle'. Only linear wave theories have this property in classical physics, and there of course we never see stable localized objects, of the sort that makes up ordinary matter.

The measurement problem put in these terms is that the state, as it evolves under the unitary equations of motion, does not correspond to any observed motion of matter or, when it comes down to it, to any *imaginable* motion of ordinary matter.

How then does quantum mechanics make contact with ordinary physical systems, of the sort that we actually see? But so far as experiments are concerned there are special, additional principles, the 'measurement postulates'. According to these, one first determines the *kind* of measurement that is about to be performed (whether, say, of particle position, or momentum, or direction of spin). The state of the system at the time of measurement is then written as a list of numbers, each of which gives the *probability* of a particular outcome. The same list can be rewritten in a number of ways, corresponding to the different types of experiments that can be performed, with well-defined rules linking the various lists (rules again involving only linear transformations). In this respect the choice of the type of experiment resembles the choice of rectilinear axes (or 'basis vectors') in Euclidean space; given these, and a vector in that space, its components can also be specified (and again, these components change linearly with change in basis). Since the state must also be "prepared"—it has to be produced by a 'state-preparation device'—the theory gives us a recipe for providing a list of probabilities, conditional on the preparation device, for each possible outcome of the measurement device. That is enough to provide the theory with empirical tests; the observed relative frequencies of outcomes are compared with the theoretically calculated probabilities. And that's it: nothing more than that is provided.

In summary, although the state seems to describe the properties of atoms and electrons and so on, in a way not so different from classical physics; and although it undergoes a complicated and interesting dynamical development in time, again similar to the classical state; it nevertheless only has a clear meaning when the state is referred to *experiments* that we do or might perform, and the probabilities of the various outcomes of those experiments.

What I have said so far is entirely uncontroversial. So far we have a kind of 'minimal' interpretation of the standard formalism—the basic method for applying it. to concrete experiments. The state is on the one hand bound up with the microscopic system, and on the other with the probabilities of measurement outcomes. At this point the problem of measurement is foreshadowed by the simple query as to how the two are to be related.

Instrumentalism

One response is to eliminate altogether the reference to the microscopic system. The state is *only* a list of numbers relating a preparation device with the probabilities of measurement outcomes, the particular list depending on the kind of final measurement to be made.

This is clearly a form of instrumentalism, particularly if no further interpretation of the formalism of quantum mechanics is on offer—if, as Bohr liked to put it, the theory is only a 'symbolic calculus'; if 'there is no quantum reality' (although Bohr was not really an instrumentalist, as we shall in a moment).

Of course, on an instrumentalist interpretation, we do not *have* to deny that there is any underlying microscopic reality. We may plead agnosticism instead. We may suppose that there is a microscopic world, but that quantum mechanics does not describe it directly. The quantum mechanical state, as a summary of the statistical relations between pairs of macroscopic experiments (preparation and detection), does give us something to go on in understanding the microscopic realm, but any puzzles here should not impact on our understanding of what the state is (so says the instrumentalist). There may be a problem of understanding the quantum world, but there is no problem of measurement.[2]

Indeed, if quantum mechanics is understood in this way, we do not so much have a problem of measurement as a problem in making precise the phenomena to which the state *does* refer, the observable preparation and detection processes. Why not describe these processes directly, as undergoing the probabilistic changes that they undoubtedly *do* seem to undergo? If we cannot find a deterministic way of doing this, why not describe them in terms of *indeterministic* dynamical equations? (Nowadays we have plenty of experience of equations like this.) Better still, why not look for a theory which describes the macroscopic quite generally, treating 'experiments' merely as certain sorts of dynamical processes among others? Of course it may be that if we do this we will have to modify or supplement the usual equations of quantum mechanics, but why not make the attempt, so as to accurately depict what we actually see?

There was a time when it was thought that there were *impossibility proofs* obstructing this kind of program. If one makes sufficiently stringent conditions on how much of the quantum mechanics of *microscopic* objects must be preserved (in terms of relationships between certain dynamical variables as given by the unitary dynamics) it is in fact quite easy to rule out any of the alternatives. But this, it was eventually made clear, is not a very convincing argument; it should never have cut any ice for an instrumentalist; even a realist would agree that it is enough to develop a theory of individual processes that agrees with the *observable* data.

Why isn't standard quantum mechanics just such a theory? But the unitary formalism fails to describe the experimental apparatus altogether. Neither do the measurement postulates (not even when supplemented by the "projection postulate", the postulate that is required to account for repeatable measurements—where, if a measured quantity takes a certain value, the state had better be replaced by one that yields that value with certainty, if the theory is to predict what is observed). The measurement postulates make no reference at all to the details of the apparatus, but only to what the apparatus is *intended to measure*—some particular microscopic dynamical variable, expressed in terms of a particular basis. Now if *this* feature of the formalism is held up as a *necessary* (or even as a *desirable*) feature, the philosophy on offer is unmasked as something much closer to idealism. It is the view that quantum mechanics does not describe any physical systems at all, but only our *investigations*, only the *state of our knowledge*.

Once put in this light, it is hard to take this sort of instrumentalism seriously. So long as there are alternatives on offer—whether a modified formalism, or an alternative interpretation of the extant formalism, which provide descriptions of observable phenomena at least—we are bound to reject it. At the very least, we can surely supplement the formalism, making use of the concepts and methods of *classical* physics, at least at the macroscopic level. In practice the latter was never in question, and we do better to clearly acknowledge it. With that the problem of measurement may be stated: what is the relationship between quantum and classical physics? How are the two theories to be reconciled with each other?

The Copenhagen Interpretation

On occasions Bohr hinted at the more idealistic form of instrumentalism just reviewed, but this was not the picture on offer in the early and critical period, when quantum mechanics was newly created, and when the question of whether or not it could be considered fundamental was a matter of urgency (a question that had to be *settled*).

The most important difference is that according to Bohr indeed the quantum mechanical state describes the individual system. It must be referred to a context of experiment, but it is not defined in terms of the statistics of preparation and detection events.

This is the absolutely crucial move: with this, there is a clear notion of 'the microscopic system' in place, the proper object of physical inquiry, no matter that—according to Bohr—there were a number of constraints on what can meaningfully be said of it. In fact Bohr insisted on using fragments of *classical* descriptions (one of a number of mutually exclusive 'complimentary' descriptions)—which fragment, on any particular occasion, to be dictated by the experimental context (and the latter too was of necessity to be described in classical terms). A context of experiment must always be in place if anything meaningful was to be said about the individual microscopic system.

Now for the measurement problem on this strategy. A first version is this: microscopic systems (and hence the macroscopic) are in some sense probabilistic. If the state says all there is to say about the microscopic, so that it is a 'complete' description of the microscopic, then just so far as there are probabilistic microscopic events, then there will be corresponding changes in the state. But the state does not evolve in this way under the unitary equations of motion. It follows that these, the unitary equations, cannot be the whole story; either that or else the state is 'incomplete'.[3]

The admission of incompleteness would be tantamount to admitting that a better, *more* complete description of the microscopic, might yet be found—and that would imply that quantum mechanics was at best an interim theory that should eventually be superseded. Bohr on the contrary insisted on the completeness of the state: its apparent deficiencies were to be attributed to a kind of *philosophical* discovery, conditional to be sure on an empirical one (the existence of Planck's constant), that there is a limitation to the classical 'mode of description'. This leads in turn to the restriction to one or other complementary descriptions, but in the first instance the limitation is this: *no theory of the microscopic, in the sense of a system of precise equations, can be applied to any objective phenomenon* (I shall give the details of this argument shortly). In particular, the unitary dynamical equations, in themselves, cannot dictate the course of events leading to any observed phenomenon.

But Bohr did not formulate the Copenhagen interpretation as a response to the measurement problem. Rather, the constraint just mentioned, what I shall call "Bohr's constraint," was supposed to follow from a more fundamental epistemological principle, namely that *an objective phenomenon is only defined relative to an observation,* where the latter must necessarily be described by means of classical concepts. I shall call the latter "Bohr's principle of significance" (or "Bohr's principle" for short); it has clear affinities with Kant's philosophy.

For Bohr it was therefore more than satisfactory that the concept of observation should enter into the measurement postulates, although he had no particular inclination to bring in its wake subjective aspects of observation, or anything purely mentalistic.[4] Chiming with this, it was a matter of indifference as to whether one introduced only the experimental apparatus, or also the observer (so long as it was described classically). Further, it did not matter very much precisely where the apparatus was supposed to leave off, and where the system under measurement begin: for Bohr the point of the apparatus was to establish a fragment of the classical mode of description (one or other complementary descriptions), to be applied to the quantum system too. (Here Bohr was on dangerous ground. It is true that the predicted probabilities are stable under changes in this boundary—the von Neumann 'cut'—but not if it is pushed too far to the microscopic.[5])

Finally, the last and most important ingredient of Bohr's interpretation was what he called "the quantum postulate." At times this sounded like a purely empirical principle (the existence of Planck's constant), but the use Bohr made of it extended well beyond any empirical evidence: the postulate "attributes to any atomic process an essential discontinuity, or rather individuality, completely foreign to the classical theories and symbolized by Planck's constant of action." Bohr used this to supplement the *classical* description of the experimental process, to describe the effect on the underlying microscopic system, and *vice versa.*

Here is Bohr's account of the matter:

Now, the quantum postulate implies that any observation of atomic phenomena will involve an interaction with the agency of observation not to be neglected. Accordingly, an independent reality in the ordinary physical sense can neither be ascribed to the phenomena nor to the agencies of observation. After all, the concept of observation is so far arbitrary as it depends upon which objects are included in the system to be observed. Ultimately, every observation can, of course, be reduced to our sense perceptions. The circumstance, however, that in interpreting observations use has always to be made of the theoretical notions entails that for every particular case it is a question of convenience at which point the concept of observation involving the quantum postulate with its inherent "irrationality" is brought in. (p. 54)

The 'irrational' element—that shows up not in the unitary dynamics, but in the marriage of quantum and classical concepts (concepts that *must* be married, according to Bohr's principle of significance)—is not to be further explained. One can of course produce a more encompassing description of the apparatus, referring it to some other experimental context, but one gains nothing by that: thereby one only shifts the von Neumann cut.

There is an 'irrational' element to nature: so stands the measurement problem on Bohr's philosophy. The unitary formalism cannot be used to illuminate the process of measurement; on the contrary, it is by appeal to the context of measurement, bringing into play the quantum postulate, that one interprets the unitary formalism in terms of one of a number of complementary descriptions.

The discrete change in the action, in multiples of Planck's constant, was also called 'the quantum jump', and, in terms of wave mechanics, 'the collapse of the wave-packet'. It can be incorporated into the measurement postulates (and it must be so incorporated for the special case of repeatable measurements) as the projection postulate. To put the conclusion of Bohr's argument in these terms, one should not expect to analyze the process of reduction of state in terms of the unitary equations (or any other precise system of equations); it is already taken care of by the measurement postulates.

The conclusion is attractive, as it solved a number of embarrassing questions about the nature of state reduction (non-local, indeterministic), which was quite unlike the unitary equations (local, deterministic). Others tried to find simpler arguments to a similar effect. A popular strategy was to view the observer in purely mentalistic terms: if state reduction ultimately concerns the mental, as something irreducibly distinct from the physical, then no wonder the equation for it is so peculiar, and without any physical criterion for when it kicks into play.[6] In less fanciful terms, the state is only to describe our *knowledge*; state reduction merely reflects *changes* in our state of knowledge (which, under the unitary equations, does *not* change). On this view the state, along with quantum mechanical probabilities, is purely epistemic. But once put in these terms, we are relinquishing the key feature of Bohr's approach: we no longer describe the individual system. It is to revert back to the instrumentalism-cum-idealism already considered. Or, on the uncomfortable thought that there ought after all to be a correlate to a state of knowledge (that our knowledge, and any change in our knowledge, is *about* something, and reflects *changes* in something) it slides over into another position entirely, namely that there are in addition goings on in atomic systems not so different from quantum jumps—'potentia', to use Heisenberg's term, that are or may be 'actualized'. But the inevitable implication of *this* point of view is the incompleteness of the state. Heisenberg, in embracing this line of reasoning, did not appear to understand how far he was departing from Bohr's philosophy.[7] On this view, there is no good reason why one should not attempt to describe this underlying reality in more detail. Any interpretation of the state as epistemic, which falls short of idealism, is likely to lead to this conclusion. This was always perfectly obvious to Einstein.

It is likely that the Kantian background to Bohr's philosophy was never much appreciated by his contemporaries; very likely they did not even understand it. But here was philosophy being used to give cover. It provided a rational to make do with the theory as it was handed down to them. Any obscurity in the interpretation could be considered a purely philosophical difficulty—someone else's problem. And of course, from a purely pragmatic point of view, none of this really mattered, for the theory (if only under the 'minimal' interpretation) was proving to be amazingly successful. For physics it was business as usual; in fact, physics had never had it so good.

The Macroscopic Quantum State

Business as usual included the thought that there are macroscopic events. Pursuit of this thought, understanding that the quantum state describes individual microscopic states of affairs, led to attempts to apply the formalism of quantum mechanics in the description of individual *macroscopic* states of affairs as well, particularly in thermal physics. This started quite innocuously, with some exciting experimental physics (superfluidity; superconductivity; the Ising model; phase transitions). The area continued to flourish. Applications of quantum mechanics to condensed matter physics soon became commonplace. This is the first stage in the unraveling of the Copenhagen orthodoxy.

At this level it is only a shift of emphasis. Nothing in the Copenhagen interpretation prohibited the application of quantum mechanics to large systems. But proceeding in this way it was found that certain classical concepts, and laws, can after all be coded into the quantum formalism, without resource to some background experimental context (of the sort that was supposed to define 'the conditions of meaningful discourse', the object as a 'phenomenon').

What was at issue with the alleged necessity of classical concepts? According to Bohr they are forced, no matter that they must be restricted by the quantum postulate:

> The recognition of the limitation of our forms of perception by no means implies that we can dispense with our customary ideas or their direct verbal expressions when reducing our sense impressions to order. No more is it likely that the fundamental concepts of the classical theories will ever become superfluous for the description of physical experience. (p. 16)

The argument is on the face of it purely pragmatic, and as such it was widely accepted. Here is how Heisenberg put the matter:

> Our actual situation in science is such that we do use the classical concepts for the description of the experiments, and it was the problem of quantum theory to find theoretical interpretation of the experiments on this basis. There is no use in discussing what could be done if we were other beings than we are. At this point we have to realize, as von Weizsäcker has put it, that "Nature is earlier than man, but man is earlier than natural science." The first part of the sentence justifies classical physics, with its ideal of complete objectivity. The second part tells us why we cannot escape the paradox of quantum theory, namely, the necessity of using the classical concepts. (pp. 55–56)

But with increasing experience in the treatment of large systems we learn that there is no real difficulty in the treatment of macroscopic systems either, at least as goes for their thermodynamic properties. In these (typically static) situations the measurement postulates had been effectively bypassed. Of course any such descriptions will still be constrained by the uncertainty relations; we do not arrive at classical properties that involve absolutely precise position and momentum (or velocity). But at the everyday level these imply no new constraints at all on what we see, or even what we (classically) judge to be the case. The uncertainties are minute for ordinary objects; they are already swamped by thermal fluctuations. It is true that there remains the problem of what it *means* to speak of uncertainty, or imprecision, but that is nothing new to philosophy: most if not all of our everyday thing-words are vague; the problem remains even if we take classical mechanics to be fundamental.[8]

Success in applying quantum mechanics to macroscopic systems is in itself only a small step, but it leads on to another. It raises a question about

Bohr's principle of significance. It may be that we don't actually have to have a context of measurement in place, in order to interpret the formalism—or that if we do, that we can do justice to Bohr's principle by modeling the context of measurement itself in quantum mechanical terms. If so, then Bohr's argument is completely undercut. We can if we wish respect his principle of significance, but it no longer implies his stricture against the application of quantum mechanics to closed systems; it no longer implies Bohr's constraint.

We can see the lacuna in the argument in its very first appearance:

> On one hand, the definition of the state of a physical system, as ordinarily understood, claims the elimination of all external disturbances. *But in that case, according to the quantum postulate, any observation will be impossible*, and, above all, the concepts of space and time lose their immediate sense. On the other hand, if in order to make observation possible we permit certain interactions with suitable agencies of measurement, not belonging to the system, an unambiguous definition of the state of the system is no longer possible, and there can be no question of causality in the ordinary sense of the word. The very nature of the quantum theory thus forces us to regard the space-time co-ordination and the claim of causality, the union of which characterizes the classical theories, as complementary but exclusive features of the description, symbolizing the idealization of observation and definition respectively. (p. 54, emphasis mine)

The argument, if sound, would show that no precise theory of the microscopic could be applied to anything other than a closed system—in which case it would no longer describe an objective phenomenon (here, an object in space and time; later, the object as phenomenon). The essential difference with classical physics is that in the latter case external disturbances can be made as small as you like, and the system still be considered an observed system; in the quantum case, because of the finiteness of the quantum of action, that is no longer the case. But the argument is not even valid: the fallacy occurs in the statement italicized, which stands in need of a missing premise: that observation is always *external* to the system, that it is never *from within* the system. But that premise appears quite arbitrary; we can perfectly well incorporate Bohr's principle by considering the observer as *internal* to the system, with the whole being modeled in terms of the unitary formalism. There is after all no *philosophical* argument, from the existence of a lower bound to the action, to the conclusion that there can be no precise description of an observed phenomenon. There is no philosophical reason not to use the equations of quantum mechanics to model the measurement process.

There is, of course, *another* reason: the problem of measurement. Specifically, it is that whilst we can interpret components of the state, without any need for introducing the observer, we cannot interpret their superposition—

and it is superpositions of such states that we arrive at by the unitary dynamics. The logic of Bohr's position is then quite different from how it first appeared. It is because of the *problem of measurement* that we cannot apply quantum mechanics to the measurement process.

Decoherence Theory

There is an important insight underlying this argument of Bohr's, however. There is a kind of coupling, introduced by 'observation' (or let us just say by the environment) that destroys interference effects in a way that is entirely independent of its strength. Interactions like this are ubiquitous; at ordinary temperatures and pressures they are also extremely rapid, occurring over timescales far smaller than even the most energetic elementary processes. If we decompose the state into components like these, we can explore the effects of the unitary equations of motion without ever having to worry about interference effects.

If so, it is a matter of indifference whether, considering one component of the state and its subsequent forward evolution in time, we bother to retain all the other components. If there are no interference effects, it will make no difference to the calculations of any of its transition probabilities. This is the reason why the probabilities are insensitive to the position of the von Neumann cut, supposing that as the cut is varied, one still has available the same non-interfering decomposition of the state. A basis like this is called a 'decoherence' basis; the study of this general field is 'decoherence theory'. It has even proved possible to set out a similar condition on the basis in the absence of a distinction between the system and its environment (as in the 'decohering histories' formalism).

At the more mathematical level, interference effects between components of the state depend on the phase relationships between these components—just as sound waves reinforce or cancel one another, depending on whether they are in phase or have opposite phase. The absence of interference effects means that a superposition of states can be replaced by a catalog of those states (a 'mixed state') with all their phase relations annulled. This catalog of states will still contain information about their relative weights, interpreted as the various probabilities that one or other of the states in the mixture is the one that *actually obtains* (these probabilities can now be viewed as *epistemic*). All along, what prevented one from interpreting a superposition of states in this way was the presence of interference effects. In other words, decoherence theory tells us when a superposition of states can be replaced by a mixture; equivalently, when a pure state can be *interpreted* as if it were a mixture.

The choice of basis, recall, is what in the instrumentalist interpretation, and what in Copenhagen philosophy, was bound up with the choice of experiment. A 'complementary' description amounted to an interpretation of the state as a mixture, when the basis was dictated by what the experiment was intended to measure. But here it is a matter of how the macroscopic world is described in quantum mechanics, including the experimental apparatus. 'Intentions' no longer have anything to do with it. The macroscopic world is treated as a whole; quantum mechanics is here applied to closed systems. Without any mention of 'the observer', quantum mechanics in and of itself has brought forth a description of the macroscopic world, all the way down to molecular levels.

The Problem of Measurement

It might now be thought that the problem of measurement has been solved; certainly decoherence theory has transformed the nature of the problem. In fact, I suggest it has only made the difficulty more immediate. What remains of the problem of measurement? Only this: with the effective washing out of the relative phases among components of the decoherence basis, it may be that interference effects are effectively eliminated; but this process is *only* an effective one. It always remains true (except in unrealistic infinite volume or infinite time limits) that there are physical quantities whose predicted values (using the measurement postulates) *do* depend on these phases. If, to get rid of these, we model the replacement of the superposition by *one or another* of the states entering into the mixture (and not by the 'effective' mixture), then something more radical is needed.

Nothing forbids us from modifying the unitary formalism; all that is needed is a mechanism that takes us from a decohering superposition of states, to one or another of those states, with the requisite probability. But this is our old friend, the reduction of state. Using decoherence theory—to be precise, decoherence theory as it arose in the study of the quantum mechanics of "open" systems—we now know how this may be done, in a way that makes no reference at all to the observer (but only to the physical nature of the environment, or the experimental apparatus, described in *quantum mechanical* terms). In effect the situation where "there can be no question of causality in the ordinary sense of the word," to use Bohr's words, has indeed been described by exact systems of equations.

In fact, it is now perfectly clear that these equations may be perfectly deterministic. The simple deterministic mechanism proposed long ago by de Broglie accomplishes this goal quite simply. Here, in the 'pilot-wave theory', the quantum formalism is supplemented by an equation, the 'guidance equation', which provides a family of trajectories each of which picks out one member of the basis at each instant of time (*which* one, we can imagine, being settled in advance, as part of the initial data).

For an indeterministic model, one of the best known is the modification of the unitary equations due to Ghirardi, Rimini, and Weber (the so-called 'GRW theory'). Here certain parameters, that in decoherence theory vary somewhat with the details of the application (as parameters of an "effective" theory) are now to be viewed as new and fundamental constants of nature.[9] Using these, one can define stochastic equations of motion.

But the existence of these alternative, deviant formalisms, and the recognition that they are perfectly adequate at least to all known *non-relativistic* quantum effects, only renders the problem of measurement more acute. For on the one hand they show conclusively that the problem of measurement *can* be solved, by modifying the physical formalism; but on the other hand they show that the modifications in question are extremely significant—that, in point of fact, the obstacles confronting the attempt to extend these sorts of theories to the relativistic domain are truly horrendous.[10] Lacking the relativistic symmetries, at least in the form in which they figure in relativistic quantum field theory, these theories cannot as yet deal with any high-energy phenomena at all. It is high-energy particle physics that now poses the problem, not 'the quantum postulate', or anything emerging from the Kantian tradition that Bohr found so beguiling. Here it seems that fundamentally new *physical* ideas are needed—including, even, the modification or abandonment of the relativity postulate itself.

The dilemma is all the more puzzling given that decoherence theory grew out of the study of the unitary formalism of quantum mechanics (a formalism which extends to relativity theory without any fundamental difficulty). The very success of this enterprise appears to have called into question the foundations of the discipline. Reflecting on the history of the problem of measurement, we see that the key developments all revolve around the notion that the quantum mechanical state is the correlate of individual states of affairs. By a natural and perhaps inevitable progression, this leads to the supposition that there is a quantum-mechanical correlate to *macroscopic* states of affairs as well. And now it seems that that must be correct; decoherence theory turns on this, its success cannot be gainsaid. We *have* obtained a probabilistic, macroscopic description, as an effective theory; we cannot turn our back on this result. But it seems we cannot push through with this program either, to make of the theory a literal one and not only an effective formalism, or not without penalty in the relativistic regime.

It is a torturous predicament. *In extremis*, then, we come to the remaining, and incredible, alternative. It is to rest with the unitary dynamics, according to which, with respect to the decoherence basis, *superpositions* of macroscopic states of affairs indeed propagate unitarily and covariantly. The entire superposition evolves in a perfectly deterministic manner, respecting the relativistic symmetries (it is only if *one* of these components is selected at each instant in time that one runs into problems with relativity). And this is a possible (but incredible) alternative because were the superposition retained, it would still *appear*, from the point of view of a system described by one of the components, as if the state were reduced on measurement. Or better (for talk of 'appearance' is suspect), *it will in fact be the case* that such a system (a macroscopic object among others) will be correlated with precisely the same environment, *whether or not* all other components of the state are killed off, so *whether or not* there is in fact any state reduction.

The remarkable implication (as first pointed out by Hugh Everett in 1957) is that the unitary evolution is in fact sufficient to account for all the observable evidence—at the price that *all* physically possible states of affairs are realized in some part of the universal state (hence the "many-worlds" interpretation, as it was called by DeWitt). And this, of course, is simply incredible. For many it is a price that is far too high to pay.

We have arrived at the measurement problem as it stands today. There are plenty of ways of solving it in the non-relativistic case; there are plenty of avenues to be explored for solving it in the high-energy case—but at the likely price of the relativistic symmetries. There is no internal *philosophical* argument against proceeding with them (unless it is the very general one that it is implausible that physicists are about to *redo* the bulk of their theorizing over the last half century). But against this, we do appear to *already* have a solution to the measurement problem, which is perfectly consistent with the basic quantum mechanical and relativistic symmetries, and which leaves particle physics intact as it is—but which few of us can believe.

Philosophy and Physics

If we hold relativistic and quantum mechanical principles to be fundamental—and we can scarcely do otherwise—then we must hold the universal state to be the fundamental object of physics. If we hold the visible universe to be the fundamental object of physics—and we can scarcely do otherwise—then these principles cannot be fundamental.

The dilemma is inescapable, and, if I am right that the universal state can only be successfully interpreted along Everett's lines, disquieting. Few in this situation can feel very sanguine in their choice. But equally, it is clear that the fundamental principles of relativity and quantum mechanics are anyway under challenge in the field of quantum gravity; there string theory and the canonical and path-integral quantization programs, theories which aim to respect the relativistic and quantum mechanical symmetries, have yet to deliver. It is entirely plausible to suppose that one or other of these symmetries will have to be anyway given up in this arena. If here there is progress— and ideally experimental discoveries—introduced by novel principles in conflict with the familiar ones, then the situation will be transformed. Better, then, as onlookers, to sit on the fence.

The actors here are the physicists: they will have to vote with their feet. If past form is anything to go by, there will be other problems that will take precedence over the problem of measurement—the problem of making any definite predictions, for example. It will be the ideas that work at this level, in the end, that will decide the matter. The dilemma as I have stated it is likely to be soon settled.

Assistance may come from another direction, however. It may be that an interpretation along Everett's lines cannot after all be sustained. There are plenty of objections that can be raised against it, quite apart from the one that it is unbelievable, but to date they all of them depend on philosophical arguments. It is perfectly possible that other objections will arise as well, depending on theoretical and experimental arguments, but the immediate objections are philosophical.

To get a sense of them, it is enough to sketch out the ideas using terms familiar to philosophy. Lewis's writings provide a ready context. We are to suppose that there is only the *superposition* of physically possible histories, determined by the choice of a decohering set of variables (and their corresponding bases). These histories are therefore effectively autonomous from each other (we do not have to consider interference effects from other histories). Using center-of-mass variables we obtain histories that are recognizably, approximately, classical; they can be described using approximately classical laws (corrected of course when it comes to quantum mechanical effects as evidenced at the macroscopic level). The essential difference, now, from Lewis's modal metaphysics, is that whilst these histories all co-exist, they are not separate worlds in his sense. They are not physically closed-off from one another. In Lewis's terms they are worlds that all *overlap* (that have segments in common); they are, in fact, worlds that branch in one direction only (towards the future – this *defines* what we mean by future). This branching involves fission, not divergence. Branching, viewed from within one of the off-shoots, appears as the quantum jump or reduction of state. It is only here that there is anything like a concept of probability coming into play. Probabilities supervene on perfectly categorical properties and relations—the relative norms of the states entering into the

branching—in accordance with Lewis's Humean supervenience thesis, as
defined by perfectly deterministic laws.

It should be evident that in the background of this interpretation is the
structural view of time and personal identity that has long been at the center
of the philosophical literature on these topics;[11] it is here being extended to
the remaining physical modalities (physical possibility, necessity, and chance).
It has long been clear that there are plenty of parallels between the modality
of time and of possibility (between 'the now', as an indexical, and 'the actual',
as an indexical, and the opposing views in both cases); more contentious is
the interpretation of probability in terms of branching.

I have said enough to make clear some of the difficulties. There are any
number of philosophical objections that can be raised against Everett's proposal, but it will be for philosophers to decide if they are fatal to it. At issue
is a question of physics, but of a metaphysical order that we have not seen
since the time of Descartes. The problem of measurement has long been
ignored by physicists; if they were right to ignore it, and the principles of relativity and quantum mechanics are after all to stay in place, then it can no
longer be ignored by philosophers.

Historical Note

The concept of decoherence has long been familiar; it already figured in Mott's
analysis of the cloud chamber in 1929. It resurfaced in the 'DLP' theory of
measurement in the early 1960s (after Daneri, Prosperi, and Loingers). More
than one champion of the Copenhagen interpretation reconsidered in consequence (Leon Rosenfeld, Bohr's faithful disciple, is an example). General
(and rigorous) treatments along these lines, taking the thermodynamic limit,
are due to K. Hepp, who supposed that the limiting procedures used were as
"natural [here] as elsewhere in microphysics." Subsequent investigators include
B. Whitten-Wolfe, G. Emch, D. Lewis, L. Thomas, and A. Frigerio, but the
most important development from the point of view of decoherence theory
was the general theory of quantum semigroups as systematically formulated
by E.B. Davies (*The Quantum Mechanics of Open Systems*, Academic Press,
1976). This was a major stimulus for the work of G. Ghirardi, A. Rimini and
T. Weber in 1986 (the GRW proposal), for whom the phenomenological model
was to be considered fundamental. Others who contributed to this program
included L. Diosi, P. Pearle, A. Barchielli, N. Gisin, and I. Percival. References to these papers can be found in the works cited below.

The same ideas, but explored in a way that was supposed to involve no
modification to the quantum formalism, were applied in a variety of concrete
physical models over the last two decades. Here results of W. Unruh, W. Zurek,

E. Joos, A. Caldera, and A. Legett were particularly influential. The notion then in vogue was that of 'environmentally-induced superselection rules', no matter that it was quite clear that the rigorous notion of superselection sectors does not permit the unitary development of the state from one sector to another. For an illustration of this debate, see the exchange between Zurek and others in the pages of *Physics Today* (October 1991; April 1993); Zurek eventually made clear that his approach is a variant of Everett's.

Different again is the decoherent histories formalism (also called the *consistent* histories formalism), beginning with the work of R. Griffiths in 1984. Contributors include R. Omnès, M. Gell-Mann, J. Hartle, and J. Halliwell; the advantage of this approach is that reference to the environment can be dispensed with, but the constraints that it imposes are significantly weaker than the dynamical decoherence theory, as was made clear by A. Kent and F. Dowker in 1994. This need not matter if the approach is intended as a supplement to Everett's interpretation, however (see my "Time, Quantum Mechanics, and Decoherence," *Synthese* 102, pp. 235–266, which also sketches parallels with the philosophy of time).

The connections between decoherence theory and the pilot-wave theory are the subject of more recent studies. In fact it is often thought that the pilot-wave theory stands quite independent of decoherence theory: so it does as a piece of speculative theorizing, but its adequacy to observed (non-relativistic) phenomena is another matter. But obviously it was not for want of attention to this aspect of the theory that it was so long ignored: on a charitable reading, it was ignored because no relativistic generalization of it could be found. (For a less charitable reading, see J. Cushing, *Quantum Mechanics: Historical Contingency and the Copenhagen Interpretation*, 1994.) Its adequacy in the non-relativistic case should have made clear what was wrong with Bohr's philosophy (for an account of why it did not, see M. Bella, *Quantum Dialog*, Chicago, 1999).[12]

7

Making Sense of Others: Donald Davidson on Interpretation

WILLIAM TASCHEK

William Taschek is an associate professor of philosophy at Ohio State University. His current research interests include the philosophy of language, the philosophy of mind, psychology, metaphysics, and the philosophy of art.

1

Over the last three decades, Donald Davidson has evolved a complex and highly original philosophical program—a program immensely rich in its implications for a wide variety of central issues in the philosophy of language, mind, action, and metaphysics. By way of bringing a few of the diverse elements of this program into sufficient focus to enable us profitably to discuss them, it may be useful at the start to locate Davidson's work within the context of a larger controversy that has concerned humanists since at least the work of Vico and Hegel—a controversy with which you will all be familiar. I have in mind what, in the late nineteenth century, emerged as the controversy over the nature of and the relationship between, on the one hand, the so-called natural sciences, *die Naturwissenschaften*, and, on the other hand, the so-called human sciences, *die Geisteswissenschaften*.

A central feature of that controversy was the question whether the aims and methodology of the human sciences—given the nature of their characteristic subject matter—was inherently distinctive from and irreducible to the aims and methodology of the natural sciences. On the one hand, there emerged what we might loosely call the 'positivist' position, which suggested either that their methods and aims were not inherently distinct or that, if they were, so much the worse for any claimed epistemological legitimacy for the methodology and aims of the human sciences. On the other hand, there emerged a myriad of anti-positivist positions. Of particular interest here—since it is within this tradition that I want to place Davidson—is that strand of opposition to the positivist position that insisted that the aim of the human sciences is not simply to explain human action and its products by subsuming them under appropriate invariant laws, but is, rather, in some distinctive sense, to make the actions, products of actions, indeed, the human beings that perform them, intelligible to us, to make sense of them. On this view, the human sciences necessarily involve an interpretive dimension; the peculiar sort of understanding that is the aim of the human sciences requires interpretation.

Davidson's own concerns and views may, I believe, usefully be understood as belonging to this tradition. In particular, the overarching concern of Davidson's program, as I understand it, is nothing less than the attempt to come to some sort of systematic understanding of the various factors that constitutively enter into and control interpretation: the particular and distinctive way in which we do make sense of human thought and intentional action—including, importantly, speech.

In the standard case, when we are puzzled by an agent's actions and want to make sense of why she acted as she did, we attempt to determine her reasons for so acting. We want it to make sense to us that she acted as she did for the reasons she did. Reflection on these cases suggests that an action (including an utterance) will be intelligible to us—in the relevant sense— only if it makes sense to us that it made sense to the agent that she did what she did. It is important that there be no equivocation here on the relevant notion of making sense.

I want to suggest that this reflexive constraint is an important (and not fully appreciated) internal constraint on the notion of making sense relevant to the interpretive enterprise as Davidson sees it. If this is right, then the following question immediately presents itself: How can whether an action makes sense to an agent make sense to us unless we suppose that the agent shares in large measure precisely those (fundamental) norms of ours, say, norms of rationality, relative to which we evaluate whether our own actions make sense?

If this question is appropriate, it leads directly to a prima facie dilemma. If we are ever in a position to suppose that an agent fails to share our most fundamental standards of intelligibility, we would seem to be precluded in principle from making sense of her actions, thoughts, and words. Alternatively, if we are ever in no position to know whether or not an agent shares our norms, we would seem to be faced with the real possibility that we are illicitly projecting our standards onto our subjects, thus only seeming to make sense of them. Does the sort of interpretation whose aim it is to make sense of others' actions, in the relevant sense, inevitably face this dilemma, or is the problem an illusion based on a misunderstanding of the nature and aims of interpretation?

Although Davidson nowhere sets up his problem in quite this way, nor is he explicit in recognizing what I have called the reflexive constraint on the relevant notion of making sense, his views nevertheless manifest an implicit sensitivity to the constraint and, while aiming to do it justice, provide the material for a compelling response to our dilemma. My hope is that seeing how Davidson might respond to this problem will bring sufficient portions of his overall program into enough focus to enable us usefully to discuss and evaluate them.

2

According to Davidson, the problem posed by our dilemma is, indeed, illusory. A correct understanding of the nature and aims of our interpretive practice will expose the illusion; it is precisely Davidson's project to provide us with just such a correct understanding. Very roughly, Davidson's proposal is something like this. Thought, language, and intentional action are inextricably interrelated; they mutually condition the possibility of one another—and are such that any attempt to understand one of them in isolation from the others is bound to fail. Indeed, it is only in the context of interpretation (of trying to make sense of other's thoughts, words, and actions) that we have whatever grip we have on such concepts as belief, meaning, intention, and so forth. Hence, we cannot make sense of some creature as a potential object of interpretation unless we can make sense of our treating that creature as a thinker, a communicator, and an actor—in other words, as a person.

If it could be argued that regarding a creature as a person—in the rather thin sense just outlined—required in some appropriately strong way the assumption of shared fundamental norms of intelligibility, our dilemma would vanish. If it were a conceptual fact about our concepts of belief, meaning, intention, and so forth that only a creature sharing in large measure our norms can even count as believers, language users, agents—that is, persons—then the purported possibilities raised by our dilemma would be exposed as unintelligible. The question of whether a creature shared our fundamental norms of intelligibility could not—as both horns of our dilemma require—arise independently of whether that creature is a potential object of interpretation, by which I mean a creature with beliefs, a language user, and an agent.

If something like this were defensible, then not only would it be permitted to interpret on the assumption of shared norms of intelligibility, but it would be required. How though might Davidson argue in defense of this position? In order to help sharpen Davidson's position a bit, let me lay out what will, no doubt, already have struck some of you as the two principle alternative responses to our dilemma.

3

The first anti-Davidsonian alternative suggests that we can intelligibly attribute specific cognitive and conative attitudes to a subject, interpret her words, identify her intentional actions, and still find ourselves in principle baffled by her actions. The idea is that we can identify her action as intentional under a certain description, that we can identify those of her beliefs and desires that constitute her reasons for acting as she did, and that, nevertheless, since her norms of intelligibility differ from ours, we are precluded in principle from making any sense of her actions. They make sense to her; but precisely because we don't share the relevant norms, it cannot make sense to us that they do so.

To take this line is, in effect, to embrace the first horn of our original dilemma. If Davidson is to defend his position, he must show that this purported possibility is unintelligible. And he will try to do precisely this by showing that it is in fact not even possible to attribute specific contentful attitudes to a creature nor meanings to its 'utterances', unless we share with it our most fundamental norms of intelligibility.

Suppose Davidson can show this. Would it suffice to establish the sort of strong connection between shared norms and 'personhood' that he requires? The second anti-Davidsonian alternative proposes that this is not enough. According to this second suggestion, we should grant that if a subject failed to share our norms of intelligibility, then we would not in principle be able to interpret her—we would not be able to identify her beliefs, her desires, or even those descriptions under which her actions are intentional; we would certainly not be able to interpret her words. This would not, however, according to the suggestion at hand, suffice to preclude the subject from being a person—a thinker, a speaker, an agent. For after all, she may simply have a radically different conceptual scheme from ours, one incorporating fundamentally different norms of intelligibility. The point here is that someone might agree that interpretability, in the sense of being able to identify the contents of beliefs, desires, and the meanings of uttered words, may require shared norms of intelligibility, but just because we are blocked—even in principle—from identifying those beliefs, desires, and so forth doesn't mean that there are no beliefs or desires, nor that his "utterances" have no meaning.

This second suggestion grants to Davidson something the first suggestion was unwilling to concede, namely, an essential connection between interpretability and shared norms of intelligibility. But it denies that just because a creature is even in principle uninterpretable by us that he isn't a thinker, language user, and agent—for, after all, he may have different norms of intelligibility. An adequate defense of Davidson's position will require that he also show that this second suggestion is unintelligible.

4

Let us begin with the first alternative. For Davidson, the coherent attributability of (propositional) thought in general, of meaning, and of intentional action, requires the attributability to subjects of beliefs (desires also, but we shall focus on beliefs). The attitude of belief plays a central role in Davidson's conception of a potential object of interpretation. For Davidson, to be a potential object of interpretation one must be a creature it makes sense to suppose has beliefs. Interpretation always involves (though is never exhausted by) the attribution of beliefs.

Of central importance, then, is the question: what are the minimal circumstances under which we can coherently ascribe and identify the beliefs of another person? Davidson will argue that it would be perverse to the point of undermining the very possibility of interpretation or communication to (try to) interpret another in such a way as systematically to attribute to her beliefs most of which are ones that one oneself would regard as absurd or manifestly false or irrationally held under the circumstances—beliefs, in other words, that in various ways violate fundamental norms that underwrite our cognitive practice.

Another philosopher, Sydney Shoemaker (in *Self Knowledge and Self Identity*, Cornell University Press, 1963), offers what I think is a telling illustration of the point Davidson wants to make. Shoemaker writes:

> Suppose that we have discovered a new people whose language we do not as yet know, and that someone has proposed a way of translating this language that involves regarding a certain class of statements (or utterances) as perceptual statements and another class as memory statements. Suppose further that we find these statements to be most commonly uttered, confidently and assertively, in circumstances in which their proposed translations would be false. For example, the expression translated by the English sentence "I see a tree" is commonly uttered, confidently and assertively, when the speaker's eyes are not open or not directed toward a tree, and the expression translated by the English sentence "I ate meat last night" is frequently uttered by vegetarians but seldom by anyone who did eat meat on the previous evening. If this happened, surely there could be no reason

for regarding the proposed way of translating their language as correct, and there would be every reason for regarding it as mistaken. (p. 232)

The point this passage makes is that we damage the intelligibility of our readings of the utterances of others when our method of reading them puts them into what we regard to be massive or inexplicable error and irrationality. In other words, we damage the intelligibility of our interpretations of the utterances of others if our method of interpretation has us usually and inexplicably disagreeing with them. But now plainly, this point, though made in the context of interpreting utterances, is inextricably connected with the correlative idea that we would likewise damage the intelligibility of our attributions of beliefs to others were our method to yield widespread and inexplicable error and irrationality. Davidson's suggestion is that if our current best efforts systematically to interpret another creature would have us attribute to her massive error, incoherence, and irrationality (by our lights of course) across the board, that is, if they made her totally incomprehensible to us, then what better evidence could we have that we have failed accurately to identify the relevant beliefs?

One must be careful not to misunderstand Davidson here. He would allow that in a perfectly ordinary sense we can and often do interpret others in ways that makes them mistaken about a great many things. But the point is that there are limits in principle to how far we can go. The reason we miss this is because we tend primarily to notice and focus on our disagreements and find little occasion to reflect on the vast reservoir of mostly trivial beliefs that we share.

Indeed, as Davidson will argue, it is precisely our agreement with respect to some such vast body of unverbalized, usually trivial beliefs that gives content to our voiced (as well as unspoken) disagreements. This is an extremely important point. According to Davidson, without this fund of agreement, there would be no comprehending the differences—we would be in no position to know what we were disagreeing about, and so we couldn't know that we were disagreeing. Indeed, according to Davidson, the very possibility of objective disagreement only makes sense against the background of a vast reserve of agreement. We can, perhaps, hear in Davidson's view an echo of a sentiment expressed by Wittgenstein in his *Philosophical Investigations*, section 242: "If language is to be a means of communication, there must be agreement not only in definitions, but also (queer as this may sound) in judgments."

The point, then, is not that we want to exclude all disagreements. Disagreements about some (perhaps many) beliefs seems inevitable. Rather, Davidson's point is that the very intelligibility of such disagreement—as well, needless to say, of agreement itself—requires a vast common ground of belief.

And this is because, according to Davidson, we cannot take ourselves to be talking about or thinking about the same things and thereby agreeing or disagreeing unless there is this background of shared beliefs.

Davidson's argument for this point runs roughly like this: Plainly, we cannot intelligibly take ourselves to be disagreeing with someone unless we can take ourselves to be talking about or thinking about the same thing or things as that other individual. In other words, we cannot intelligibly take ourselves to be disagreeing with someone unless we can identify her beliefs and recognize that they concern the same subject matter about which we hold a differing opinion. But now, according to Davidson, we cannot intelligibly suppose that we and another are talking about or thinking about the same things—that the subject matter of our beliefs is relevantly the same—unless there is a substantial background of shared beliefs involving the very concepts or notions in terms of which the dispute is couched. And why is this? The primary reason has to do with the holistic way in which, according to Davidson, the contents of thoughts are individuated and the centrality that beliefs in particular play in this. The idea is that any thought, including a belief, is identified and described only within a dense pattern of other thoughts—especially other beliefs. This is what Davidson has in mind when, in "Thought and Talk", he writes:

> It is doubtful whether the various sorts of thought can be reduced to one, or even to a few: desire, knowledge, belief, fear, interest, to name some important cases, are probably logically independent to the extent that none can be defined using the others, even along with such further notions as truth and cause. Nevertheless, belief is central to all kinds of thought. If someone is glad that, or notices that, or remembers that, or knows that, the gun is loaded, then he must believe that the gun is loaded. Even to wonder whether the gun is loaded requires the belief, for example, that a gun is a weapon, that it is a more or less enduring physical object, and so on. There are good reasons for not insisting on any particular list of beliefs that are needed if a creature is to wonder whether a gun is loaded. Nevertheless, it is necessary that there be endless interlocked beliefs. The system of such beliefs identifies a thought by locating it in a logical and epistemic space. (in S. Guttenplan, ed., *Mind and Language*, Clarendon, 1975, p. 156)

Davidson is suggesting here that any thought has the content it does in virtue of its location in a pattern of beliefs and thoughts—not the least important of which is its standing in various epistemic and logical relations (that is, norm-governed relations) with vast numbers of other beliefs that in relevant respects share features of the content of that thought. In other words, my thought that the gun is loaded could not plausibly count as just that thought unless I also believed, for example, that guns were weapons, that they were relatively enduring physical objects, that they can be used to shoot people, that pistols and rifles and plausibly cannons are guns, that their efficacy depends upon their being loaded, that loading involves adding bullets or something that counts as ammunition, that guns are not the sort of thing you swallow to get rid of a headache, that guns are not good to eat, that guns aren't afraid of the dark, and so on, and so on. It is in virtue of having this, or some relevantly similar, open-ended, interlocking collection of beliefs and other thoughts that make it the case that the thought in question is plausibly a thought about guns anyway. Lots of these beliefs are trivial and would hardly bear mentioning, and yet if most of them were not held, if instead we supposed their contraries to be held, then the plausibility of counting the original thought a thought about guns would quickly evaporate.

This example helps to illustrate two points. First, it makes plausible the claim that the content of any particular belief is importantly a function of its place in, and essentially depends upon there being, a vast network of other thoughts—most importantly other beliefs—the contents of which themselves concern features of the subject matter of the original thought. And second, it suggests that the intelligibility of attributing a particular thought to someone rests upon the possibility of attributing to him lots of other thoughts, lots of other beliefs—but beliefs, notice, most of which importantly must be true and intelligibly held by our lights. To assume that a person has only or mostly false beliefs about guns is to undermine the intelligibility of the assumption that any of his beliefs are about guns! It is just this set of ideas that, for Davidson, underwrites application of the so-called 'principle of charity' in interpretation: interpret another's utterances so as to minimize inexplicable error and irrationality.

To be sure, in practice we individuate and identify beliefs, as we do desires, intentions, and meanings, in a great variety of ways. But according to Davidson, consideration of the pattern of relations among beliefs (and among beliefs and the other attitudes) always plays a decisive constitutive role. And reflection makes it clear that the guiding principles of appropriate pattern identification derive ultimately from normative considerations—in particular, from our fundamental norms of intelligibility.

The conclusion, then, is that we can only understand the beliefs, thoughts, and words of another if we can suppose that her beliefs are incorporated in a pattern that is in essential respects like the pattern of our own beliefs, which is to say, a pattern essentially governed by our norms of intelligibility. If this is right, then the first anti-Davidsonian suggestion proves to be unintelligible. However, even if we accept this much, we are still left with the second anti-Davidsonian possibility suggested earlier: the possibility of radical conceptual difference grounded in radically different norms of intelligibility.

5

Before directly examining Davidson's argument against this possibility, I want very roughly to outline those considerations that, according to Davidson, show that propositional thought requires language, that only interpreters can be thinkers. Though this is a bit of a detour, it will, I believe, eventually help clarify an otherwise obscure feature of Davidson's "official" argument against the possibility of radical conceptual difference.

The present argument proceeds in three stages. First, we argue that propositional thought requires belief. This will have been established if we accept Davidson's views, just rehearsed, concerning the centrality of belief in the holistic determination of thought content. Next, we argue that having beliefs requires, in some sense, possessing the concept of belief. And finally, we argue that possessing the concept of belief, in the relevant sense, requires being an interpreter, a language user.

Davidson very succinctly lays out this argument in two paragraphs toward the very end of "Thought and Talk" (p. 170). The argument is explored in more detail in his "Rational Animals" (reprinted in *Actions and Events: Perspectives on the Philosophy of Donald Davidson*, ed. by E. LePore and B. McLaughlin, Blackwell, 1985, pp. 473–480). A propos the second step of the argument, Davidson writes:

> Can a creature have a belief if it does not have the concept of belief? It seems to me it cannot, and for this reason. Someone cannot have a belief unless it understands the possibility of being mistaken, and this requires grasping the contrast between truth and error—true belief and false belief.

And a propos the final crucial stage, he writes:

> We have the idea of belief only from the role of belief in the interpretation of language, for as a private attitude it is not intelligible except as an adjustment to the public norm provided by language. It follows that a creature must be a member of a speech community if it is to have the concept of belief. And given the dependence of other attitudes on belief we can say more generally that only a creature that can interpret speech can have the concept of a thought. Though there are many questions that could be raised concerning both the first and second steps of this argument, the principal interpretive difficulty, I believe, concerns just how we are to understand this last step. How exactly is having the concept of belief, or better, of objective truth, supposed to depend on the possibility of interpretation?

At the end of "Rational Animals" (p. 372), after presenting an analogy concerning the apparent impossibility, for an individual bolted to the earth, of giving content to the concept of an object's being located a certain distance from him, Davidson writes:

> Not being bolted down, I am free to triangulate. Our sense of objectivity is the consequence of another sort of triangulation, one that requires two creatures. Each interacts with an object, but what gives each the concept of the way things are objectively is the base line formed between creatures by language. *The fact that they share a concept of truth alone makes sense of the claim that they have beliefs* [my emphasis], that they are able to assign objects a place in the public world.

The conclusion of these considerations is that rationality (by which, in this context, he means possessing propositional attitudes) is a social trait. Only communicators have it.

The gist of Davidson's point here would seem to be something like this. Having beliefs requires understanding the possibility that what one takes to be the case may not in fact be the case. To understand this possibility just is (as far as Davidson is concerned) to have the concept of belief. Perhaps one need not admit this possibility with respect to all one's beliefs—say, one's beliefs in simple and obvious logical truths—but unless one admitted it with respect to some, if not most, of one's beliefs, one could not properly be said to have the concept of belief, nor, indeed, attitudes we should be willing to call beliefs. Understanding the possibility that what one takes to be the case may not in fact be the case is tantamount to having a conception of objective truth. So according to Davidson, having a conception of objective truth is constitutively tied to being what we might call a self-conscious believer: having the concept of belief or of objective truth involves the recognition that the way I take things to be may be mistaken.

As a self-conscious believer, in this minimal sense, I must understand the distinction between my merely taking something to be the case and something in fact being the case. One might suppose that all that I ever have at my disposal, so to speak, is what I take to be the case, the way things seem to me. But without an appreciation of the distinction between how I take things to be and how they are it seems impossible for me even to have a conception of things seeming to me to be any particular way, for evidently the notion of a thing's seeming to be a particular way only makes sense in the context of a possible contrast to the way things actually are. Now what is required if we are to make sense of my appreciating that there may be a difference between the way things seem to me and the way they are?

Davidson's suggestion seems to be that I cannot have a conception of the relevant contrast unless I can understand the possibility of another subject entertaining the same thought as my own, though significantly disagreeing with my attitude toward it—that is, where I believe it, she does not. In other words, Davidson is arguing that belief requires the conception of another and potentially contrary point of view on the same subject matter. This would seem to be what Davidson is driving at when in the "Rational Animals" passage (quoted earlier) he writes that it is the fact that creatures "share a concept of truth [that] alone makes sense of the claim that they have beliefs, that they are able to assign objects a place in a public world." The claim, then, seems to be that this conception of another point of view on the same subject matter can only emerge in the context of interpretation.

Davidson admits that these considerations (of which I have given only the roughest outline) do not amount to an airtight argument for the claim that only communicators can be self-conscious believers and hence thinkers. Nevertheless, if one finds them persuasive at all, it should now seem that the burden of proof will be on Davidson's opponent, who will need to show exactly how something short of, or other than and not presupposing, communication suffices to underwrite a conception of objective truth, of the contrast between the way things seem to me and the way they are.

For our present purposes, the important consequence of Davidson's argument, if we accept it, is this: if it is indeed the case that it is only in the context of interpretation that the relevant contrast emerges, then it will follow that the only concepts of truth and objectivity that we have are precisely those that emerge in the context of interpretation. It is just this consequence that we shall want to keep in mind when we consider Davidson's argument against the possibility of radically alternative conceptual schemes—to which we now return.

6

The second anti-Davidsonian possibility that we noted earlier depended upon accepting the possibility of radical conceptual difference. Davidson has argued, in "On the Very Idea of a Conceptual Scheme," that reflection on the conceptual demands of interpretation will suffice to demonstrate the impossibility of radically different conceptual schemes—indeed, if Davidson is right, such reflection will suffice to undermine much of the temptation we might have to speak of conceptual schemes at all.

In order adequately to understand Davidson's argument, we need first to be clear about what his target is. What exactly is Davidson denying the possibility of? What would it be for there to be a radically different conceptual scheme in any interesting sense—in particular, in a sense capable of subserving the aims of the second anti-Davidsonian proposal? Plainly, to suppose that some other person or culture has a radically different conceptual scheme from our own, it won't do merely to suppose that they have concepts or words for which we haven't got any direct word-for-word translation. (Also compare Davidson's remarks on Quine, the Sapir-Whorf hypothesis, and Kuhn's "paradigm shifts," in "On the Very Idea of a Conceptual Scheme"— henceforth referred to as OVICS—as reprinted in his *Inquiries into Truth and Interpretation*, Clarendon, 1984, p. 184.) Rather, a radically different conceptual scheme of any interesting sort would seem to require a more fundamental incompatibility, incommensurability, or incomparability. If a conceptual scheme is to be radically different from our own, in the relevant way, it seems that it must in some sense be in principle inaccessible to us and incommensurable with our own.

That someone has a radically different conceptual scheme from our own (in the relevant sense) would seem then to require either that he is in massive disagreement with us about beliefs—that is, relative to our view of the world most of his beliefs are mistaken; or, alternatively, that most of his beliefs are such that not only don't we share them—in the sense that our beliefs don't overlap with his—but somehow in principle we couldn't come to share them while preserving most of our current beliefs.

Let's identify these two conceptions respectively as the 'conflict' conception of radical difference and the 'non-overlapping in principle' conception of radical difference. Two individuals would count as having radically different conceptual schemes in the 'conflict' sense just in case they are in massive disagreement about their beliefs; that is, relative to one, the other's beliefs would be counted mostly in error. Two individuals would count as having radically different conceptual schemes in the 'non-overlapping in principle' sense just in case the one not only failed to share most of the other's beliefs, but also could not in principle come to share those beliefs without giving up most of her current beliefs.

In OVICS, Davidson is primarily concerned with the latter conception of radical conceptual difference, though it should be clear that he would also dismiss the conflict conception as unintelligible. On what basis? Well, if we suppose that Davidson has already successfully argued that the possibility of disagreement only makes sense against a background of massive agreement, it will follow that the situation described in the conflict conception could never arise.

Assuming that Davidson has thus efficiently dispatched the conflict conception of radical conceptual difference, what about the more interesting non-overlapping in principle conception? The suggestion here is that two individuals would differ radically in their conceptual schemes just in case their beliefs failed in principle mostly to overlap. The idea is not that their beliefs are false, by our lights; rather, we are encouraged to suppose that their beliefs are likely to be mostly true—as true as ours are. But even so, we can't, even in principle, share those beliefs without giving up most of our own. Unlike with the conflict conception, our inability simultaneously to entertain both sets of beliefs does not result from their being in conflict—after all, we're supposing that both sets of beliefs, ours and our radical alien's, are mostly true.

We can bring our problem into line with Davidson's discussion by supposing that associated with a conceptual scheme will be a language, or a set of inter-translatable languages. (This suggestion will be justified by considerations in support of the interdependence of thought and talk of the sort previously discussed.) We can then understand the claim that there can be radically different conceptual schemes as amounting to the claim that there can be natural languages supporting and supported by beliefs that are mostly true but in principle untranslatable by us. Plainly, it will follow from Davidson's own principles that, were it intelligible to suppose that there could be a creature or culture most of whose beliefs were both true and in principle not sharable by us, then the language of that creature or culture could not be translated by us.

Davidson's central claim is that we cannot make sense of such a total (or massive) failure of translation. But how does he argue for this? As Davidson says (OVICS, pp. 185–86):

> It is tempting to take a very short line indeed: nothing, it may be said, could count as evidence that some form of activity could not be interpreted in our language that was not at the same time evidence that that form of activity was not speech behavior. If this were right, we probably ought to hold that a form of activity that cannot be interpreted as language in our language is not speech behavior. Putting matters this way is unsatisfactory, however, for it comes to little more than making translatability into a familiar tongue a criterion of languagehood. As fiat, the thesis lacks the appeal of self-evidence; if it is a truth, as I think that it is, it should emerge as the conclusion of an argument.

What is this argument?

According to Davidson, the question of whether the notion of a radically alternative conceptual scheme is intelligible is just the question of whether or not the idea of an in principle untranslatable language, supporting and supported by mostly true sets of beliefs, is intelligible. And the question of whether this is intelligible depends, according to Davidson (OVICS, p. 194) on:

> how well we understand the notion of truth, as applied to language, independent of the notion of translation [interpretation].

And Davidson's claim is that we don't understand it independently at all [cf. previous discussion]. The sense in which this is true is, evidently, supposed to provide the basis for the claim that the possibility of an in principle untranslatable language is unintelligible.

In an especially enigmatic passage (OVICS, pp. 194–95), Davidson sets out his argument in this way:

> We recognize sentences like ' "Snow is white" is true iff snow is white' to be trivially true. Yet the totality of such English sentences uniquely determines the extension of the concept of truth for English. Tarski generalized this observation and made it a test for theories of truth: according to Tarski's Convention T, a satisfactory theory of truth for a language L must entail, for every sentence s of L, a theorem of the form 's is true iff p' where 's' is replaced by a description of s and 'p' by s itself if L is English, and by a translation of s into English if L is not English. This isn't, of course, a definition of truth, and it doesn't hint that there is a single definition or theory that applies to languages generally. *Nevertheless, Convention T suggests, though it cannot state, an important feature common to all the specialized concepts of truth. It succeeds in doing this by making essential use of the notion of translation into a language we know* [my emphasis]. Since Convention T embodies our best intuition as to how the concept of truth is used, there does not seem to be much hope for a test that a conceptual scheme is radically different from ours if that test depends on the assumption that we can divorce the notion of truth from that of translation.

What is the argument here? It is obviously important that, according to Davidson, Convention T "embodies our best intuition as to how the concept of truth is used," and that Convention T makes essential or ineliminable use of the idea of translation (interpretation). But it's not just that it makes ineliminable use of the idea of translation, but rather, according to Davidson, that it makes "essential use of the notion of translation into a language we know (interpretation *by us*)" [my emphasis]. Where does this latter claim come from, and how is it used against the radical conceptual relativist?

Before addressing this claim directly, let me first clarify the larger strategy of the argument, at least as I understand it. Davidson wants to undermine the claimed intelligibility for us of an untranslatable language. He wants to do this first by revealing certain conceptual commitments one has just insofar as one is willing to countenance something as a language—irrespective of the question whether it can be translated or interpreted by us or not.

He then wants to argue that the very conditions that make it possible to regard something as a possible natural language at all preclude its being wholly untranslatable/uninterpretable. The idea is just this. If I am going to suppose that an untranslatable language is possible, then I am supposing two things:

I am supposing that something is both a language and untranslatable. Davidson's point will be that the very conditions for my coherently supposing that something is a language at all are inconsistent with the possibility that it might be in principle untranslatable by me. How are we to understand Davidson's remarks in the quoted passage as instantiating this general strategy?

Clearly, the notion of truth plays a central role in Davidson's implementation of the strategy. Recall that our picture of this radically alternative conceptual scheme is one relative to which someone is capable of entertaining mostly true beliefs that we ourselves are precluded from entertaining. The language coordinated with this scheme will, consequently, have to be one in which a multitude of non-translatable truths can be expressed. This way of understanding the situation is in effect forced on us by the fact that nothing would even count as a conceptual scheme in the relevant sense—a point of view on the world—unless it were a point of view relative to which many true beliefs could be entertained. And correlatively, nothing would count as a language unless it were such that speakers of that language would be capable of expressing truths in it.

In other words, to have a conceptual scheme in the relevant sense is at least to be in a position to have beliefs about the world—attitudes with respect to which the question of truth or falsity arises; and to be a language in the relevant sense is at least to be something in which claims about the world can be made—something some of the sentences of which are evaluable as true or false. Consequently to have a language in the relevant sense is at least to be able to express and interpret one's own and others' beliefs about the world. This should make it relatively clear then that there is an essential connection between being a language and the notion of truth. Nothing will count as a language in the relevant sense unless it is capable of expressing truths.

Needless to say, the concept that we express with the word 'language' is our concept, as is the concept we express with the word 'truth'. The question is whether it is coherent to suppose that there could be a language capable of expressing truths—where, recall, the concept expressed by that term is ours (whose else would it be?)—which, however, cannot in principle be expressed in our language or some suitable expansion of it. (Hereafter I will leave off making this important qualification explicit.)

Davidson wants to argue that it is not possible both to conceive of a language capable of expressing truths (which is just to say, to conceive of a language) and to conceive of that language as incapable in principle of being translated/interpreted by us. To imagine a language as capable of expressing true sentences is to imagine our truth predicate significantly applying to its sentences—which, importantly, is different from imagining our actually applying our truth predicate to its sentences. In order to imagine this latter possibility, we would have to imagine having satisfied ourselves that, at the very least, what we were predicating truth of was indeed an indicative sentence in the other language. But in the case of a radically untranslatable language, it is difficult to see how we could satisfy ourselves of even this much. So let me repeat: to imagine a language as capable of expressing true sentences is to imagine our truth predicate significantly applying to its sentences. It is to imagine that some of its sentences belong to the extension of our truth predicate. But now what is required in order coherently to imagine our truth predicate significantly applying to a sentence?

It is at this point that Davidson's appeal to Convention T becomes relevant. Davidson writes that "Convention T embodies our best intuition as to how the concept of truth is used." Clearly, Davidson's argument is going to be that whatever that best intuition is, it will be a consequence of it that we will be able coherently to imagine our truth predicate significantly applying to a sentence of a language only if we can coherently imagine the possibility of translating that sentence into our own language, that is, interpreting it. What, then, is the content of this "best intuition," and how does it follow that it makes no sense to imagine our truth predicate applying to a radically untranslatable sentence? The relevant passage is this:

> according to Tarski's Convention T, a satisfactory theory of truth for a language L must entail, for every sentence s of L, a theorem of the form 's is true iff p' where 's' is replaced by a description of s and 'p' by s itself if L is English, and by a translation of s into English if L is not English.

Davidson's claim here seems to be that our understanding of the truth predicate and our grip on its possible extension—that is, our grip on what is to count as an item to which it might genuinely apply—is essentially captured by Convention T. In other words, it seems to be Davidson's view that it is a necessary condition on the possibility of some sentence s belonging to the extension of the truth predicate that it be an s for which there could be in English (or an appropriate extension of English) a T-sentence of the form s is true iff p, where s is a sentence in some language and "p" is replaced by a translation of that sentence into English. The suggestion is that it is an essential part of our understanding of the truth predicate that its extension is uniquely fixed by the totality of true instances (in our language) of the T-schema.

If this is right, then plainly we cannot make sense of anything belonging to the extension of the truth predicate unless it is a sentence in principle translatable into our language. But then we cannot make sense of the truth predicate's applying to the sentences of a language radically different from our own. But then we cannot make sense of the possibility of such a language at all.

But is this right? Well, the sense in which it is right (if it is) is revealed, I would suggest, by reflection on the important consequence, noted previously, of Davidson's "Rational Animals" argument. I earlier said that if we accept that argument, then it will follow that the only concepts of truth and objectivity we have are ones that emerge in the context of interpretation. Consequently, where and only where interpretation is conceivable will the concepts of truth and objectivity find significant application. If this is right, it is not possible to make sense of any seriously radical conceptual relativity. Consequently, the second anti-Davidsonian proposal is unintelligible.

If we can assume that Davidson has indeed successfully countered both of the original anti-Davidsonian suggestions, then he will, it seems, have successfully established a strong sense in which in interpretation we must presume some shared fundamental norms of intelligibility. And, it will follow from the peculiar strength of this that how we must interpret someone (viz., as in large measure sharing our fundamental norms of intelligibility) is how in fact they are.[1]

8

Analyticity and Holism in Quine's Thought

PETER HYLTON

Peter Hylton is a professor of philosophy at the University of Illinois at Chicago and received his Ph.D. in Philosophy from Harvard University. He has published essays on the history of analytic philosophy, and Russell, Idealism, and the Emergence of Analytic Philosophy. *His most recen book is* Propositions, Functions, and Analysis: Selected Essays on Russell's Philosophy.

I. The Nature of the Question

More than fifty years after the publication of "Two Dogmas of Empiricism," more than forty years after the first appearance of "Carnap and Logical Truth," there is no sign of agreement about the lessons that we should draw from Quine's writings on analyticity.[1] More alarming, there isn't even agreement about what Quine's *claims* are. As evidence here I offer a passage from an essay of Paul Boghossian's. Boghossian is discussing a notion which he calls "Frege-analyticity": a sentence is Frege-analytic just in case it is "transformable into a logical truth by the substitution of synonyms for synonyms."[2] Commenting on what he takes to be Quine's attitude towards this idea, Boghossian says:

What form does Quine's resistance take? We may agree that the result being adver-
tised isn't anything modest, of the form: There are fewer analytic truths than we
had previously thought. Or, there are some analytic truths, but they are not important for the purposes of science. Or anything of a similar ilk.[3]

Now this on my view is not simply misleading, or wrong; it is *completely*
wrong, almost the reverse of the truth. It would be much nearer the mark to
say that Quine's view is precisely that "[t]here are fewer analytic truths than
we had previously thought" and that "they are not important for the purposes
of science."

So the task confronting us is not only to say what Quine's views really
are, but also to say why they are so susceptible of misunderstanding.[4] A helpful way in is to ask the following meta-question: what sort of question is at
issue? In particular, is the question of the reality of the analytic-synthetic distinction a straightforward Yes-or-No question? Or is it a more complex sort
of question, calling for a less straightforward answer? Boghossian, and others, take it that it is a Yes-or-No question that is at issue; they take this to be
a question about the existence or the objectivity of meaning; and they see the
negative answer they attribute to Quine as rather obviously absurd.

Now the answer to my meta-question is itself a complex one; it is by no
means straightforward even to say what sort of question Quine is trying to
answer. Sometimes it does seem as if we face a single Yes-or-No question; at
other times a far more subtle and nuanced picture seems to emerge. My suggestion is that both appearances are to some extent correct. There *is* a Yes-
or-No question, which is sometimes at the centre of Quine's attention (especially
in "Two Dogmas"). Boghossian is not wrong about that, though he is wrong
to suppose that the negative answer is obviously absurd. More to the present
point, however, he is also wrong to think that this is the only question at issue.
With Quine's (negative) answer to that question in place, other questions
emerge, requiring more complicated sorts of answers.

To explain this, let us suppose that there were a notion of meaning, sufficiently clear and robust to serve as the foundation for a philosophical system. More particularly, let us suppose that we could make sense of an atomistic
notion of cognitive meaning. "Atomistic" because it is a notion of meaning
that is supposed to apply to sentences taken one by one; "cognitive" because
Quine's concern, as always, is with epistemology, and with the sort of meaning relevant to knowledge. We may think of the cognitive meaning of a sentence as, roughly, the claim that that sentence makes upon reality. Given this
supposition, we could define the analytic sentences as those that are true in
virtue of meaning. More precisely (eliminating the "in virtue of") we could
say: analytic sentences are those sentences that make no claim on reality,

which say nothing about it either way, and which therefore cannot fail to be true.

Notice that a notion of analyticity defined in such a way is fitted to play the role of the a priori in two crucial respects. First, the notion thus explained will have the right *scope*. It will include all those sentences for which we have a use that do not make a claim upon reality; those that do make a claim upon reality will, presumably, not be plausible candidates for being a priori.[5] Second, the notion is also bound to have *epistemological significance*, since it distinguishes those sentences that make a claim upon reality, and are thus subject to confirmation and disconfirmation by evidence in the usual way, from those that make no such claim, and to which notions of evidence and justification therefore do not apply, or at least not in anything like the usual way.

Now our supposition highlights the Yes-or-No question that I take to be at issue in some of Quine's discussions. The question is simply: is there an atomistic notion of cognitive meaning that can play this role? Quine's answer, of course, is No; his reason is holism, a rejection of the atomism of our assumed notion of meaning. Let us briefly consider this point.

Let us agree, if only for the purposes of illustration, that some sentences make claims that are more or less directly answerable to sensory experience. (Quine's version of this idea is his notion of an observation sentence; the point here, however, is independent of this particular way of making sense of the more general idea.) Other sentences have implications for experience because they imply sentences of this kind. In very many cases, however, no such implications hold between an individual sentence, taken by itself, and sentences of the more observational kind. Various classes of sentences containing the given sentence will have implications for experience, but the sentence taken alone will not. Hence, as Quine puts it, "the typical statement about bodies has no fund of experiential implications it can call its own."[6] This is holism: the view that many of our supposedly empirical sentences have implications for experience only when they are taken together with a larger or smaller body of other sentences. It is the more inclusive theory that has such implications, not the individual sentence by itself.

Now it is a direct consequence of Quine's holism that the notion of a "claim upon reality," at least if we interpret it in experiential terms, is not in general happily applied to sentences taken one by one. Bodies of sentences taken together make claims that cannot be parceled out among the individual sentences, hence the idea of a "claim upon reality" does not fit with our taking individual sentences, rather than wider theories, as the relevant units. Hence there is in general no such thing as the cognitive meaning of an individual sentence. (The "in general" here leaves room for the idea that there may be *some* sentences to which the idea of cognitive meaning can be applied. Most obviously, it will apply to those sentences directly answerable to experience, assuming that there are such. But it will not be applicable to all sentences, and we can never simply assume that it is applicable to a given sentence.)

In Quine's view, holism thus negates any notion of atomistic cognitive meaning. Yet the intuitive appeal that the idea of analyticity may have is, he holds, largely due to the fact that we tend, uncritically and illegitimately, to assume a notion of meaning of that sort.[7] Much of "Two Dogmas of Empiricism," as I see it, is an attempt to make this assumption explicit, and to undermine it. Clearly there is much more that could be said about this matter, but I shall not go further into it here.

If, with Quine, we conclude that we cannot simply assume a notion of cognitive meaning, universally applicable to sentences taken one by one, then where are we? One kind of notion of analyticity becomes untenable; it is not clear, however, that this is the only thing that might reasonably be meant by the word 'analyticity'. So we are left with various questions, which might be phrased like this: First, is there any tenable notion that might be more or less accurately described as 'truth in virtue of meaning', and if so, what? Second, what will be the scope of such a notion? To find an account according to which certain paradigm sentences about bachelors or vixens come out as analytic is one thing; to show the analyticity of the whole complex structure of mathematics is quite another. Third, what will be the epistemological significance of such a notion? In what ways, if any, will the epistemological status of sentences that are analytic in this sense differ from that of other sentences? These are complex questions, which are unlikely to have simple Yes-or-No answers; focusing on these questions will show that it is quite misleading to think of the analyticity issue as a single straightforward question.

In spite of the complexity of the questions, we may state, very roughly and by way of preview, Quine's answers. To the first question: Yes, we can find something that might be reasonably called analyticity. (This is a view that is much clearer, at least, in Quine's later work than earlier. I am inclined to think that it is quite consistent with what is important—from Quine's own point of view—in the earlier work, but this is certainly a point that is open to argument.) To the second: the scope of such a notion will fall short of what Carnap and others had hoped for. In particular, Quine sees no prospect for an understanding of analyticity that encompasses mathematics. The third question is the most crucial from Quine's perspective. Here his answer is that there will be no real epistemological significance to the notion. As Quine says it, "I recognize a notion of analyticity in its obvious and useful but epistemologically insignificant applications."[8] This negative answer to the third question gives rise to a further issue: if the status of apparently a priori subjects such as logic and mathematics is not to be understood in terms of analyticity, how should we understand what Quine himself calls "the palpable surface differences" between those subjects and the clearly empirical subjects?[9] We shall also briefly address this issue.

II. Quinean Analyticity and the Question of Scope

What sense *can* be made of the notion of analyticity, given Quine's assumptions? Quine rejects the idea that we can usefully approach meaning by beginning with the assumption that meanings are introspectible mental items; this is the view that he deplores as mentalism. His starting point, in thinking about meaning, is the *use* of language—both the use that is actually made of it, and the uses that *would* be made of it under various counterfactual circumstances. In particular, since his focus is always on the cognitive or theoretical language in which our knowledge is embodied, his focus is on the assertoric uses of sentences.[10]1

Now what sort of sense can be made, in these terms, of the notion of cognitive meaning? Early on Quine says, "In point of *meaning* . . . a word may be said to be determined to whatever extent the truth or falsehood of its contexts is determined."[11] He reiterates the point later; in "Carnap and Logical Truth," he says, "Any acceptable evidence of usage or meaning of words must reside surely in the observable circumstances under which the words are uttered...or in the affirmation and denial of sentences in which the words occur."[12] Suppose—*per impossibile*—that we had the totality of sentences of the language spread out before us, and along with each sentence an account of the circumstances under which it would be correct to assert it. Then we would have, on Quine's account, all the evidence relevant to meaning.

Two points need to be made immediately about this imaginary, and impossible, situation. First, it might be thought to give comfort to the Carnapian because he could then define the analytic sentences as those that would be correctly assertable in *all* situations. But in fact there is no comfort of this sort. The proposed definition would make out the analytic sentences to be those that are true under any circumstances, true come what may. As we shall see shortly, however, Carnap would reject such an understanding of analyticity; he holds, with good reason, that there are no such sentences. (Very roughly, his view is that any sentence might be abandoned under some circumstances, but in the case of the analytic sentences such a move involves abandoning the language in favor of another. Carnap's analyticity is language-relative.) Second, for most sentences, an account of the circumstances under which an utterance of the sentence would be accepted as correct would be a very long way from an account of its meaning, in any ordinary understanding of that word. The point here is holism. The chemist might accept the sentence, "There is copper in it," upon seeing a greenish tint in a test-tube, but that does not show that this sentence *means* that there is a greenish tint, or anything of that sort.[13] What it shows is, rather, that evidence of the greenish tint bears on a theory, a body of sentences of which the given sentence is one—perhaps the one that is salient at a given moment, but not the only one. Many sentences are more deeply theoretically embedded than this one, so that the observable circumstances that affect our acceptance or rejection of them may be extremely remote from anything that would ordinarily be thought of as their meaning. Holism implies that, even given our impossible assumption, meaning is not a straightforward matter. Nevertheless, the imagined situation represents all that there could be to cognitive meaning on a Quinean view.

For the cognitive meaning of a word, then, we look to its contexts—the sentences in which it occurs, and the truth-value of each sentence, or the way the truth-value of each varies with variations in the observable circumstances. But then the question is: *which* of the contexts of a word must be determined in order to determine its meaning? Without some reason to discriminate, we have no reason to treat one context as more definitive of a word's meaning than any other. But then no true sentence in which the word appears would have any better claim to be analytic than any other such sentence; it seems unlikely that any useful analytic-synthetic distinction can be erected on that basis.[14] If we are to obtain any reasonable version of the distinction, we must be able to discriminate among contexts and say that the truth of some is constitutive of the meaning of a given word, and that those sentences are therefore true in virtue of the meaning of that word.

What sort of thing might give us reason to discriminate among contexts in this way? If mastery of some very small subset of a word's uses gave one mastery of its use as a whole, then there would be reason to say that those uses, those contexts, constituted its meaning. And clearly this happens in some cases. A child who otherwise has a fair degree of linguistic sophistication but does not know the word 'bachelor' can be given a mastery of that word all at once, at a single stroke, by being told that bachelors are unmarried men. This fact gives us every reason to say that 'bachelor' *means* 'unmarried man', and hence also to say that the sentence 'All bachelors are unmarried' is analytic—which Quine would certainly not deny.[15] Very much along the same lines, Quine claims that in some cases one learns the truth of the sentence in coming to understand it. Socializing this idea, he suggests, will yield a suitable criterion for analyticity: "a sentence is analytic if *everyone* learns that it is true by learning its words."[16] And he has expressed some sympathy with a suggestion that goes further in the same general direction, that we should count a sentence as analytic if failure to accept it indicates that the speaker is not a competent user of one or more of the words in that sentence.[17]

It is useful here to compare the position I have attributed to Quine and that defended by Putnam in "The Analytic and the Synthetic," perhaps the most insightful of the early responses to "Two Dogmas."[18] Putnam takes it that Quine in "Two Dogmas" straightforwardly denies that there is any distinction at all between the analytic and the synthetic. He argues that this view is mistaken, that the analytic-synthetic distinction cannot be wholly denied; Quine in fact agrees on this point, at least in *Word and Object* and later. More importantly, Putnam also argues that the distinction will not in fact do any epistemological work, because all analytic truths are trivial and uninteresting. Certain concepts, Putnam points out, are single-criterion concepts: the only criterion for being a bachelor is being an unmarried man; the only criterion for being a vixen is being a female fox, and so on. These are the concepts that give rise to analytic statements. In such cases we have only one criterion for the application of the word, and we have reason to think that this situation will not change. A statement such as "All vixens are female foxes" has, as Putnam says, "little or no systematic import. . . . There could hardly be *theoretical* reasons for accepting or rejecting it."[19] For this reason, analytic sentences will all be trivial. Interesting concepts, by contrast, have multiple criteria for their application. The theoretical concepts of science, in particular, are what Putnam calls "law-cluster concepts:" their identity is given not by a single criterion of application but rather by a multitude of laws and inferences into which it enters. To separate these laws into the analytic and the synthetic, Putnam claims, would be misleading: even if some are called "definitions," still all are involved in our learning the term concerned. Here again, Quine is in agreement with Putnam.[20]

Now let us consider what I have called the issue of the *scope* of analyticity. How extensive is the notion of analyticity, on the sort of understanding of it that is acceptable to Quine and to Putnam? Initially one might think that it is very limited indeed. All of the sentences that count as analytic by any criterion of the sort suggested above, it seems, will be trivial (in the ordinary and literal sense of that word), and not subject to dispute. But in fact Quine, at least in his later writings, takes a somewhat broader view of the matter. He counts certain inference-patterns as analytic (or as analyticity-preserving), and argues that we should count as analytic "all truths deducible from analytic ones by analytic steps."[21] On this understanding of the matter, he claims, first-order logic will count as analytic. We might come to repudiate the law of the excluded middle, say, but our doing so would involve a change of meaning.

Crucially, however, there is no prospect of arguing on the same or similar basis for the analyticity of mathematics as a whole. Quine takes Gödel's incompleteness theorem to show that mathematics as a whole is *not* deducible by obvious steps from obvious truths.[22] For any philosopher, perhaps, and for a scientifically-minded philosopher quite certainly, mathematics is the central and most important kind of knowledge that is usually classified as a priori. An account of analyticity that does not extend to mathematics will not perform the central function of the traditional conception of the a priori.

III. An Epistemological Distinction?

We now turn to the issue of the significance of the distinction between the analytic and the synthetic. Quine himself, in his later work, came to see this issue as the crucial one in discussions of analyticity. In a work published in 1986, he wrote, "I now perceive that the philosophically important question about analyticity and the linguistic doctrine of logical truth is *not* how to explicate them; it is the question rather of their relevance to epistemology."[23]

Here, and in what follows, it will be helpful to contrast Quine's views with those of Carnap. (Remember, however, that our concern is to understand the former, not to do justice to the latter.) Unlike more traditional conceptions of the a priori, analyticity in Carnap's philosophy is not an absolute notion; it is language-relative. So to call a sentence analytic is not to say that it is (absolutely) unrevisable: we may cease to accept a sentence that up to that point we had counted as analytic, or we may come to accept a sentence whose negation we had, up to that point, counted as analytic. As Carnap says, "No statement is immune to revision."[24] The point of Carnap's distinction between the analytic and the synthetic is not that sentences of the former kind are unrevisable; it is, rather, that any revision of an analytic sentence is a change of language. If the language changes then certainly a sentence that was once held to be true, and analytically true, may now be held to be false; and for Carnap we can change the language as we please. (Here it is perhaps helpful to think of the informal characterization of analytic sentences as those that are true in virtue of the meanings of the words they contain. Then the point is simply that the meanings of words may change, giving rise to changes in the status of sentences that were previously analytic.) So on Carnap's account an analytic sentence, we might say, *is* "immune to revision" *provided that* there is no change of language.

One way of marking the distinction between the analytic sentences and the synthetic sentences is thus to say that the revision of an analytic sentence must be a change of language, while the revision of a synthetic sentence is a change of belief or of theory within a language. We can, accordingly, raise the issue of the epistemological significance of the distinction by asking: what *epistemological* difference is there between a change of mind that involves an analytic sentence and one that involves a synthetic sentence? Is there a clear and systematic difference in the way the two kinds of revision are to be justified? At least in some of his writings, Carnap seems to offer an answer to exactly this question.[25]

Let us speak of an *internal revision* when we have a revision involving a synthetic sentence (and thus no change of language); and of an *external revision* when an analytic sentence (and therefore also a change of language) is involved. On Carnap's account, there seems to be a clear epistemological distinction between the two. In the former case, a synthetic sentence is involved, and there is a question of the justification for the revision, of the evidence that can be brought to bear for or against making it. In the latter case, by contrast, there is no question of justification or of evidence. The very concepts of justification and evidence, for Carnap, are language-relative; to speak of a sentence as justified or not presupposes a particular language, a framework that gives sense to those concepts.[26] So an internal revision can be evaluated as more or less justified; because no change of language is involved, we have those concepts to draw on. But an external revision is another matter. Here no one language is presupposed: the question is precisely one of shifting from one language to another. Since no particular language is presupposed, there is no notion of justification in terms of which the change can be evaluated.

Similarly, an internal revision—a change of theory within a language—is correct or incorrect; the (synthetic) sentence under consideration is either true or false. Correctness and truth, however, are also, for Carnap, language-relative concepts: they apply only when a particular language is presupposed. When an external revision is under consideration, therefore, they do not apply. An external revision is, properly understood, a proposal that we should use a different language (though the difference may be very minor). This sort of proposal, however, suggests that we shift our concepts of justification and of truth (since these concepts are language-relative). Evaluating a proposal of this kind, therefore, is not a matter of deciding on its correctness, or even its justification (not, at least, in anything like the sense in which a synthetic sentence may be justified). It is, rather, a pragmatic question: what is at stake is not truth but convenience. "The acceptance [of a new language] cannot be judged as being either true or false because it is not an assertion. It can be judged as being more or less expedient, fruitful, conducive to the aim for which the language is intended."[27]

There is a kind of circularity in this Carnapian picture. Analytic sentences are to have a different kind of epistemological status from others. (Since epistemology presupposes a language, and the analytic sentences of that language, it might be said that their status is not really an *epistemological* status at all, that epistemological questions simply do not apply to them. We shall return to this point shortly.) This epistemological difference rests on the idea that within a language (at least of the appropriate kind) there is a clear concept of justification, while no such concept is applicable to the choice of language. But the idea that there is a clear concept of justification within a language rests, in turn, on the claim that rules of language have an epistemological status different from that of synthetic sentences. Carnap attempts to reconstruct—to explicate—the notion of justification, and these attempts presuppose that rules of language, and sentences that follow from them, belong to an epistemically privileged class of sentences. So it seems that to arrive at the conclusion that analytic sentences are epistemologically different from others, we must be explicating the concept of justification in a way that already presupposes this conclusion.

Circularity is not always a philosophical vice. For Carnap, I think, the kind of circularity sketched above indicates that if we wish to view analytic sentences as epistemologically different from others—if, for example, we find it a useful way of attaining a philosophical understanding of how scientific knowledge progresses—then we are free to do so. He might claim that his view is part of a consistent and, so to speak, self-reinforcing conception: perhaps we are not forced to such a conception, but if it gives interesting results, or appeals to us for other reasons, we may adopt it.[28] How can Quine break into the circle so as to undermine the Carnapian picture? The answer depends on the parenthetical point deferred in the previous paragraph. For Quine, epistemological questions apply to all sentences, the analytic as well as the synthetic; they cannot simply be rejected. It is, at most, the kind of answers to those questions that may differ when the sentence is analytic rather than synthetic.

Given this interpretation, the Carnapian picture depends upon the contrast between the sort of justification available within a language and the sort of justification (or: 'justification') available when no language is presupposed. As Quine sees the matter, Carnap's contrast is that the former is rule governed, with rules of the language setting out the relation of each sentence to the observations that would justify it; the latter is not rule governed, and is a matter of convenience and of vague pragmatic factors (hence it is 'justification' only by a stretch of that word). On this reading of Carnap, it is for the philosopher to explicate the notion of (internal) justification that applies to this or that language. But there is no guarantee that the attempt to do so for any language will succeed and will in fact capture a concept that comes close to doing justice to our actual epistemic practices. Seen in this way, Carnap's view is vulnerable at this point. There simply may be no clear contrast between internal revision, where a relatively straightforward notion of justification applies, and external changes, where nothing of the sort is true. (We should note, however, that a more sympathetic reading of Carnap might take his view to reject the epistemological question as entirely inapplicable to analytic sentences. If that is correct, then the gap between Carnap's views and those of

Quine is larger than I have perhaps suggested, and debate between them more clearly a missing of minds. But my concern here is, again, with Quine's views.)

It is, I think, a crucial part of Quine's view that there is no clear-cut contrast between internal revision and external revision. We do not in fact have rules setting up that sort of tight relation between theory and evidence. Attempts to formulate such a 'confirmation relation' governing internal revisions quickly proved inadequate except in relatively constrained situations. As Quine says in "Two Dogmas:" "I am impressed . . . with how baffling the problem has always been of arriving at any explicit theory of the empirical confirmation of a synthetic statement."[29] It is important here that Quine is talking about synthetic statements quite generally. Locally, in particular cases here and there, we do seem able to give fairly precise accounts of the extent to which given evidence confirms a given claim. We can perhaps say with some confidence to what extent the statement that the parents of a child are blue eyed justifies the prediction that the child itself will also have blue eyes. Presupposing a background theory enables us to make precise statements about the degree of confirmation of some sentences by others. But if we turn our attention to the background theories themselves, then the prospect of anything similar seems implausible; when we consider our system of beliefs as a whole, it seems out of the question. We have no reason to expect a rule-governed notion of justification for synthetic statements in general.

Holism, in Quine's view, gives us principled reasons to think that no such theory of confirmation is available. According to that doctrine, the relation of justification does not, in general, hold between experience and individual sentences, but rather between experience and theories, more or less sizeable groups of sentences. We cannot in general think of an individual sentence as being confirmed or disconfirmed by experience at all. The justification of a sentence is, in general, that it is part of a theory that, taken as a whole, does a better job of predicting and explaining sensory experience than any other. In practice this means, very roughly, that the theory predicts experience at least as well as any rival, and that it is better than any rival in being simpler, more fruitful, easier to work with, and so on. These factors can no longer be thought of as mere matters of convenience, or as merely pragmatic. For theories in general, they are all that we have to go on.

As Quine reads Carnap's views, then, they depend upon an epistemological contrast: internal questions are to be settled by rule-governed procedures of justification, procedures that are obviously unavailable for external questions. Given holism, such rule-governed procedures of justification are not in general available, even for what anyone would count as synthetic sentences. (They are not *in general* available: as we indicated, they may be in special cases.) If a given sentence at some level of theoretical abstraction is at issue, all we can do is to compare the theory that we have if we accept that sentence with the theory that we have if we accept some alternative. And the choice between the two theories is to be settled by seeing which of them better enables us to cope with experience. This is in part a matter of yielding correct predictions; it is also in part a matter of simplicity, convenience, fruitfulness, and so on. In short: justification—even internal justification, even of supposedly synthetic sentences—is to some extent a matter of just those vague 'pragmatic factors' that Carnap says play a role in connection with external questions—choice of language—but *not* in connection with internal questions. Quine argues that the same pragmatic factors also play a crucial role in internal questions and advocates, as he famously says, "a more thorough pragmatism."[30]

In light of this, consider the external side of the (alleged) distinction. Carnap holds that the choice of language is not a matter we can be right or wrong about, not a matter for justification: hence the Principle of Tolerance. The language of Newton's physics and the language of Einstein's physics, say, differ in expressive power: what can be said in the one cannot, in all cases, be said in the other. Some choices of language, however, are more efficient than others, more conducive to the construction of successful and fruitful theories. Why should we apply the Principle of Tolerance to questions of language-choice? Why should we not think of this as a matter about which we can be right or wrong? If adopting one language rather than another enables us to formulate better theories of the world, why should we not speak of the choice of that language over the other as *correct*? From a Quinean perspective, the only reason not to do so would be if talk of correctness goes together with a relatively strict conception of justification, a conception that makes it more than merely a matter of efficiency. But if in fact such strict notion of justification is not available anywhere, then justification everywhere must, perforce, be seen as in part a matter of efficiency— and this is clearly a notion that will apply to Carnap's 'external' revisions as well as to his 'internal' revisions. In other words the epistemological contrast between the two kinds of questions will have broken down. We would thus no longer have a reason to say that one sort of question has no right or wrong answer while the other does.[31]

For Quine, then, even if one grants the distinction between analytic sentences and synthetic sentences, and thus also the distinction between choice of language and choice of theory, this does not seem to mark a significant *epistemological* difference. The sorts of considerations that might lead us to change from one language to another are not in principle different from the sorts of considerations that might lead us to make a change from one theory within a language to another theory within the same language: in each case the most we can say, generally and in the abstract, without detailed exami-

nation of the particular case, is that the new theory is simpler, or m ore ele-
gant, or more fruitful, than the old—whether the new theory is within the same
language or involves adopting a new language. On this reading, Carnap's picture depends on a distinction between the vague pragmatic factors that operate in choice of language and the more rigid rule-governed justification that
operate within a language. But if we accept Quinean holism about justification we must also accept that the idea of such a rigid notion of justification is
a myth: pragmatic factors operate everywhere. In Quine's view, therefore, there
is no epistemological cleavage between the analytic and the synthetic, or
between change of language and change of theory within a language.

IV. Explaining the A Priori

Quine's views as we have discussed them so far are negative: we have been
considering his objections to (what he takes to be) Carnap's use of the notion
of analyticity. The negative point, however, is supplemented by a positive one:
that we have no need for Carnapian analyticity, because we have no need for
a substantive notion of a priori knowledge. As we have said, Quine takes it
that epistemological questions are everywhere applicable; in particular, that
they are applicable to what Carnap counts as analytic sentences as well as to
those that he counts as synthetic. He sees analyticity as Carnap's attempt to
answer those questions.[32] On that view, the notion is needed because certain
truths—most notably those of mathematics and logic—seem to almost all
philosophers just evidently different in kind from ordinary empirical truths;[33]
Quine himself, as we have seen, accepts at least that there are "palpable surface differences" here.

Quine's negative point is thus incomplete without an alternative account
of our knowledge of these truths, the supposedly a priori, as we might call
them. And he does, indeed, offer such an account. The crucial point, again,
is holism, or the denial of the dogma of reductionism. Quine puts it like this:

> The second dogma of empiricism, to the effect that each empirically meaningful
> sentence has an empirical content of its own, was cited in "Two Dogmas" merely
> as encouraging false confidence in the notion of analyticity; but now I would say
> further that *the second dogma creates a need for analyticity as a key notion of
> epistemology, and that the need lapses when we heed Duhem and set the second
> dogma aside.*[34]

Quine takes holism to cast doubt not merely on Carnap's distinction between
the analytic and the synthetic but also on the more general distinction between
the a priori and the empirical.[35] Some supposedly empirical claims are related

to experience only very indirectly, via much other theorizing. The claims of the Theory of General Relativity, say, can be tested by experience, but only if we accept (at least provisionally, for the purposes of the experiment) a large body of other theories—including a good deal of mathematics. It would be absurd to take one sentence from Einstein's theory and ask of that sentence, in isolation from everything else we take ourselves to know, what are *its* empirical consequences. In thinking of such a sentence as empirical—as having observational or experiential consequences that enable us to test it—we are not thinking of it in isolation; we are thinking of it rather as an integral part of a large body of theory that, taken as a whole, has such consequences. In *this* indirect and holistic sense, Quine claims, the supposedly a priori may also have observational consequences. Mathematics can be thought of as having the same kind of indirect confrontation with experience as the hypotheses of a very abstract theory of physics has.

Quine thus claims that the supposedly a priori claims of logic and mathematics are epistemologically on a par at least with the more abstract claims of physics. In each case, a given claim taken by itself has no consequences for experience; in each case, however, the given claim is an integral part of a more general theory that, taken as a whole, does have such consequences. Logic and mathematics are thus not wholly free-standing theories, independent from the rest of our knowledge. They are, rather, integrated with our knowledge as a whole; it is in their role within our wider system of beliefs that their ultimate justification lies.

Does this mean that Quine takes logic and mathematics to be *empirical*? No: in denying the distinction between the a priori and the empirical, he is not simply consigning everything to one side of the distinction. If one says that for Quine all truths are empirical, one must immediately add that he is reconceiving this latter notion, along holistic lines. Quine explicitly denies the sort of view often attributed to J.S. Mill, that our knowledge of the truths of arithmetic, say, is directly based on observation, in the same sort of way in which my knowledge of the truth of "There is a desk in front of me" is directly based on observation. Arithmetic is not empirical for Quine in that sense:

> The kinship I speak for is rather a kinship with the most general and systematic aspects of natural science, farthest from observation. Mathematics and logic are supported by observation only in the indirect way that those aspects of natural science are supported by observation; namely, as participating in an organized whole which, way up at its empirical edges, squares with observation. *I am concerned to urge the empirical character of logic and mathematics no more than the unempirical character of theoretical physics; it is, rather, their kinship that I am urging, and a doctrine of gradualism.*[36]

The problem, as Quine sees it, is to explain the status of mathematics along lines acceptable to an empiricist, that is, in a way compatible with the idea that all real knowledge has to do with the prediction of sensory experience. As we have indicated, Quine explains one aspect of this status, the fact that mathematics counts as knowledge at all, along holistic grounds: it plays a crucial role in a theory that, taken as a whole, is used in the prediction of experience. The other crucial aspect of the status of mathematics is the way in which it is unlike other branches of knowledge: its claims are answerable to proofs rather than to experiments; such claims, once firmly established, are never in fact abandoned, whatever experimental results we find; and the falsity of such claims is often said to be not merely unlikely but unimaginable. A Quinean explanation of these features is to be found not in the mere fact that mathematics plays a role in our knowledge as a whole, but rather in the nature and peculiarities of that role.

We shall not linger over the details here, but it is clear that it is the generality of logic and mathematics, their centrality to our knowledge as a whole, that is responsible for their special status. Abandoning or greatly modifying established mathematics would require us to reconceive our system of knowledge from the ground up. No wonder such a thing is beyond imagination, and no wonder we have every reason to avoid it. Quine appeals to exactly these sorts of factors to explain why logic and mathematics are often thought of as sharply distinct from other branches of knowledge and why, in particular, they are taken to be a priori and necessary:

> At the end of *Philosophy of Logic* I contrasted mathematics and logic with the rest of science on the score of their versatility: their vocabulary pervades all branches of science, and consequently their truths and techniques are consequential in all branches of science. This is what had led people to emphasize the boundary that marks pure logic and mathematics off from the rest of science. This is also why we are disinclined to tamper with logic and mathematics when a failure of prediction shows that there is something wrong with our system of the world. We prefer to seek an adequate revision of some more secluded corner of science, where the change would not reverberate so widely through the system.
>
> This is how I explain what Parsons points to as the inaccessibility of mathematical truth to experiment, and it is how I explain its aura of a priori necessity.[37]

V. Holism and Analyticity

Our sketch of Quine's views on analyticity has invoked holism at a number of crucial junctures: to explain his rejection of the atomistic notion of cognitive meaning that figured in our initial supposition; to explain Quine's reasons for thinking that analytic sentences do not differ from others in any epistemologically significant way; and, finally, to explain how an empiricist can accept mathematics and logic as part of our knowledge. The final point I want to make in this essay is that I don't think that the best way to think of the issues we have discussed is as a number of distinct arguments, each of which happens to have holism as a crucial premise. Certainly it would be quite wrong to think that it is somehow a matter of chance that a single doctrine is involved here.

To the contrary: Quine's holism is part and parcel of his reconception of knowledge in a way that leaves neither room for, nor need for, a serious notion of the a priori. The crucial result of this reconception, from the present perspective, is that *all* claims to knowledge can be judged by a single criterion: whether the given sentence is part of a theory that, taken as a whole, is superior to any available rivals. This criterion applies to individual sentences by taking them as integral parts of wider theories; there is not, in general, going to be any criterion that is applicable to sentences taken one by one, in isolation from the theory in which they figure. The criterion is, of course, exceedingly abstract and general. At a more concrete level, there will be various things to say about various sentences. What Quine denies, however, is that there is an interesting or useful bifurcation into very general sorts of points that apply to analytic sentences and very general sorts of points that apply to synthetic sentences. At the most general level, justification is monistic: there is one very general criterion applicable to sentences of all kinds. Our point about epistemological significance follows immediately from this statement: even analytic sentences are judged by this same criterion, hence they are not on a different epistemological footing from others. The lack of need for a separate account of the a priori also follows as soon as we see that the criterion applies to the putatively a priori, to logic and mathematics, in particular.

Essentially the same point is involved in Quine's rejection of an atomistic notion of cognitive meaning as a basis for analyticity. We might put it like this. If we consider cognitive meaning atomistically, as applying to sentences one by one, then very many of our sentences lack cognitive meaning entirely, since taken by themselves they have no implications for experience. These will include many sentences no one wants to call analytic. This consequence may lead us to use a more liberal notion, and say that a sentence has cognitive meaning just in case it plays a crucial role in a theory that, taken as a whole, has implications for experience. In that case, however, we have a notion that applies equally to logic and mathematics. The underlying point, however, is that for almost all sentences a workable notion of justification, and hence of cognitive meaning, must apply not to the individual sentence but rather to the theories in which it figures; and that any notion of this sort will apply to the supposedly a priori as well as to the supposedly empirical.[38]

REFERENCES

Barrett, Robert, and Roger Gibson, eds. 1990. *Perspectives on Quine*. Oxford: Blackwell.

Boghossian, Paul. 1996. Analyticity Reconsidered. *Noûs* 30, pp. 360–391.

Carnap, Rudolf. 1950. Empiricism, Semantics, and Ontology. First published in *Revue Internationale de Philosophie* 4, pp. 20–40; reprinted in *Meaning and Necessity*, pp. 205–221.

———. 1956. *Meaning and Necessity*, second edition. Chicago: University of Chicago Press.

Creath, Richard, ed. 1990. *Dear Carnap, Dear Van*. Berkeley: University of California Press.

Floyd, Juliet and Sanford Shieh, eds. 2001. *Futures Past: The Analytic Tradition in Twentieth-Century Philosophy*. New York: Oxford University Press.

Hylton, Peter. 1982. Analyticity and the Indeterminacy of Translation. *Synthese*, pp. 167–184.

Hahn, L.E. and P.A. Schilpp, eds. 1986. *The Philosophy of W.V. Quine*. La Salle: Open Court.

Putnam, Hilary. 1962. The Analytic and the Synthetic. In Herbert Feigl and Grover Maxwell, eds., *Minnesota Studies in the Philosophy of Science*, III (Minneapolis: University of Minnesota Press); reprinted in Putnam, *Mind, Language, and Reality* (Cambridge: University of Cambridge Press, 1975), pp. 33–69.

Quine, W.V. 1960. *Word and Object*. Cambridge, Massachusetts: MIT Press.

———. 1961 [1953]. Two Dogmas of Empiricism. In *From a Logical Point of View* (Harvard University Press), pp. 20–46.

———. 1969. Epistemology Naturalized. In *Ontological Relativity and Other Essays* (New York: Columbia University Press), pp. 69–90.

———. 1970. *Philosophy of Logic*. Englewood Cliffs: Prentice-Hall.

———. 1974. *The Roots of Reference*. La Salle: Open Court.

———. 1976 [1966]. Carnap and Logical Truth. In *The Ways of Paradox* (Harvard University Press), pp. 107–132.

———. 1976. Truth By Convention. In *The Ways of Paradox*, pp. 77–106.

———. 1991. Two Dogmas in Retrospect. *Canadian Journal of Philosophy* 21, pp. 265–274.

———. 1994. *In Conversation: W.V. Quine*. London: Philosophy International, Center for the Philosophy of the Natural and Social Sciences, London School of Economics.

Richardson, Alan. 1998. *Carnap's Construction of the World*. Cambridge: Cambridge University Press.

Schilpp, P.A., ed. 1963. *The Philosophy of Rudolf Carnap*. La Salle: Open Court.

Skorupski, John. 1998. *John Stuart Mill*. London: Routledge.

9

On Wanting to Say, 'All We Need Is a Paradigm'

RUPERT READ

Rupert Read is a lecturer in philosophy at the University of East Anglia. He is the editor of The New Wittgenstein *(with Alice Crary) and* The New Hume Debate *(with Kenneth Richman). His recent publications include* Kuhn: Philosopher of Scientific Revolution *(with Wes Sharrock) and "Perspicuous Presentation: A Perspicuous Presentation," in* Philosophical Investigations.

Can the *philosophy* of the social sciences do what it most centrally wants to do, namely, to specify how the social sciences ought to work?

What normative recommendations, if any, can philosophers and methodologists actually make or state (coherently and groundedly) on the question of how to correctly *constitute* a social *science?*

The great Cambridge (Harvard and MIT) philosopher, Thomas Kuhn, is widely thought to have offered or implied very particular answers to these questions, answers which have been taken up with enthusiasm by some social scientists, and regarded with dismay by some philosophers.

If we want to know more, the most profitable way to proceed initially may be by looking at those who have attempted to employ or 'oppose' Kuhn in this regard.

The Question of Social Scientists'
Appropriation of Kuhn

When one starts to look closely at Kuhn in relation to the *social* sciences, a question, indeed a *conundrum,* strikes one. Because Kuhn is, without much doubt, the most apparently-influential post-Popperian philosopher of the social sciences. And yet he wrote almost *nothing* directly on the topic. How come?

Kuhn has been enthusiastically taken up by some postmodernists, by some apologists for the social sciences, and by some major social theorists. They've read him as systematically licensing the thought that if only social scientists were able to get to agree on a 'paradigm' within which to focus their research, then that would be enough—the social sciences would genuinely *be* sciences.

Meanwhile, Kuhn has been viewed with alarm by Popper, by Feyerabend, and by mainstream Realist philosophers of science, for just the same reason—he apparently legitimates the pretensions of the social sciences and much more, when what should be happening (according to these critics) is the remorseless exposure of the social sciences' non-scientific status, unless and until they adopt an acceptable methodology etc. (such as, for the Popperians, Falsificationism).

The conundrum here is sharpened when we note that Kuhn himself wondered rather irritatedly what all the fuss was about. He evidently felt that both his 'fans' and his 'foes' had got the wrong end of the stick in supposing his views to have these drastic implications for the social sciences. I want to explore here the possibility that he might have been right about his own work—the possibility, that is, that observers of science tend to have the wrong image of (what Kuhn implied about) the scientificity of the non-natural sciences.

This standard yet, I think, *wrong* image of Kuhn is, in outline, as follows: The way to scientificity is simply the *establishment of* the dominance of a *paradigm* in one's discipline. One needs to professionalize one's discipline around the central focus of the doctrines of one of its schools, and that's all. The pro-Kuhn camp takes the message of this to be 'We just need a paradigm—if we enforce agreement on a paradigm, then we can be a proper science. There's nothing more to being a proper science than that'. The anti-Kuhn camp takes the message to be 'Kuhn legitimates relativism and mob rule, because any group of people can "get" a paradigm in that sense—the genuine sciences will not be able to distinguish themselves from pseudo-sciences, if Kuhn's ideas are accepted'.

But has either camp caught onto what Kuhn was actually saying? What in fact *is* the nature and force of his 'paradigm' idea?

An Approach to This Question Via the Feyerabendian Critique of Kuhn

It has recently begun to be noted that this may all involve a huge misconstrual of Kuhn.[1] But those who have so suggested, such as Fuller and Hollinger, have tended to just reverse the image of Kuhn that they find in his conventional foes and fans: rather than finding Kuhn to be a quasi-political apologist for social science, they find him to be a quasi-political apologist for *natural* science, instead.

I wish to see if there is a reading of Kuhn available on which he is neither of these—but simply a philosopher of science trying to put the history and sociology of science on a secure footing, trying to free it up from the fetters of particular normative methodologies or political agendas. I can think of no better way of beginning this task in earnest than by looking at the strong words said to Kuhn by someone often thought to be one of his allies: Paul Feyerabend.

Here is Feyerabend, in a letter to Kuhn which sounds unmistakable notes of warning, and of negativity:

> I more than ever think your essay [*The Structure of Scientific Revolutions*] is quite unique as regards the contribution it makes both to the history and to the philosophy of science. On the other hand my impression of danger, and my misgivings[,] have been very much increased. What you are writing is not just history. It is *ideology covered up as history*. Now please, do not misunderstand me . . . [I do not] pretend that in history a nice distinction can be drawn between what is regarded as a factual report, and what is regarded as an interpretation according to some point of view. But points of view *can* be made explicit. . . . Nobody will think that the history of crime justifies crime, or shows that crime possesses an inherent 'reason' or an inherent morality of its own. In the case of the sciences or of other disciplines [for] which we have respect the situation is much more difficult and the distinction cannot be drawn with equal ease. But in these cases it is of paramount importance *to make the reader realize that it still exists*. You have not done so. Quite on the contrary, you use a kind of double-talk where every assertion may be read in two ways, as the report of a historical fact, and as a methodological rule.[2] You thereby take your readers in. . . . I do not object to your [having the] belief that once a paradigm has been found a scientist should not waste his time looking for alternatives but try working it out. . . . What I do object to most emphatically is the way you present this belief of yours; you present it not as a *demand*, but as something that is an obvious consequence of historical facts. Or rather, you do not even talk about this belief, you let it as it were emerge from history as if history could tell you anything about the way you *should* run science.[3]

And here is a more indirect but nevertheless significantly anti-Kuhnian remark, also from the early 1960s:

It is very important nowadays to defend . . . a normative interpretation of scientific method . . . even if actual scientific practice should proceed along completely different lines. It is important because many contemporary philosophers of science seem to see their task in a very different light. For them actual scientific practice is the material from which they start, and a methodology is considered reasonable only to the extent to which it mirrors such practice.[4]

For "actual", one can (I think) read Kuhn's own term "normal" without much disturbing the sense.

Now I wish to consider in some detail whether the kind of critique being made here *actually and fully* applies to Kuhn, as an effective means of considering the more general question of whether the widespread, indeed almost *standard* reading of Kuhn, as meaning to legitimate or at least as in fact legitimating (whether he explicitly meant to or not) the general recipe of the establishment of dominance of one paradigm as the road to scientificity, is itself a legitimate reading (of Kuhn). That is, I will endeavor to establish what Kuhn's text actually entails and supports—what it actually *can* support and *wishes to* support—and I will distinguish this from the kinds of misreadings and over-dramatisations which Kuhn's *followers* (such as social scientists wanting to be able to say, 'We just need a paradigm!') and *foes* (such as those who have worried that Kuhn is depicting science as saturated with power, as 'mob rule' or at best 'elite or institutional rule') *alike* have tended to impose upon him (albeit sometimes with Kuhn's unwitting help).

Are Feyerabend's Criticisms Valid?

So then, *what of Feyerabend's claims here?* To evaluate them we will need to look in some detail at the relevant sections of Kuhn's work. Those are Kuhn's discussions of the 'road', if there is one, to normal science, and in particular his comments on where on that road the social sciences might be.

Kuhn writes of 'pre-paradigmatic' sciences. And of the emergence of a paradigm through the establishing by one of the schools of thought that exist in 'pre-paradigmatic' disciplines of a hegemony, a dominance. This can sound awfully like what Kuhn's followers and foes (mentioned above) find in his text. But does what Kuhn writes about this in fact imply a prescription for what social scientists ought to do? Let us focus in on one of Kuhn's rare direct remarks on the social sciences in this context:

In parts of biology—the study of heredity, for example—the first universally received paradigms are [really quite] recent; and it remains an open question what parts of social science have yet acquired such paradigms at all. History suggests that the road to a firm research consensus is extraordinarily arduous.[5]

It is worth paying quite close attention to this quotation. Does it imply that social sciences must be on the road to a research consensus, if they are to be doing anything worthwhile? Does it license the thought, 'obvious' to positivists but also attractive to any who look to put a social science, or their social science, on a 'secure' or 'scientific' footing, that what is really required is a paradigm to bring the social science in question together 'under one roof', to put it firmly on "the route to normal science"?

The use of the word "yet" might imply such a teleological vision. And likewise the phrase that Kuhn uses elsewhere, "pre-paradigmatic". But just because certain disciplines have become . . . disciplines, have become sciences, surely cannot imply that *all* will. For example, here is one possibility: that the social sciences will eventually come to appear to most of us as astrology appears to most of us now—as a pathetic attempt to ape science, failing due to its failure to have a genuine tradition of research, a genuine actionable set of problems and puzzles.[6] Here is another possibility: that the social sciences might 'stay' in what Kuhn describes (misleadingly perhaps again) as the " 'early' fact-gathering" stage. That they might remain 'disciplines without a paradigm' (a phrase deliberately lacking the imaginable teleological consequences of "pre-paradigmatic"). Here is a third possibility: that the social sciences might be best understood as already in some degree operating in a manner which is ill-captured by the formula of "fact-gathering", but not in a manner akin to that of a science—for example, perhaps they have a systematically 'hermeneutic' structure.

I think there is reason to think that all of these three possibilities have *something* to be said for them. But the immediate point is this. I hope it will not be taken as a redundant vacuity if I remark that Kuhn describes for us the structure of normal science and of scientific revolutions—*in those disciplines which do in fact fit the description.* In disciplines which 'find themselves' with paradigms. He lays down no advice or prognostication for disciplines without a paradigm. There is *nowhere* in Kuhn—not in the quote given above, nor anywhere else—a *claim* that one can confidently predict that in a discipline with schools, the eventual victory of one school can be confidently predicted. I do not mean simply: the victory of one particular named school. No, I mean the victory of any school, ever. Kuhn's claim concerning the emergence of paradigms is purely a *retrospective* claim. *He is talking about the structure of the emergence of those disciplines that have become sciences.* Not providing a manual for the creation of new sciences. He is, at least by implication and omission, pretty clear that that there can never be a guarantee that a discipline without a paradigm will acquire one, and thus no sense in which it can be obvious and perspicuous that (for example) the social sciences are well-conceptualized as on the road to normal science.

For the victory of a school, the construction of certain types of institutions is perhaps necessary. And certainly afterward. But this does not imply that it is a good idea to construct such institutions at any particular time. Nor that the construction of same will ever be *enough*. One needs to have sets of agreed-upon exemplars, common methods or ways of acting, and an absence of ongoing foundational disputes. There are strict limits to the extent to which any of these can be imposed upon others in the discipline unwilling to be imposed upon. One can try to suppress foundational disputes—for example, through hegemony in a professional association or in educational institutes in a discipline—but this is liable to be to some extent self-defeating, especially in any climate valuing academic freedom. Whichever way you cut the cake, it looks as if scientificity just ain't in the institutions (alone). And the struggle of schools for hegemony, the attempt to turn a school prematurely into a paradigm, can be the most self-defeating move of all.

An Example

This last point can be nicely illustrated by means of an example from Mary Midgley. She is discussing the attempts to transform psychiatry, for example, into a scientific discipline, with normal problems and an agreed research agenda. Someone who had read Kuhn, and who as a consequence of such reading had come up with the popular thought that what one had to do was indeed to try to get the methods of one's own school to triumph as *'the* scientific method' in psychiatry, would then presumably wage an essentially political campaign to demonstrate and enforce this, replete with accounts of how the beliefs of their school alone could enable psychiatry to understand itself and refine its methods and get lots of government money and be respectable among the medical community, etc. etc. The question is, would this be likely to be a productive thing to do? Would it be likely to hasten the advent of a truly scientific psychiatry?

Midgley addresses these thoughts by means of querying in particular whether Materialist schools of psychiatric thought are pursuing their efforts to scientifise their discipline in a way that ultimately makes much sense:

> [T]he reduction of mind to body is now seen as a major factor in determining diagnoses and methods of treatment. As two concerned practitioners in this field have put it, "Despite the ambiguity and complexity of psychiatry, it is striking that many students begin its study with the appearance of having solved its great-

est mysteries. *They declare themselves champions of the mind or defenders of the brain* . . . The unfortunate result is that many of them become partisans—and needless casualties—in denominational conflicts that have gone on for generations and that they scarcely understand." [Emphasis Midgley's]

As the authors point out, this metaphysical issue cannot be ignored. . . . It is "more than a question of taste whether we think about schizophrenia as a clinical syndrome . . ., as a set of maladaptive behaviours, a cluster of bad habits that must be unlearned, or as an 'alternative life style', the understandable response of a sensitive person to an 'insane' family or culture. Each of these proposals makes different assumptions about the phenomenal world and its disorders, and each has different consequences for psychiatric practice and research. . . . The result of ignoring the fundamental differences between perspectives is not to diminish sectarianism but, in the end, to encourage it."

Their quite long list . . . of possible ways in which schizophrenia might be seen shows plainly what tends to be wrong with reductive, exclusive approaches to large-scale problems. All these suggestions seem clearly worth taking seriously. One might reasonably expect that even the wildest of them might play some part in a proper understanding of this very obscure complaint. It seems reasonable to suggest that they would best be seen as viewpoints belonging to investigators encamped round the mountain of mental trouble. *Yet the temptation to choose one and to take sides is extremely strong for a profession that feels the 'scientific' imperative compelling it to choose only one approach.*"[7]

Thus Midgley is claiming that the idea that one of the existing schools ought to triumph in order to commence a glorious new age of normal science within a discipline which as yet lacks it . . . is part of the *problem,* not part of the solution. The effort to make one's discipline scientific may well encourage sectarianism, rather than diminishing it, and to no productive end. One might go so far as to say that in the human sciences, ironically, schools have tended to emerge and to firm themselves up—thus pre-empting perhaps the possibility of a unified account of their subject-matter sooner rather than later—precisely from and as a result of an effort to reach a point where they could become 'normal sciences', in Kuhn's terms. . . . That's bad—even, shocking—news, if it's true. It would take us too far afield to consider the point further in detail, but the reader might think of the current state of Literary Theory or of Sociological Theory as potential illustrations. Does not the advent of 'Theory' imply a would-be *telos* of dominance for one or another theoretical school? And does this actually help at all in constituting the discipline of (for example) sociology as a science? Or does it rather stand in its way?

I take this point that I have expanded upon from Midgley to be *highly consonant* with Kuhn's analysis. The attempt to *force* a victory of one school, the forced establishment of some dominant exemplars, and thus the imposition of a disciplinary matrix for the first time will normally result, not in a surer road to science, but in a surer continuation of the reign of 'schools'! That is, dogmatic efforts to transform a discipline into a science will normally have *just the opposite result* from that intended. One will instead foster ongoing hostility and foundational disputes.

A discipline will only become a science à la Kuhn if that is, as it were, its fate. And there is simply no telling in advance of the facts, in advance of the success of a new exemplar or some such, whether any particular discipline is destined to go down that road. And after all, doesn't this make sense? If we knew where economics or literary criticism or what-have-you were going, wouldn't we all be there already?

To generalize, paraphrasing the sometime remark of a famous jazz musician: If we knew where 'pre-paradigms' were going, we'd be there already. This is surely what the sensible Kuhnian must say to the over-keen social studies-ists (or whoever) who search out a recipe in *The Structure of Scientific Revolutions* for putting their conflicted discipline onto the true path of a science.[8]

More of Feyerabend on Kuhn

Thus we must conclude provisionally that Feyerabend—a 'foe' of Kuhn on normal science and by extension on social science—has, like many others (including many apologists for social science, who hope for precisely what Feyerabend and the Critical Rationalists fear), importantly misread Kuhn on this point, on Kuhn's supposed recipe for the switch from 'pre-paradigmatic' activity to normal science. *Kuhn ought neither to be praised nor buried for having apparently given 'pre-paradigmatic' sciences a road or a menu toward normal science.* Because, appearances to the contrary, he simply did not do so. Careful reading indicates that he did not even attempt to provide such a road or recipe.[9]

If we now return for a moment to the quotation from Feyerabend with which I began this section, then his strong misreading of Kuhn becomes more obvious in retrospect. For Kuhn aims to record primarily not what scientists say they do, nor what others say they do, nor what they think they should do, nor what others think they should do, but *what they actually do*. Thus it is off-target for Feyerabend to refer to Kuhn as having the "belief" that scientists "should not waste . . . time looking for alternatives" to a working paradigm; and for him to claim that Kuhn is saying that history can tell you the way science *should* be run science rather drastically misses Kuhn's point.[10] Kuhn is simply trying to give an account of what history tells us about how science has actually been run, and as a consequence to question certain popular and philosophical normative philosophies of science.

However, we should also take care not to *over*-emphasize the extent to which Feyerabend's position on Kuhn on science is negative, and thus to overemphasize the extent to which Feyerabend unequivocally held the (mis)reading of Kuhn in question. In particular, it should be borne in mind that:

(i) Feyerabend, much more than the orthodox Popperians, found Kuhn's concrete accounts of scientific *revolutions* impressive and highly suggestive—suggestive of the extent to which such events are 'non-rational',[11] and even also, very importantly, have an aspect worth calling 'incommensurable' about them;

and

(ii) Rather more surprisingly, there can also be found in Feyerabend, if one searches it out, a different strand—namely, a *limited* but real defence or explication of Kuhn's *normal* science. Here is Feyerabend again:

[In the analysis of science] historical research and not rationalist declarations must now determine the nature of the entities used, their relations and their employment in the face of problems and...a *general* theory of science *must make room* for these specific parameters. It must leave specific questions unanswered and it must refrain from premature and research-independent attempts to make concepts 'precise'. Kuhn's account perfectly agrees with these desiderata. His paradigms are 'obscure and opaque'[12] not because he has failed in his analysis but because the articulation changes from case to case. The relation between theories and paradigms remains unresolved because each research tradition resolves it in its own way, in accordance with the cosmological, normative, empirical elements it contains. There is little specific advice concerning the treatment of anomalies because each paradigm deals with these matters in its own way. [Larry] Laudan's accusation [against Kuhn] of incompleteness (which he takes over from a host of bewildered philosophers of science who have read a few logic books but have never seen science from nearby) shows that despite his severely historical posture he still shares the rationalists' dreams for clear, well-defined and history-independent conceptual schemes.[13]

So now, rather than seeing 'normal science' and 'paradigm' simply as concepts that Kuhn unjustifiably leaves under-exemplified in his account, we might try seeing them as *themselves* 'paradigms' (exemplars), waiting for more applied uses which will *change* them, and necessarily general at the stage when Kuhn proposed them, in the service of a revamped sociology/history/ philosophy of science which would *develop its own examples* (and simultaneously—crucially—in the service of displacing and overtaking a monstrous prior philosophy of science). Thus Kuhn's account can—

thanks to Feyerabend's highly-insightful (and in this instance, in this insistence, highly-laudatory) perspective on it—perhaps be rendered compatible *with itself.* And, to repeat, this will involve a gestalt-switch to seeing the concept of 'paradigm' *as itself* a paradigm (an exemplar—albeit an unusually abstract one).

This highly-sympathetic (as opposed to highly negative) Feyerabendian interpretation of Kuhn *even on normal science* is to be found actually at a handful of important points in Feyerabend's work; for example, compare also the following:

> Understanding a period of science [according to Kuhn] is similar to understanding a stylistic period in the history of the arts. There is an obvious unity, but it cannot be summarized in a few simple rules and the rules that guide it must be found by detailed historical studies (the philosophical background is explained by Wittgenstein . . .). The *general* notion of such a unity or 'paradigm' will therefore be poor and it will state a problem rather than finding a solution: the problem of filling an elastic but ill defined framework with an ever-changing historical content. It will also be imprecise. Unlike the sections of a theoretical tradition which all share basic concepts the sections of historical traditions are connected only by vague similarities. Philosophers interested in general accounts and yet demanding precision and lack of ambiguity . . . are therefore on the wrong track; there are no general and precise statements about paradigms.[14]

This seems among other things a good reason for thinking that there will be an unjustified misreading going on if, without it being made plain that they are extending Kuhn's terms and adapting them for different purposes, someone takes Kuhn's terminology and outline abstract tentative necessarily-imprecise counter-hegemonic philosophical sociology to license a set of methodological rules[15] for transforming any discipline at any time from a set of studies to a science. What I have been trying to do is to see if Kuhn could be right in being angry about people reading him as legitimating the "We just need a paradigm!" idea. The answer is: to a large extent, if not quite completely (largely because of his easy-to-misread rhetoric), 'Yes'.

Feyerabend then does two things to or for Kuhn: He alerts us cleverly to the 'dangers' of normal science; *and* he makes clear how Kuhn's account of normal science is nevertheless useful, if applied with a selective philosophical sensibility, as opposed to formulaicly.

Do You Need a Paradigm to Catch a Paradigm?

What were folks expecting when they expected that Kuhn's *Structure* should show them a way forward for the human sciences, for their own social discipline, along the sure road of science? These sociologists and political scientists and psychologists and anthropological linguists, and perhaps also literary and art critics and historians and students of religion, were presumably expecting that Kuhn was pointing them toward something beyond his own practice. But if they had looked at that practice rather harder or longer, they might not have been so expectant that it would provide them with something radically new, with the outline of how to get hold of a paradigm *for their* use.

For one is struck, if one notes the listing of disciplines just made, that *Kuhn himself* borrows something from each of them. That is, one could well bear in mind his use of metaphors from religious studies and politics, his analogies to art history, his use of methods from textual criticism, his borrowings from gestalt psychology and from Sapir-Whorf, not to mention his straight history (and sociology). So: Kuhn's own practice draws far more on the practices of the human sciences and the humanities than does that of any other major philosopher of science. Kuhn is to some considerable extent *himself* a human scientist. Kuhn is doing philosophy, and is doing it after the fashion of interpretive human science far more than most philosophers of science (some of whom attempt to draw more on Logic, or 'Cognitive Science', or to build their own '[philosophical] *theories'* of science, for example).

And what does Kuhn's practice show us? By means of applying a historically-'based' approach to problems in the philosophy of science, it shows the existence of paradigms in natural science, it shows us the nature of normal science and of scientific revolutions. Thus Kuhn, looking at the behavior of certain human beings (principally scientists), finds in their practice paradigms—disciplinary matrices, and exemplars (whatever exactly you want to call them). He attempts to 'capture' how science works through employing the concept of 'paradigm'. And one hopes that what Kuhn is finding is not wholly of his own invention. In other words, one hopes that 'paradigms' are actually already there in the social practices of the communities which Kuhn is talking about. That, as Peter Winch would have it, a reasonable scientist could actually be brought to formulate her own experience in the kinds of terms that Kuhn offers. Kuhn is keen to reflect some important aspects of how scientists conceptualize their own practice when they do so reflectively— presumably he would hope to do so never more than in this key respect. In other words, Kuhn encourages one to look at the sciences and to see if one finds paradigms there. Paradigms are already objects of Kuhn's philosophical sociology. Exemplars and disciplinary matrices are both constitutive of the order of scientists' practices in a normal science situation. And again, they pre-exist Kuhn's description of them, they are not just artifacts of Kuhn's writing (unless Kuhn is quite wrong—in which case no-one would need worry about his lessons for the social sciences).

Now, what is it that human scientists more generally do? Is it not something very similar? For example, a sociologist looking at any set of practices, be they what they may, or an anthropologist looking at an 'alien' society; are they not in search of the beliefs, methods of acting, tacitly agreed norms *etc.* among the people they are looking at? Are they not in the business...of describing these?

I am suggesting the following: that, rather than taking inspiration from the *content* of Kuhn's descriptive history of the natural sciences, rather than looking for a paradigm to guide and enforce limitations on their own practice *qua* social scientists (an enterprise liable to be useless or even counterproductive as argued earlier in this section), social scientists could profitably look instead to Kuhn's version of their practice *as he himself employs it.* As he himself employs, that is, much the same method: in describing the history and sociology of science (sometimes fairly abstractly) and in teasing out their meaning for the philosophy of science. Social scientists could usefully think through the sense in which their own practice is *already* the searching out and describing of paradigms and their ilk. Do they *need* a separate paradigm of their own to do that properly? Might it not rather hinder their task? Take our sociologist, looking (say) at some set of religious practices and beliefs. Isn't the Wittgensteinian philosophers of social science, Peter Winch, right in saying that "the sociologist of religion will be confronted with an answer to the question: Do these two acts belong to the same kind of activity?; and this answer is given according to criteria which are not taken from sociology, but from religion itself."[16] Why? Because:

> The concepts and criteria according to which the sociologist judges that, in two situations, the same thing has happened, or the same action performed, must be understood *in relation to the rules governing sociological investigation.* But here we run against a difficulty: for whereas in the case of the natural scientist we have only to deal with one set of rules, namely those governing the scientist's investigation itself here *what the sociologist is studying,* as well as his study of it, is a human activity and is therefore carried on according to rules. And it is these rules, rather than those which govern the sociologist's investigation, which specify what is to count aas 'doing th same kind of thing' in relation to that kind of activity.
>
> An example may make this clearer. Consider the parable of the Pharisee and the Publican (Luke 18:9). Was the Pharisee who said "God I thank thee that I am not as other men are" doing the same kind of thing as the Publican who prayed "God be merciful unto a sinner"? To answer this question one would have to start by considering what is involved in the idea of prayer; and that is a religious question. In other words, the appropriate criteria for deciding whether the actions of these two men were of the same kind or not belong to religion itself." (p. 87)

Similarly: the appropriate criteria for deciding whether two people are engaged in the same kind of activity—are both testing a particular hypothesis or not, say—belong to that activity—say, the specific science in question—itself. At times of paradigm-shift, there may suddenly be divergent decisions among scientists on such issues, such decisions. That normally there are not is if you like a condition of possibility for the stability of the sciences as institutions at all. And that normally there are not is another way of saying: there are paradigms, *in* science.

Let us sum up the above. Kuhn's 'fans' say: Social science needs a paradigm (that doesn't exist yet). I say: Social science is about, among other things, finding paradigms *that exist already,* in social settings. (And what one surely needs to do in relation to such paradigms is to describe them, to be responsive to them as they already exist, not to impose an alien theory onto them.)

None of the above *proves* that social or human scientists are wrong to look to Kuhn for a blueprint. It *might* be that one needs a paradigm in order to look most effectively for paradigms; though that does sound rather like putting a cart in front of a horse.

But the above argument *does* imply that students of society should not think of the practice of finding paradigms and exploring their nature descriptively as radically new. Kuhn did what they have *already* been doing, to a considerable extent (and vice versa, now). And what they do looks very different from what natural scientists do—for the latter, unlike the former, do not have as their business *anything like* the description of paradigms. If they 'explore' paradigms, it is in an utterly different sense—through theorisation, experimentation, and so forth. And the point is that we have no particular reason to think that the human sciences will profit from aping such methods. For they need essentially to explore something like paradigms *which already exist,* rather than creating a new one. They need to effect a description of a set of human practices, a set of practices which do not necessarily need to have a paradigm or a set of categories or such like imposed upon them in order to become interpretable, for they already *embody* such a set of categories. They may even be argued to be correctly describable in principle in a sense unavailable to natural scientific inquiries, because there is no such thing as describing the non-human-world in a way that the latter prefers. Whereas perhaps the human world truly can be 'cut at its joints' (!)—by a description that respects it and (simply) gets it right, gets it in terms accurately reflecting participants' self-understandings and ordered activities. Paradigms and their ilk already exist—*in* social action (for instance, of scientists). No new terms or concepts or theories are necessarily required. As was brought out above in connection with Peter Winch, one loses sight of this aspect of the human sciences at one's peril.

The 'Kuhnian' apologists for social science may, in their desperation for respectability, be overlooking this possibility, the possibility that careful description of social action, of paradigms and so forth, may, as Mary Midgley among others suggests, already be possible ('even' in disciplines—the social studies—without a paradigm), *provided* one doesn't get sidetracked into fighting for dominance of a would-be social *science*. And the wish of Kuhn's cruder fans or appliers to ape natural science by means of 'getting' a paradigm, finding their own Newton, is deeply ironic. These people, who think that Kuhn has proven a kind of Relativism to be true, are still—at the very same time—wanting to have the kudos of being recognized as scientists, by means of having a paradigm to unify them and the paraphenalia of professionalism to maintain and enforce the unification. But this shows that they are still vulnerable to the attractions of Positivism. If they really had the confidence of their Relativist convictions, they wouldn't care about how the natural sciences conducted themselves, they wouldn't try to ape science as described by Kuhn or whoever—they would boldly strike out in their own direction, they would rest content with self-generated criteria for how, if at all, to distinguish between good and bad ways of structuring their discipline, good and bad work within their discipline. It is in fact a sign of deep disciplinary insecurity that one calls upon a philosopher of science to supposedly legitimate one's own discipline as being 'just as good' as the natural sciences. It makes no difference, whether one hopes to do that by pulling one's own discipline up to their level or pulling their discipline down to one's own level.

What I am saying can even be put thus: those who feel a need to argue that their discipline is as good as the natural sciences (or at least could be, if only it had a paradigm) are *ipso facto* still utterly in thrall to the prestige of the natural sciences. That's a very poor man's relativism!

The alternative of course is for 'the social sciences' to regard themselves as truly *sui generis,* as not needing to look to methodological aspects of the sciences with paradigms in order to validate themselves. This can only be done if more or less one accepts the current state of one's own discipline, ducks out of endless methodological debate (except insofar as it is necessary to puncture the aspirations of those who have been criticized above) and *gets on with* doing what good work can be effectively done within that discipline. For example, perhaps: in sociology, good ethnographies or descriptions of very diverse social practices. Including (but only as one case among many) of scientific practices.

Toward a Conclusion

The above discussion provides a final and, I think, decisive sense in which the message of Kuhn is utterly misunderstood if, for good or for ill, it is taken to be, "Social science can make itself just the same as, as good as, as effective as natural science, if only it gets itself a paradigm."

And so to sum up my discussion: The basic point of the concepts 'normal science' and 'paradigm' is to point up a distinction between disciplines where many of the participants are always tearing everything up and starting again, and disciplines where that doesn't happen. That distinction happens (and perhaps it is not mere happenstance!) at this point in history to coincide roughly with the divide between the social and the natural sciences.

After spending some time at the Center for Advanced Studies in the Behaviourial Sciences, while working on the ideas which would eventually become *The Structure of Scientific Revolutions*, Kuhn wrote the following words, which are there for all to see on p. vii of the "Preface" to *Structure*:

> I was struck by the number and extent of the overt disagreements between social scientists about the nature of legitimate scientific problems and methods. Both history and acquaintance made me doubt that practitioners of the natural sciences possess firmer or more permanent answers to such questions than their colleagues in social science. [*Kuhn is saying that it's not as if natural scientists have a superior explicit grasp on proper scientific methodology than social scientists. That's not the clue to the difference between them.*] Yet, somehow, the practice of astronomy, physics, chemistry or biology normally fails to evoke the controversies over fundamentals that . . . often seem endemic among, say, psychologists or sociologists. Attempting to discover the source of that difference led me to recognize the role in scientific research of what I have since called paradigms. These I take to be universally recognized scientific achievements that for a time provide model problems and solutions to a community of practitioners.

So: in astronomy, physics, chemistry—or increasingly nowadays, in subspecializations of those disciplines—scientists have a unifying idea *which comes from a certain impressive result or theory*—as, for example, Newton's laws were for a long time a universally agreed paradigm for physics.

Kuhn's concept of paradigm *comes* then from a distinction between disciplines like physics—disciplines with a paradigm, with one paradigm—and disciplines like sociology—disciplines without a paradigm; or, what comes to the same thing as not having a paradigm, disciplines with loads of competing paradigms, forming incompatible *schools* of thought. That our image of Kuhn may well have been quite wrong starts to become very clear when we realize that Kuhn *isn't* saying that enforcing the victory of one school *via* professionalization will do the trick of putting one's discipline on the secure road to being a science. The community of practitioners has to actually be impressed by, has to actually pretty much universally recognize a scientific achievement, and take it for a paradigm. If that doesn't happen, then too bad— *you don't have a science.*

Kuhn's main topic in his work is 'mature' sciences—or, better, 'disciplines with paradigms'. It's in *them* that we have actual examples of paradigms and paradigm-shifts. He doesn't dwell as much on transitions from 'pre-paradig-matic' to 'paradigmatic' states, and when he does so, it is only in cases where the transition has been made—disciplines with paradigms, the natural sci-ences—not surprisingly, for a historian of science!

Nor does Kuhn dwell very much on borderline cases of (mature) sciences. One extrapolates to these cases at one's peril—the interpretation given here of the true (and small, if you like) impact that Kuhn should have on the phi-losophy of the social sciences is far less perilous a way to go. And we have been clear that Kuhn was not in the business of laying down norms for how to *get* paradigms, nor saying that 'getting' a paradigm is always possible.

Especially in light of the fact that Kuhn was very mad at the appropria-tion by him of relativists, post-modernists and apologists for the social sci-ences. My policy is to at least *try* to read Kuhn such that he understood himself, understood his own work, was *not* badly confused or stupid—in this, I fol-low Kuhn's own hermeneutic, famously applied by him to cases like those of Aristotle and Carnot. On the topic of this paper at least, I think that that fol-lowing this hermeneutical approach is in fact not too difficult to do—and that Kuhn's 'foes' and 'fans' alike have more or less demonstrably got it wrong. I think that Kuhn could be quite-reasonably said to be mostly in the right in his righteous anger at those who saw him as trying to legitimate the "All social sciences need to be real sciences is to give themselves a paradigm" idea. To think that 'getting' a paradigm is sufficient to guarantee one's discipline real—normal—science is to put the cart before the horse again. For if we have a paradigm, then we have normal science, but a paradigm is something one has only if one actually *has* it, not if one fantasizes it or attempts to impose it. Again, for Kuhn a paradigm can't be forced on an area of investigation, it must emerge 'naturally.'

The clinching piece of evidence for my interpretation is from Kuhn's longest, if still fairly brief, consideration of an example from the social sci-ences in *The Structure of Scientific Revolutions*. (This passage develops the thoughts which were so influential in the very development of his ideas, as expressed in the quotation given above, from the Preface to *Structure*.) Here Kuhn addresses explicitly the question of what if anything the social sciences can learn from methodological reflection concerning the scientificity of their own disciplines:

> Why should the [scientific] enterprise . . . move steadily ahead in ways that, say, art, political theory or philosophy does not? Why is progress a perquisite reserved almost exclusively for the activities that we call science?

Notice immediately that part of the question is entirely semantic. To a very great extent the term 'science' is reserved for fields that do progress in obvious ways. Nowhere does this show more clearly than in the recurrent debates about whether one or another of the contemporary social sciences is really a science. . . . Men argue that psychology, for example, is a science because it possesses such and such characteristics. Others counter that those characteristics are either unnecessary or not sufficient to make a field a science. Often great energy is invested, great passion aroused, and the outsider is at a loss to know why. Can very much depend upon a *definition* of 'science'? Can a definition tell a man whether he is a scientist or not? If so, why do not natural scientists or artists worry about the definition of the term? Inevitably one suspects that the issue is more fundamental. Probably questions like the following are really being asked: Why does my field fail to move ahead in the way that, say, physics does? What changes in technique or method or ideology would enable it to do so? These are not, however, questions that could respond to an agreement in definition. Furthermore, if precedent from the natural sciences serves, they will cease to be a source of concern not when a definition is found, but when the groups that now doubt their own status achieve consensus about their past and present achievements. *It may, for example, be significant that economists argue less about whether their field is a science than do practitioners of some other fields of social science. Is that because economists know what science is? Or is it rather economics about which they agree?*[17]

In this passage, Kuhn, unlike his 'foes' and his 'fans', is proclaiming the uselessness of *defining* science.

Now, one could take issue with Kuhn's characterisation of economics here, and it might be quite interesting to do so—there are, I think, serious questions about whether economics is actually substantially different from other social sciences in the regard mentioned by Kuhn.[18] But the passage is pretty decisive so far as *interpretation* of Kuhn goes. For Kuhn's claim about economics is *hypothetical*; what he plainly implies here is that *if* economics has managed to take on some of the characteristics that we find in the natural sciences, it's not because of good philosophy or methodology of science. It's not because of 'following' Kuhn's philosophy of science, for instance, and 'getting' a paradigm—rather, it's simply that economists have been fortunate enough to be able to *agree*, to achieve a research consensus, *on matters of economics*. Economists, Kuhn is tentatively surmising, don't worry about fundamentals, but neither have they all explicitly agreed about methodology—they just get on with it.

Here is the crucial difference—the difference, which perhaps I have labored, but only because it is so crucial for understanding Kuhn aright, between *naturally acquiring* something like a paradigm, and merely *striving deliberately* to get the *trappings* of one. Kuhn's 'followers' and his 'anatagonists' alike confuse the latter with the former.

Returning then to the questions with which we began, we can note that Kuhn actually shows us that it's very questionable whether there can be anything that a normative philosophy of science can succeed in stating. In particular, the philosophy of social science wants to say things like, "All you need is a paradigm—let us specify to you how to get one" (or alternatively "What you need is a proper falsificationist scientific methodology")—but none of these prescriptions can be given any basis. Philosophers up to now have wanted to *change* science; however, according to Kuhn, the point is to *interpret* it, to understand it.

The positive point of all this, perhaps, is as follows: we can avoid confusion, avoid wasting time, and *see the social sciences as they actually are* more clearly, if, rather than taking the standard prescriptivist approaches, we take this genuinely Kuhnian approach. And we need to be quite clear that that approach has very little to do with the hopeless hopes of Kuhn's purported followers or with the wildly exaggerated fears of his purported foes. The conundrum presented at the opening of this paper is resolved when we realize just how systematically Kuhn has been misread by both sides here. When we realize that the popular conception of him as having grand consequences for social science is a castle built on just a few handfuls of sand. The completely discrepant accounts of the nature of the castle are a consequence of how small and loose the foundations of it are.

Kuhn's philosophy of science is in actuality fundamentally descriptive[19]— and prescriptive philosophy of science by contrast has little if anything to say.

Conclusion

In conclusion then, the drastic consequences for the social sciences—positive or negative, depending on whether you are an 'advocate' for the 'coming' scientificity of the social scientists, or a traditionalistic defender of the uniqueness of the natural sciences (in which category at present we can place the Popperians)—these drastic consequences that are supposed to follow from Kuhn's philosophy of science just do not follow, *on a correct reading of Kuhn.* The whole debate about the 'implications' of Kuhn for the theory and practice of social science has been misconceived from the start.

10

Causation and Ceteris Paribus Laws

NED HALL

Ned Hall is a professor of philosophy at Harvard University. He works mainly on metaphysics and philosophy of science, with a special emphasis on philosophical problems associated with the foundations of quantum physics.

Introduction

I am going to connect three topics: causation, causal relevance, and ceteris paribus laws, focusing mostly on the first and last. I am going to do so in a way that aims to solve—or at any rate, make some progress on—a long-standing problem about ceteris paribus laws to which the philosophical literature about them has devoted considerable attention. The problem, roughly, is to say exactly what is meant by the ceteris paribus clause in such laws, so as to clarify what exactly it is that such laws say, and in the process protect them from charges of vacuity and non-testability.

But of all this more later. To help fix ideas, let's start with a concrete example:

Suzy throws a rock at a window. Her rock flies through the air and strikes the window, breaking it. Focus on three distinct features of this situation. First, there is the fact that Suzy's throw is a *cause* of the window's breaking. Second, various parameters that characterize the situation at the time of Suzy's throw *matter* to whether that throw causes the window to break, and various other ones *don't*. For example, the mass of the rock is causally relevant in this way, but its color is not. Third, suppose we have managed to make an inventory of all the causally relevant parameters; then we might hope to find some *law* that expresses whether or not the window breaks as a function of these parameters: that is, some law that says, roughly, that when a rock is thrown at a window, the window breaks if and only if the values of such-and-such parameters (the mass of the rock, its velocity at the time of the throw, the distance between the thrower and the window, and so forth) are related in such and such a way.

Let's pause over this rock-throwing law. It is evident that it cannot be a *strict* law—by which I mean, a law that holds in any nomologically possible world—since there will be nomologically possible situations that satisfy the antecedent, but that also contain some interfering factor that prevents the window from breaking (there are other reasons, as well; we'll look at them shortly). Imagine for example that a rock is thrown at a window, and that all the relevant parameters have appropriate window-breaking values, but that a thermonuclear device is detonated in the vicinity while the rock is mid-flight. Or, less drastically, imagine that something intercepts the rock mid-flight. So we retreat, and say that the law that "covers" our example will be a *hedged* law, or, to use the more common but misleading term, a *ceteris paribus* law (more, shortly, on why this term is misleading).

So the three topics I'm concerned with—causation, causal relevance, and ceteris paribus laws—all make a straightforward appearance in this example. As I indicated, I'm going to argue that these topics are connected. Surprise, surprise. Who would have thought otherwise? But the surprise, such as it is, will come in my claims about how they are connected, and in the lessons that can be drawn from this connection for understanding the content of ceteris paribus laws.

Here is one very common conception of the connection, and of the problem that is widely taken to beset ceteris paribus laws. What is it for one event—for example, Suzy's throw—to cause another—for example, the window's breaking? It is, so the story goes, for those two events to instantiate some law (or perhaps for the cause, together with all those other events contemporaneous with it that are also causes, together with the effect, to instantiate some law). Similarly, what it is for certain of the parameters that characterize the causes to count as causally relevant is for those to be the parameters that are mentioned in the appropriate "covering" law. But, so the story continues, only in very rare cases will such covering laws be the kind of strict, absolutely exceptionless laws to which we look to fundamental physics for examples. More likely, especially in garden variety cases such as our example of Suzy and the window, they will be ceteris paribus laws of the kind that figure centrally in the 'special sciences'.

It is at this point that the story takes a rather unhappy turn, for there is supposed to be a special and rather serious problem about ceteris paribus laws. Our example already suggests that such laws need, minimally, to be qualified by some clause to the effect that nothing interferes. A moment's reflection will convince you that the range of possible interferences is vast, perhaps even infinite, perhaps even, as some philosophers are wont to say, 'unspecifiable in principle'. And that is supposed to be bad, for two main reasons. First, it is supposed to show that ceteris paribus laws are exposed to a charge of vacuity: the worry is that there is no way to precisely specify the content of the needed ceteris paribus clause that will not give it the sort of 'whatever it takes' character that will render the resulting law trivially true (for instance, 'ceteris paribus, conditions of type C are followed by conditions of type E' comes out as 'conditions of type C are followed by conditions of type E, except in those cases where they aren't'). Second, it is supposed to show that ceteris paribus laws are exposed to a charge of untestability: the worry is that unless and until the content of the ceteris paribus clause is made clear, we won't have any criterion for distinguishing between apparent counter-instances to a ceteris paribus law that are *genuine* counter-instances (because not covered by the ceteris paribus clause) and those that are *merely* apparent (because they are so covered).

I will say more shortly by way of trying to sharpen up these alleged problems about ceteris paribus laws. For now, I just want to make two broad observations. First, the standard conception of the connection between our three topics is exactly backwards. At the very least, it suggests a wrongheaded order of investigation, namely, that in order to get clear on what causation and causal relevance are, one first needs to get clear on what laws are, and in particular on what ceteris paribus laws are. That is back to front. Causation comes first: once we are clear on it—more exactly, as we will see, once we are clear on how to solve the most outstanding problem for giving an account of it—a natural account of causal relevance and ceteris paribus laws drops out. Second, the account of ceteris paribus laws that emerges yields a relatively clean and straightforward understanding of the "no interference" clause that must, apparently, accompany any such law; and in light of this understanding we will be able to see that the charges of vacuity and non-testability are empty.

Here is the picture, laid out in a little more detail, and beginning with a slight retraction. What I've called the standard conception of the connection between our three topics is really not at all standard—indeed, pretty clearly out of favor—among the small group of fanatical philosophers (like me) who work full-time in the causation industry. That is, if one surveys the range of currently popular approaches to giving a philosophical account of causation, one finds, for example, counterfactual approaches, probabilistic approaches, 'singularist' approaches, approaches that stress the existence of some sort of proprietary physical connection between cause and effect, and so on. One does not find, any more, too many partisans of the kind of regularity approach that might be thought to most straightforwardly embody what I've called the standard conception of the connection between laws, causation, and causal relevance. So it's really more accurate to say that the 'standard' conception is standard (to the extent that it is) in the *rest* of the philosophical world.

Never mind. What I really want to focus on is, first, that the causation literature is driven by obsessive (which is not to say misplaced) attention to certain canonical examples and by the need to handle those examples; and, second, that by far the most important of these examples are cases of asymmetric causal overdetermination. Rather than characterize them abstractly, I will just give a paradigmatic instance. Suppose that at the moment Suzy throws her rock at the window, her friend Billy likewise throws a rock at it. His is just a bit slower, however, and so reaches the location of the window a split second after the window has already shattered as a result of Suzy's throw. Then in a clear sense the shattering is overdetermined by Suzy's throw and Billy's throw: intuitively, each throw is *enough* to guarantee the shattering. But, equally clearly, the overdetermination is asymmetric: Suzy's throw gets sole credit as cause of the shattering, Billy's throw gets none. The problem for a whole swath of theories of causation—and it is quite a serious problem—is to explain this asymmetry.

Again, I will go into more detail about this problem shortly. But first the big picture: I think there is a right way to go about giving an account of causation, which is to understand it, broadly speaking, in terms of the counterfactual structure of the world (as we will see, that does not mean that I endorse anything like a Lewis-style counterfactual analysis of causation). I also think that cases of asymmetric overdetermination are a really serious, bloody painful thorn in the side of any such approach. But there is a clearly best way to handle them, a way that in fact succeeds in handling them. Applied to the case at hand, the solution goes roughly as follows: Suzy's throw counts as a cause of the window's breaking, even in the presence of Billy's backup throw, because there is a process connecting her throw to the breaking that is intrinsically similar, in relevant respects, to what would have happened if Suzy alone had thrown. By contrast, Billy's throw does not count as a cause of the window's breaking, because, even though there are many processes connecting Billy's throw to the breaking (understanding a process simply to be an arbitrary sequence of events), none of these processes is intrinsically similar in relevant respects to what would have happened if Billy alone had thrown.

That's a mouthful, but its intuitive force can be seen more clearly if we approach it from another angle. Start with the case where Suzy alone throws, and nothing else is happening. The sequence of events connecting her throw to the shattering has a certain intrinsic character. All that happens when we include Billy and his throw is that we add stuff to the environment of this process which does not alter its intrinsic character—or at least, not in any relevant respect. That is why Suzy's throw still counts as a cause of the shattering. Now, by contrast, start with a case where Billy alone throws. When we add Suzy and her quicker throw, we *do* alter the intrinsic character of the sequence of events connecting Billy's throw to the shattering: a spatiotemporal gap opens up where before there was none. And that is a relevant alteration. In short, if we want to map out the causal characteristics of some messy situation—as it might be, a situation involving the asymmetric overdetermination of one event by some earlier ones—we need to do so by making explicit reference to certain 'clean' situations.

Quite obviously, this approach is going to need further motivation, elaboration, and defense. What we will see is that once we have done so, and in particular once we have said how to pick out "clean" situations and how to discern the relevant and irrelevant respects of comparison between them and any given situation, a very natural story about ceteris paribus laws will drop out. They will be seen to be, strictly, *about* the clean situations. And once this is clear, any worry that they are, at bottom, vacuous or untestable will dissolve.

Basic Metaphysical Commitments

So much for a broad overview. Getting down to details requires, first, that I lay out some basic metaphysical commitments that I'm going to take on board.

I will assume that every fact about our world, and in particular facts about what causes what, what is causally relevant to what, and what ceteris paribus laws there are, do not merely *supervene on*, but *reduce to*, first, the sum total of purely non-modal or categorical facts about our world, and, second, the facts about what the fundamental laws are that govern our world. It is worth emphasizing, especially in the present context, that I am assuming that there is a sharp and profound distinction between the fundamental laws of our world—which I take to be the sorts of laws that fundamental physics aims to discover—and any other laws (for instance, those of the special sciences). Putting the point another way, while I am happy to grant that it is a truism that all sciences aim to discover laws, I think it is a misleading truism, since it glosses over an extremely significant difference between the aims of fundamental physics and the aims of the special sciences. They are not hunting at all the same sort of game.

Not surprisingly, my conception of what fundamental physical laws are is heavily informed by physics: I think of them as fixing how complete physical states of the world evolve into successive physical states. But that is really giving them more structure than is necessary for my purposes here. All I require is that whatever the fundamental physical laws are, they fix a sharp distinction between those worlds that are nomologically possible relative to ours, and those that are not. For they will thereby fix the counterfactual structure of the world, and it will emerge that causal facts and facts about ceteris paribus laws are in a fairly direct sense *facts about that structure*. At any rate, there are a number of philosophical analyses of laws that differ quite dramatically in their details, but that all deliver a conception of fundamental laws that draws the needed distinction, and for my purposes it won't matter which one if any of those one assumes to be correct. Note that I will make one further assumption about the laws, but only in order to simplify the discussion: I will take it that they are deterministic, and permit neither backwards causation nor action at a temporal distance.

Causation as a Nomological Entailment Relation

Given these background metaphysical commitments, it seems to me that by far the most promising approach to causation is to analyze it in terms of some sort of 'nomological entailment' relation. What do I mean by this? Roughly, that the analysis seeks to treat causation as, at bottom, consisting in some kind of entailment relation holding between cause and effect (more precisely: between the propositions that the cause occurs, and that the effect occurs), where this entailment is mediated by the fundamental laws. If that's *too* rough, let me try ostension instead; herewith some examples:

Crude sufficient condition account: c causes e iff c and e both occur, and in any nomologically possible world in which c occurs, e occurs.

Crude necessary condition account: c causes e iff c and e both occur, and in any nomologically possible world in which e occurs, c occurs.

Mackie-style regularity account: c causes e iff c and e both occur, and from the fact that c occurs, together with some suitable auxiliary premises describing contingent facts about the circumstances in which c occurs, together with the laws, it follows that e occurs; but this fact does *not* follow from the auxiliary premises and the laws alone. (This is roughly Mackie's view: causes are necessary parts of sufficient conditions for their effects.)

Simple counterfactual account: c causes e iff c and e both occur, and had c not occurred, e would not have occurred. (The role the fundamental laws play in deter-

mining the truth-values of the relevant counterfactuals is what earns this and kindred counterfactual accounts the name "nomological entailment" accounts.)

There are many, many other accounts that could be mentioned, but these
will do to give the flavor. Note that while nomological entailment accounts
cover a lot of ground, they still leave some influential approaches out in the
cold. For example, I would reject so-called singularist approaches, which treat
causation as a metaphysically primitive relation, not merely because they conflict with my basic metaphysical commitments, but because they do so in a
way which strikes me as pathetically defeatist. And I would reject the kind
of physical process oriented approach championed by Phil Dowe among others both because it is far too crude to capture causal relations in the messy
macroscopic world (and probably too crude even for causation at the most
microphysical level), and because it is defeatist in another way, declining to
say anything about what causation would be like in worlds with very different laws from our own.

The Problem of Asymmetric Overdetermination

At any rate, that is a battle for another day. For now, having singled out nomological entailment relations for attention, we can see a bit more clearly why
cases of asymmetric overdetermination pose such a problem. Pick your favorite
nomological entailment relation. It is pretty much just a homework exercise
to design a variant on our Billy and Suzy case such that both the genuine
cause and the would-be cause are on a par; either both or neither bear the target relation to the effect. For example, in the case as we gave it, the shattering counterfactually depends on neither throw, either throw is sufficient in
the circumstances for it, neither throw is connected to it by the ancestral of
counterfactual dependence (compare Lewis 1973), and so forth.

The literature is chock full of attempts to get around this difficulty by
designing ever more subtle entailment relations. Counterfactual dependence
won't do? Try insisting that causation is not a matter of bare counterfactual
dependence alone, but also a matter of how the exact manner in which the
effect occurs depends on the exact manner in which the cause occurs (Lewis
2000). Or maybe we add more complicated conditions, as Ramachandran
does in his 1997 "M-set" analysis: event c is a cause of event e iff there is
some set of actual and merely possible events such that (i) c is the sole actual
member; (ii) if none of the events in the set had occurred, then e would not
have occurred; (iii) the same is not true of any proper subset. Or maybe we
go back to the simple counterfactual approach, but beef up the antecedent in
certain ways: Suzy's throw is a cause of the breaking because, *holding fixed*

that Billy's rock did not strike the window, had Suzy not thrown the window would not have broken; whereas Billy's throw is not a cause because . . . hmm, rather difficult to fill in the details (let alone give coherent truth-conditions to the counterfactual that is supposed to bear witness to the causal status of Suzy's throw—though see Yablo 2002 and Hitchcock 2001 for attempts).

It will be apparent that I don't think much of these approaches, popular though some of them are, nowadays. In fact, I don't think that any reasonable nomological entailment relation will distinguish genuine causes from would-be alternatives across the board, in cases of asymmetric causal overdetermination. And yet I think that a nomological entailment approach is the right approach. How's that, exactly? We'll have to wait and see, when I sketch how I think the problem posed by these cases ought to be solved. But first we have one more preliminary, which is to make some distinctions by way of sharpening up the problems posed for the special sciences by their apparent reliance on ceteris paribus laws.

Caeteris Paribus Laws: Targeting the Problem

There seem to be two basic ways you can go wrong in trying to give an account of the generalizations of the special sciences. One is to think that they are all of a type; the other is to think that even when one has singled out a particular type, there is only one way in which generalizations of that sort need to be hedged, in order to make contentful true claims. Let's take these issues in turn, with the aim of zeroing in on a single kind of ceteris paribus law, and a single job (one among several, as will emerge) that the ceteris paribus clause is supposed to perform.

There appear to be a variety of different kinds of generalizations that crop up in special sciences, and it would certainly be a mistake, at the outset anyway, to assume that they have anything deep in common. There are for example *idealizations*, such as the ideal gas law. And *type-causal claims*, such as the claim that smoking causes lung cancer. And *generics*, such as the claim that carbon in organic molecules has four bonds. I'm not going to be considering any of these, but will rather narrow my focus to claims of the following form:

Ceteris paribus, for any time t, if conditions of type C obtain at t, then conditions of type E obtain at future time $f(t)$.

Two quick points. First, this form is a little bit too restrictive, for I also mean to cover cases where the conditions E are asserted to obtain within some specified *interval* after time t. Second, I am in fact going to narrow my focus further to cases where it is understood that, at least when we have a genuine instance of the ceteris paribus law, the conditions C *cause* the conditions E to obtain. Our example of the rock-throwing law is like this. Contrast such laws with ones that proceed, as it were, from effect to cause, such as the following: ceteris paribus, when the mercury in a thermometer rises, the temperature in the surroundings increased shortly beforehand. And, with laws that assert a relationship between joint effects of a common cause: ceteris paribus, if you and I are watching television, and our televisions are tuned to the same station, then whatever you see, I see. And, finally, with laws that assert a relationship between a condition and something that it doesn't necessarily cause, but that it causally guarantees: ceteris paribus, when the first input to an or-gate is switched on, the output will be switched on shortly thereafter. (It might be that cases where *both* the first and second inputs are switched on count as instances of this law, even if, given the inner workings of the or-gate, it is only the second input that *causes* the output to switch on.) For short, I will be considering just 'cause to effect' ceteris paribus laws. It will, however, be more or less obvious that the techniques for dealing with them can be extended to other cases. More speculatively, it may be that these techniques can be extended in certain ways to cover generics, and to cover type-causal claims. At any rate, I'll leave the development of those speculations for another day.

Now that we have picked out a target kind of generalization, we need to consider the reasons why any such generalization needs qualification by a ceteris paribus clause. I think the best way to do this is to consider the strict law associated with any ceteris paribus law—that is, the law shorn of any qualifications, and taken to hold with nomological necessity. What we will see is that there are a *variety* of distinct ways in which these associated strict laws can fail; the idea that there is some *single* ceteris paribus qualification is therefore inapt. We will also see that for most sorts of failure, hedging against them is *not* accomplished by adding the clause, 'other things being equal'—another respect in which talk of a 'ceteris paribus' qualification is seriously misleading.

In the abstract, the strict laws we are considering have the following form: In any nomologically possible world, for any time t, if conditions of type C obtain at t, then conditions of type E obtain at time $f(t)$. I can think of six different ways in which such a strict law might fail.

First, it might involve an element of idealization in virtue of which it cannot hold strictly, but at best only approximately—even in cases that are meant to be canonical instances of it. Thus, a law that says that objects dropped near the surface of the earth accelerate downwards at a rate of 32 feet per second per second incorporates the (strictly false) idealization that the force of gravity is constant throughout the duration of the fall.

Second, it might be that all that is strictly true is that the C-conditions raise the probability of the E-conditions to very close to one. Thus, suppose we have a law about sealed containers with partitions in them, on one side of which is a gas, and on the other side of which is vacuum. Our law says that if the partition is removed at a time t, the gas will expand to fill the entire chamber within a short period of time after t. We know from statistical mechanics that that stands in need of a probabilistic qualification, since it is possible, if astronomically unlikely, that the particles of the gas have such a configuration of positions and velocities that when the partition is removed, the gas stays put.

Third, it might be that while the law is clearly intended to state more than a merely accidental generalization about our world, it cannot be claimed to hold with nomological necessity, but perhaps only across a restricted range of the nomologically possible worlds. As a fanciful example, imagine that it turns out that the chemical properties of atoms and molecules depend in subtle ways on fundamental physical parameters that could, as far as the fundamental physical laws are concerned, have had different values. We don't think that the chemist should have to care about such details, and correspondingly we might allow that the chemist, when announcing the discovery of some chemical law, should be charitably understood as including a rider that restricts the scope of the law to nomologically possible worlds in which the relevant parameters have their actual values.

I think one can accomplish something of the same effect by building, as it were, a lot into the essences of the kinds mentioned in a ceteris paribus law. Suppose, for example, that there is a nomologically possible alternative course of evolutionary history which would have produced humanoid creatures built a lot like us, with brains a lot like ours, but not *so* much like ours that the psychological generalizations that hold (ceteris paribus) for us hold for them. It might be that the psychologists, in stating ceteris paribus laws of their discipline, intend them to be laws of *human* psychology—and that these nomologically possible critters don't count as human.

Fourth, it might be that a law has, straightforwardly, *exceptions*—which is okay, as long as such exceptions are in some reasonable sense atypical (which should mean, at the very least, statistically rare, but may well have to mean more than this). Thus, carbon in organic compounds has four bonds. Well, typically, at any rate: there are exceptions, such as carbon monoxide. And perhaps there are other sources of exceptions. For instance, David Lewis, in "Mad Pain and Martian Pain," argues that it is possible for someone to be in excruciating pain that never causes them to exhibit typical pain behavior—so that they violate various psychological laws relating pain to pain behavior—not because they are an incredible stoic, but rather because they have a bizarre sort of functional organization. Why say that they are in pain, then, as opposed to some other state? (For if they are in some other state, then we don't have a violation after all.) Because, says Lewis, the state they are in is intrinsically similar to the states that play the functional role of pain in typical members of their kind. In a similar, but frankly more sensible vein, Jerry Fodor has argued, roughly, that we might have a functional role picked out by a large number of psychological laws, and we might have a particular realization of that role that counts as such because it conforms to *almost all* of these laws; this allows the realization to be an exception to *some* of the laws.

Onward. The fifth way that our strict law might fail is that the conditions mentioned in the antecedent are inadequately specified. And this shortcoming, in turn, might have a number of different sources. One might be sheer laziness. I say, for example, that it is a law that when dry matches are struck, they light, failing to mention the need for an adequate supply of oxygen in the vicinity. Next, it might be simply obvious that the law is intended to hold throughout a range of cases with certain constant background conditions. Our rock-throwing law, for example, might not be faulted if it does not explicitly mention that the rock is thrown at or near the surface of the earth. Somewhat more interestingly, it might be that certain parameters don't get mentioned in the antecedent not because those parameters are causally irrelevant, but because only for certain extreme values of them do they make a difference. Consider our rock throwing law again. Clearly, the temperature of the rock is in *some* sense causally relevant—after all, if the rock were hot enough, it would *melt* the window before it had a chance to break it. But it seems silly to mention the temperature of the rock explicitly in a statement of the law, roughly for the reason that in the range of cases we mean to be considering, the temperature of the rock makes no interesting contribution to whether or how the window breaks.

More interestingly still, it might be that certain parameters fail to get mentioned in the law simply because we don't know what they are. Thus, to take an example that is depressingly close to home, it seems to be a physiological law that one's blood cholesterol level is determined by, among other things, the levels of saturated fat in one's diet. But there are lots of other parameters that matter, and they haven't been sorted out yet. In a case like this, we are not of course in a position to state the ceteris paribus law in the form given. Rather, we will use a contrastive form: ceteris paribus, increased levels of saturated fat in one's diet lead to increased levels of blood cholesterol. The contrast that is intended is first and foremost not a temporal one, but a modal one. What's intended, that is, is not the claim that for any times t_1 and t_2, with $t_2 > t_1$, if the level of saturated fat in one's diet is higher at t_2 than it is at t_1, then the level of one's blood cholesterol shortly after t_2 is higher than it is shortly after t_1. That may well be right, but what is intended is rather a contrast between two *possible* situations, one in which the time t saturated fat levels are one thing, and the other in which the time t saturated fat levels are some other, higher value. What's more, this is one of the rare cases in which the 'other things being equal' reading of the ceteris paribus qualification is truly warranted; for what is *also* intended in making the contrast is that all other causally relevant factors, whatever they are, are held fixed between the two cases.

To sum up: So far, we've canvassed five different ways in which the strict version of a ceteris paribus law can fail, and so five different ways in which it needs to be qualified. I think it is obvious that these ways are related in interesting and subtle ways, and raise complex and important philosophical questions both about the content of ceteris paribus laws, and about the methodology for testing them. But these questions, fascinating as they are, are not going to be my concern. My concern, rather, has to do with the sixth and final way that such strict laws can fail: namely, because some factor independent of the conditions C can be present that acts to *interfere* with the C-to-E connection. And so it looks inevitable that all ceteris paribus laws will need, as *one* of their qualifications, some 'no interference' clause—that is, they will need to be understood as saying that C-conditions are followed by E-conditions, *provided nothing interferes*.

This point is worth stressing, partly because it seems occasionally to be misunderstood in the literature. Thus, Earman and Roberts hold that if a purported law of a special science needs a no interference clause, that simply shows that it is not a proper law all, but rather something like a way station on the road to finding a proper law:

> ... we wish to make the following suggestion. 'Ceteris paribus laws' are not what many philosophers have taken them to be, that is, they are not elements of typical scientific theories that play the same kinds of roles in the practice of science that less problematic statements such as strict laws or near-laws ... play. Rather, a 'ceteris paribus law' is an element of a 'work in progress', an embryonic theory on its way to being developed to the point where it makes definite claims about the world. It has been found that in a vaguely defined set of circumstances, a given generalization has appeared to be mostly right or mostly reliable, and there is a hunch that somewhere in the neighborhood is a genuine, well-defined generalization, for which the search is on. But nothing more precise than this can be said, yet. (1999, pp. 465–66)

That would be a nice result, since then we could all stop worrying, at least, about the revealed-to-be-pseudo-problem of ceteris paribus laws. But it won't look plausible, if in mature scientific theories that have already undergone a good deal of gestation, we find that laws standing in need of a no-interference clause are rife—and if the scientists in question do not appear particularly concerned to scour the neighborhoods of these laws in search of refinements that need no such qualification. So it is important for their purposes that Earman and Roberts make the case that laws that are held up as solid, upstanding citizens by the scientific disciplines that employ them do not, typically, stand in any need of the troubling 'no interference' qualification.

Earman and Roberts do not do this, but their discussion of one example suggests that they don't see any great difficulty, here:

> The ragged character of the philosophical literature on this topic is explained in part by the fact that it tries to treat under one umbrella several different usages. For example, there is the *lazy sense* of ceteris paribus, as in Lange's example of "cp: (if a metal bar is heated uniformly, its expansion is directly proportional to the difference in temperature before and after heating)." We contend that when physicists assert the heat expansion law they are implicitly assuming that there are no external stresses acting on the bar. If so, this assumption can be explicitly incorporated into the generalization, *obviating the need for a ceteris paribus qualification.* (1999, p. 461; last emphasis mine)

I think they would hold that any mature law that *looks* as if it needs a no-interference clause counts as a ceteris paribus law only in the lazy sense: for, just as in this case the surrounding theory provides a bit of proprietary vocabulary—'external stress'—that can be used to state a perfectly precise condition whose incorporation renders the no-interference clause otiose, so, in general, the mature theory in which the mature law is embedded will provide some such vocabulary, and some such condition.

But this is all confusion, because one can *of course* imagine other ways that the normal process by which heating a metal bar leads to its expansion is interrupted that don't involve the application of any 'external stress' to the bar. Suppose for example that the metal in question is sodium, and that while being heated up it is also brought into contact with a large quantity of water. If so, the bar and water will undergo an extremely violent chemical reaction, at the end of which the sodium will all be in the form of sodium hydroxide. Or maybe it's sodium hydride. I can't remember. At any rate, the metal bar will *not* expand in the way described by the law in question. Perhaps this is just the sort of thing Earman and Roberts have in mind as a paradigm example of an 'external stress', but I doubt it. What is more plausible is that, in issuing their critique, they have merely suffered from a minor failure of imagination. The moral I draw is that on this point at least the philosophical literature, "ragged" though it may be, is perfectly correct: even the most mature laws will typically need to be understood as carrying a 'no-interference' rider.

So it looks as if we need to understand our ceteris paribus laws in the following way. Bracketing the need for *further* qualifications having to do with restrictions on nomological scope, idealization, the possibility of exceptions, probability, and uncertainty about the relevant conditions, such laws say that in any nomologically possible world, at any time *t*, if conditions of type C obtain at *t*, and if there are at time t no interfering conditions, then conditions of type E will obtain at later time f(*t*).

Now, why exactly is the inclusion of such a 'no interference' clause supposed to pose a problem—indeed, a problem so serious as to threaten the legitimacy of every special science? It is not, frankly, at all clear. But for what it is worth, here is what seems to be the prevailing wisdom on the matter. The no interference clause is, as it stands, unacceptably vague. If it cannot be replaced with something more precise, then, first, we will have no assurance that a typical ceteris paribus law even makes a contentful claim—since, for all we know, the phrase 'there are no interfering conditions' might simply mean 'other conditions are such that the E-conditions will obtain.' And at any rate, even if we are confident that the clause does not have this trivializing meaning, its content remains too unclear for it to be possible to test any law qualified in this way—we do not know what could count as evidence for against the claim that no interfering factors are present.

On a purely autobiographical note, I have to confess that I find it hard to be gripped by either of these problems. It seems to me plain as day that the no interference clause does not have the trivializing meaning. Furthermore, I doubt very much that scientists are ever all that confused about what could count as evidence for or against the claim that there are interfering factors. Still, there seems reason enough to at least pretend to take the problem seriously, if only because 'solving' it promises to enhance our understanding of the content of ceteris paribus laws, and how exactly evidence for or against them works. In my own case, there is an extra motivation, since, as noted earlier, the way to go about trying to solve this problem will, I hope, expose interesting and unnoticed connections between causation, causal relevance, and ceteris paribus laws. Time now to turn to these connections.

How to Solve the Problem of Asymmetric Overdetermination

Back to causation. Let's remind ourselves what the problem is. We need to find some way to distinguish genuine causes from would-be causes in cases of asymmetric causal overdetermination. I have already indicated which strategies I don't recommend; let me now sketch the strategy I *do* recommend.

It begins with the idea that the causal structure of a process is intrinsic to it—fixed, that is, by the intrinsic character of that process, together with the governing laws (by which I mean *fundamental* laws). Now, that is too loose a statement to get us anywhere. The following somewhat more cumbersome formulation is better (see Hall 2004 for a detailed explanation and defense):

> *Intrinsicness:* Let S be a structure of events consisting of event *e*, together with all of its causes back to some earlier time t. Let S′ be a structure of events that intrinsically matches S in relevant respects, and that exists in a world with the same laws. Let *e′* be the event in S′ that corresponds to *e* in S. Let *c* be some event in S distinct from *e*, and let *c′* be the event in S′ that corresponds to *c*. Then *c′* is a cause of *e′*.

In a moment, I will get to why that suspicious word "relevant" is there. But first let me try to bring out the intuitive force of this principle. Suppose you have identified some event *e*, and you have also identified all of its causes back to some earlier time *t*. The structure constituted by all of these events has a certain intrinsic character, fixed by the exact manner in which its constituent events occur, and by their exact spatiotemporal relations to one another. Then the principle says, in effect, that the fact that the events in this structure distinct from *e* are all *causes* of *e* is invariant under alterations of the environment of that structure, or at any rate under alterations that leave the intrinsic character of the structure unchanged in all but irrelevant respects. Again, it will become clear soon enough why mention of relevant and irrelevant respects is intruding—and how to cash these notions out. But first let me sketch the strategy for applying this intrinsicness thesis to the problem posed by asymmetric overdetermination.

Take the case of Billy, Suzy, and the broken window. Suppose we have a provisional analysis of causation that does not get this case wrong, but that does not get it right either—our analysis simply falls silent about it. To fix ideas, here is an example: Our analysis says that when some events—call them the C's—occur at time *t*, and some other event *e* occurs at a later time *t′*, then the C's are all and only the causes of *e* occurring at time t if (not, note, only if) the following conditions are met:

1. the C's are *sufficient* for *e*, in the sense that if no *other* events had occurred at time *t* (but the C's still had), *e* would still have occurred;

2. the C's are *minimally* sufficient for *e*, in the sense that no proper subset of them meets condition *(1)*;

3. the C's are *uniquely* minimally sufficient for *e*, in the sense that no distinct set of events occurring at a time *t* meets conditions 1 and 2.

That analysis falls silent about our case, because the sufficient condition spelled out in it is not met: there will be a minimally sufficient set for the breaking of the window that includes Suzy's throw but not Billy's, and likewise one that includes Billy's throw but not Suzy's.

So far, not so good. But now consider a variant of our case, in which Billy is wholly absent, and the only thing that happens is that Suzy throws, in just the same way that she does in the hard case. Then it looks as if our provisional analysis will successfully identify Suzy's throw (together with the presence of the window itself, if we're willing to call that an 'event') as a cause of the shattering. What's more, it looks like it will be able to successfully identify, for each intermediate time between the time of the throw and the time of the shattering, the events that are the causes of the shattering. And so our analysis will be able to tell us about *that* situation, at least, that such and such a structure of events culminating in *e just is* a structure consisting of *e* together with all of its causes back to the time of Suzy's throw. It is exactly at this point that the intrinsicness thesis comes into play. For it allows us to say that in the hard case—the case where Suzy and Billy both throw—Suzy's throw counts as a cause of the shattering precisely because it belongs to a structure of events that intrinsically matches the foregoing 'reference' structure. Since the same is not true of Billy's throw, we close out the analysis by saying that his throw is therefore *not* a cause of the shattering.

Wait a minute. Who says the same is not true of Billy's throw? After all, consider a situation in which Suzy is wholly absent, and Billy alone throws, and in just the way that he does in the hard case. In that situation, the window breaks, and we can use our analysis to pick out a structure consisting of the breaking of the window, together with all of its causes back to the time of Billy's throw. These will, of course, include Billy's throw. Now return to the hard case. Here is a sequence of events connecting Billy's throw to the shattering: it consists of the throw, together with the flight of his rock through the air, together with the shattering. Yes, there is a spatiotemporal gap in the structure, but this does not matter; and at any rate we can fill it in by the interpolation of some arbitrary events—for example the passage of a photon from Billy's rock to the window, a photon that strikes the window at the exact moment that it shatters. Now, *that* structure is certainly highly intrinsically similar to the reference process exhibited in the situation in which Billy alone throws. So why doesn't our thesis tell us that Billy's throw, in the hard case, is a cause of the window's breaking after all? Well, because the structure in question is not similar to the reference process *in relevant respects*, whereas in the case of Suzy's throw it *is*. Better not stop there, or else it will look like "relevant" is being used as a weasel word, to mean whenever it has to in order for the account to come out true.

But in fact we need not stop there. Go back to the simple case where Suzy alone throws and nothing else is happening at the time of her throw. Consider all the ways we might tweak the parameters of the case: we might change the distance between Suzy and the window, or the strength of the window, or the speed or mass of the rock, or its color, or its temperature, or any combination of these at once, and so forth. All that matters is that we respect a distinction between tweakings that introduce something novel into the environment at the time of Suzy's throw, and tweakings that merely alter the values of pre-existing parameters; it is the latter sort that we are focusing on. Some of these tweakings will, intuitively, leave the causal structure of the process with which we began unchanged: that is, we will be able to match up the constituent events in the original process with the constituent events in the 'tweaked' process in a way that preserves intrinsic similarity (events are mapped to intrinsically similar events), spatiotemporal relations, and, crucially, causal relations.

For example, suppose we increase the mass of the rock a little bit. In that situation, it flies through the air in pretty much the same way, strikes the window, and the window breaks in pretty much the same way. On the other hand, some tweakings will significantly alter the causal structure. They might do so because they result in a situation in which the window does not break at all: for example, we increase the velocity of the rock so much that it flies over the window. In other cases, they might do so because they result in a situation in which the window breaks, but in which the way in which it breaks is dramatically different. For example, we increase the velocity of the rock so much that it passes through the sound barrier, and even though it flies over the window, the resulting shock wave breaks the window. Glossing over such details, we can see that there is a distinction between ways of ringing changes on the situation we began with that leave its causal structure invariant in the manner indicated, and ways that do not. Focusing on the former, we now have not just *one* reference process, but a *set* of reference processes: the one we began with, together with all the possible variations causally isomorphic to it. These reference processes differ, of course, in any number of ways. But the way they are picked out guarantees that they differ only in ways that are irrelevant to the fact that the throw is a cause of the shattering, and moreover irrelevant to the nature of the process by which that throw causes the shattering. And that allows us to define 'relevant respects of similarity' by means of the reference processes, as follows: In the hard case, a structure of events connecting Suzy's throw to the shattering counts as relevantly similar to the reference process exhibited in a situation where she alone throws, just in case it is similar to that process in those respects in which that process and its variants are similar to one another. One such respect of similarity, constant throughout the field of reference processes, is that the rock strikes the window. And that fact blocks the attempt to show that the intrinsicness thesis also counts Billy's throw as a cause of the shattering.

Let's back up, and take stock of the key points in the discussion so far. I suggested that the right way to go about analyzing causation is in terms of some basic nomological entailment relation, perhaps the one sketched above, perhaps some other one. Cases of asymmetric causal overdetermination pose a serious problem, however, since for any entailment relation we choose, such a case can always be constructed in which the genuine cause and the would-be alternative are symmetric with respect to that relation. But all is not lost. When circumstances are 'nice', we might successfully use our entailment relation to map out the causal facts. For example, in circumstances in which Suzy throws a rock at a window *and nothing else is happening*, the analysis sketched earlier seems to succeed in mapping out the causal relations that hold between Suzy's throw, the intermediate events, and the breaking of the window. What's more, it may be that we can discern, in a range of such nice cases, isomorphic causal structures. If so, then we can use a set of such causally isomorphic processes to pick out, by means of the intrinsicness thesis, a distinctive type of process, as follows: some arbitrary structure of events X instantiates this type just in case it is similar to the 'reference' processes in those respects in which they are similar to one another. (Note that it is exactly at this point that we can begin to frame a notion of *causal relevance*. Very roughly, a parameter will be causally relevant just in case sufficient variation in it would, holding other parameters fixed, take one outside the range of the reference processes.) And then we can say, finally, that in the hard case Suzy's throw is a cause of the shattering because it belongs to a structure of events that is of the right type—that has the right sort of intrinsic character—whereas Billy's throw does not.

We can put the matter another way, in terms of a 'decision procedure' of sorts for finding causes. Doing so will make it easier to see how all this connects to ceteris paribus laws. Suppose we've got some event e, and we have some earlier events—call them the C's—all occurring at a time t. We want to decide whether the C's are all and only the causes of e occurring at time t. In light of the foregoing discussion, we do so as follows:

First, we consider what would happen if, at time t, the *only* events that occurred had been the C's, understanding that they occur in exactly the same way as they actually do. If, in such a situation, e does not occur, then we're done: the C's are not the t-causes of e. But even if e does occur, it does not follow, of course, that we have found its t-causes—after all, the C's could have included *all* of the events actually occurring at time t. So we add some further requirement, as it might be this one: the C's need to be *minimal* with respect to the first condition; that is, not only is it the case that if they alone had occurred at time t, *e* would still have occurred, but the same is not true of any proper subset of them.

But we're still not done, of course: remember that Billy's throw and Suzy's throw both belong to such minimally sufficient sets. So we ask, in the counterfactual situation in which the C's occur at time t but nothing else does: What are the causes of *e* (back to time *t*)? Let's just assume that our analysis of causation can tell us—presumably because the 'nothing else occurs' clause renders the situation tractable enough. And let's also assume that, given that the C's form a set minimally sufficient for *e*, our analysis counts them as all belonging to this slice of *e*'s causal history. If so, then we will have succeeded in picking out a reference process that includes the C's: a process consisting of *e*, together with all of its causes back to the given time *t*. We now ask, of the *actual* situation, whether there is any structure of events connecting the C's to *e* that is intrinsically similar to this reference process. If not, we're done: the C's are not the *t*-causes of *e*. But even if so, there is one further step, which is to check to see whether the given structure of events is similar to the reference process in the *relevant respects*. To do this, we consider variants on our reference process—counterfactual situations in which the C's alone occur at time *t*, but do so in a slightly different manner from how they actually occur—counting on our analysis to discern which of those variants yield processes culminating in *e* that are causally isomorphic to the reference process with which we began. We thus arrive at a whole set of reference processes, and can ask the final question: in the actual situation, is there a structure of events connecting the C's to *e* that is similar to the original reference process in those respects in which it and its variants are similar to one another? If the answer to this final question is yes, then we have found the t-causes of *e*.

How to Explain the 'No-Interference' Clause

Now let's switch gears, and for the moment forget about the analysis of causation and how to carry it out in the face of the problem posed by asymmetric overdetermination. For if the story I've been telling with respect to that issue is right, something of independent interest emerges. Suppose we have some event *e*, and suppose we have at some earlier time *t* all the causes of *e*; call them the C's. Then there is, associated with the C's, a reference process: namely, the process that unfolds from the C's in a counterfactual situation in which they are the *only* events occurring at time t. What's more, this reference process lies in the middle of a wide range of variants causally isomorphic to it: processes that unfold from different ways that the C's could occur at time *t* (but that all lead to *e*, by way of appropriately similar intermediate stages). These reference processes will all bear some systematic similarities to each other (what I've been calling the "relevant respects"). Maybe there is some relatively simple way to describe these similarities, some compact expression, that is, of what the reference processes have in common. *That* will be a ceteris paribus law. In short, what ceteris paribus laws *do* is to articulate the structure of a range of reference processes. What's more, the way the reference processes are picked out guarantees that the no-interference clause will be satisfied.

Consider our example: Suzy throws a rock at a window, and the window breaks. Never mind what else is going on. There are, at the time of Suzy's throw, some causes of the window's later breaking: Suzy's throw itself, the very presence of the window, and so forth. Collect them together. Consider a situation in which they alone occur at some given time t. A certain process unfolds, culminating in e. Consider variants on the situation, arrived at by altering the conditions of the throw, the window, and so forth, in all possible ways that leave the causal structure of the resulting process unchanged. What our rock-throwing law does is to map out this range of processes, exactly by delineating the common features of the boundary conditions: what it says is that the parameters that characterize these boundary conditions are related in just the way they need to be to result in a window-shattering. Finally, in this range of cases the no-interference clause is idle, since its work has been done by the stipulation that, at the given time t, the *only* events occurring are the causes of the window's shattering. Since by stipulation nothing else is happening, there is, a fortiori, *nothing else that could interfere* with these conditions.

Here it is again from another direction, and spelled out in more detail. Consider a ceteris paribus law that says that in any nomologically possible world, at any time t, if conditions of type C obtain at time t, and nothing interferes, then conditions of type E obtain at future time $f(t)$. How should we understand the "no interference" clause? In light of the foregoing, I suggest we understand it as follows: First, take the law to be primarily *about* nomologically possible situations in which C-conditions occur at some time t, and *nothing else is happening* at that time; the law says of those situations that E-conditions obtain at the appropriate future time. (Call these the *canonical situations* for the given law.) But I do not mean to imply that "nothing interferes" just means "nothing else happens" (although the latter is certainly *sufficient* for the former—which point dispels, all by itself, any worries about vacuity). Rather, what is meant by an interference can be explained by reference to these canonical situations. For, looking across them, there will be systematic similarities in the processes that unfold from the C-conditions and culminate in the instantiation of the E-conditions. In virtue of these similarities, these processes will pick out a process *type* by means of the now-familiar formula: a structure of events instantiates the type just in case it is similar to these processes in those respects in which they are similar to one another.

(What if there are no such systematic similarities? What if, for example, the processes culminating in the E-conditions unfold in one distinctive way in certain of the canonical situations, and in an entirely different distinctive way in certain other of the canonical situations? Then, I suggest we have a 'law' that is too disjunctive to really deserve the name, and that ought to be split up into two or more laws as needed. As an example, imagine that it is a law of human physiology that people with a certain disease D are cured by administration of a certain medicine M. But imagine further that the biochemical mechanisms by which the medicine effects a cure are *completely different* in males and females (though similar within each sex). I think that the appropriate taxonomic verdict, in such a case, would be to say that we have one lawful regularity underwritten by *two* distinct physiological laws.)

Then in any ordinary (presumably, non-canonical) situation we can say exactly what it is for there to be an interference: the C-conditions obtain, but they do not belong to any structure of events that instantiates the type of process that is associated with the given law. Note that it does not follow, from the claim that something interferes, that the E-conditions don't also obtain; and that shows, contra certain authors, that 'nothing interferes' cannot be replaced by 'nothing prevents the E-conditions from obtaining'. For example, suppose that Suzy throws a rock at a window, and the parameters characterizing her throw, the strength of the window, the distance between her and the window, and so forth, all fall within the range covered by the rock-throwing law. But suppose that Billy throws faster, so that his rock breaks the window; or suppose that some outside factor comes along and speeds up Suzy's rock to the point where it passes through the sound barrier, with the resulting shock wave breaking the window. In both cases, we have the window breaking. But in neither case is Suzy's throw an instance of the rock-throwing law, and that is because the process unfolding from her throw does not have the right character; it does not have the features distinctive of the canonical instances of the rock-throwing law.

If this account is right then I think we can quickly dispense with the two main charges that are so often leveled against ceteris paribus laws. As to the charge of vacuity, I suppose it will be obvious that on my account it is misguided. For the truth of the ceteris paribus law stands or falls with the truth of the range of counterfactuals describing what would happen in nomologically possible situations in which the conditions specified in the law are realized, and in which nothing else happens at the time of their realization. Such counterfactuals can easily fail to hold. Consider the following lame window-breaking law: ceteris paribus, if you glare at a window, it will break—and imagine a defense of this 'law' that insists that the only reason windows *don't* break when we glare at them is that something (who knows what) interferes. The defense fails: for, obviously, in a circumstance in which you glared at a window and nothing else happened, the window would not break. As for the charge of untestability, I do not see any way of making it stick that does not just turn into a very general skepticism about scientific methodology. That is, it seems to me a truism about science (and about ordinary life, for that matter) that we somehow, and in many cases quite easily, cotton on to the truth of various counterfactuals by taking stock of what *actually* happens. One might doubt that this is so, and more generally doubt that empirical evidence can *ever* be evidence for or against the truth of a counterfactual (with a false antecedent); but unless one embraces such a radically skeptical position, I do not see that there is any problem about finding evidence for or against ceteris paribus laws. And at any rate, this would not be a *special* problem for such laws.

More should be said, since there are really a couple of separate issues here. They can be illustrated, once again, by reference to our rock-throwing law. Consider, in the abstract, how one might go about testing this law in the most empirically simple-minded way. Suppose we have at our disposal tools for measuring every possible physical parameter that characterizes the given rock-thrown-at-a-window situation. Suppose we set up a whole bunch of these situations. In some of them, the window breaks; in others, it doesn't. Focus on the ones in which the window breaks. Even if we set things up very carefully, we certainly *won't* be able to say, of any of these situations, that the *only* thing that happens at the time of the throw is the throw itself (we are watching, over on the other side of the field our colleagues are conducting a different experiment, George Bush happens at the time to be conducting another inept press conference, and so on). But, if we are careful *enough*, then we should be able to say that for anything else that occurs at the same time, the following counterfactual is true: If it hadn't occurred (if in place of it nothing happened), then the window would still have broken, and furthermore the process connecting the throw to the breaking would have unfolded in almost exactly the same way. (For example, dispiriting as it was, the press conference didn't make any difference to the outcome of the throw, and so forth.)

Do I have a story about how we come by knowledge, or at any rate justified belief, about such counterfactuals? No. But as noted, if there is no such story, then ceteris paribus laws are the least of our worries. At any rate, if we are in a position to judge that all such counterfactuals are true, then I think we are also thereby in a position to conclude—not as deductive inference, to be sure—that in the situation that would have obtained had only the throw occurred at the given time, the window breaks, and the process leading to its breaking unfolds in almost exactly the same way. And that means that we have, in each of our actual experimental situations, an instance of something that very closely approximates a canonical situation—and approximates it *well enough* to serve as a fully adequate test case.

That is step one. Step two on the road to articulating the full rock-throwing law simply involves the familiar—which is not to say philosophically unproblematic—process of extrapolating from some limited set of data points to a more complete set. Now, no doubt both of these steps hide a host of philosophically interesting problems. My only point is that to the extent that this is so, the problems in question have nothing in particular to do with ceteris paribus laws.

REFERENCES

Earman, John, and J. Roberts 1999. 'Ceteris Paribus', There Is No Problem of Provisos. *Synthese* 118, pp. 439–478.

Hall, Ned. 2004. The Intrinsic Character of Causation. In Dean Zimmerman, ed., *Oxford Studies in Metaphysics,* Volume 1 (Oxford University Press, 2004).

Hitchcock, C. 2001. The Intransitivity of Causation Revealed in Equations and Graphs. *Journal of Philosophy* 98, pp. 273–299.

Lewis, David. 1973. Causation. *Journal of Philosophy* 70, pp. 556–567.

———. 2000. Causation as Influence. *Journal of Philosophy* 97, pp. 182–197.

Ramachandran, Murali. 1997. A Counterfactual Analysis of Causation. *Mind* 151, pp. 263–277.

Yablo, Stephen. 2002. De Facto Dependence. *Journal of Philosophy* 99, pp. 130–148.

11

The Mysteries of
Self-Locating Belief and
Anthropic Reasoning

NICK BOSTROM

Nick Bostrom is a British Academy Postdoctoral Fellow and a Research Fellow in Philosophy at Oxford University. His research interests include philosophy of science, foundations of probability theory, and ethics of technology and science. His first book, Anthropic Bias: Observation Selection Effects in Science and Philosophy, *came out in 2002. His other recent publications include "Self Locating Belief in Big Worlds,"* Journal of Philosophy *and "Are You Living In a Computer Simulation?"* Philosophical Quarterly.

1

How big is the smallest fish in the pond? You take your wide-meshed fishing net and catch one hundred fishes, every one of which is greater than six inches long. Does this evidence support the hypothesis that no fish in the pond is much less than six inches long? Not if your wide-meshed net can't actually catch smaller fish.

The limitations of your data collection process affect the inferences you can draw from the data. In the case of the fish-size-estimation problem, a *selection effect*—the net's being able to sample only the big fish—invalidates any attempt to extrapolate from the catch to the population remaining in the water. Had your net had a finer mesh, allowing it to sample randomly from *all* the fish, then finding a hundred fishes all greater than a foot long would have been good evidence that few if any fish remaining were much smaller.

In the fish net example, a selection effect is introduced by the fact that the instrument you used to collect data sampled from only a subset of the target population. Analogously, there are selection effects that arise not from the limitations of the measuring device but from the fact that all observations require the existence of an appropriately positioned observer. These are known as *observation selection effects*.

The study of observation selection effects is a relatively new discipline. In my recent book *Anthropic Bias*, I have attempted to develop the first mathematically explicit theory of observation selection effects. In this article, I will attempt to convey a flavor of some of the mysteries that such a theory must resolve.

The theory of observation selection effects may have implications for a number of fields in both philosophy and science. One example is evolutionary biology, where observation selection effects must be taken into account when addressing questions such as the probability of intelligent life developing on any given Earth-like planet. We know that intelligent life evolved on Earth. Naively, one might think that this piece of evidence suggests that life is likely to evolve on most Earth-like planets, but that would overlook an observation selection effect. No matter how small the proportion of all Earth-like planets that evolve intelligent life, *we* must be from a planet that did (or we must be able to trace our origin to a planet that did, if we were born in a space colony) in order to be an observer ourselves.

Our evidence—that intelligent life arose on our planet—is therefore predicted equally well by the hypothesis that intelligent life is very improbable even on Earth-like planets, as it is by the hypothesis that intelligent life is highly probable on Earth-like planets. The evidence does not distinguish between the two hypotheses, provided that in both hypotheses intelligent life would very likely have evolved somewhere.

2

Another example comes from cosmology, where observation selection effects are crucial considerations in deriving empirical predictions from the currently popular so-called 'multiverse theories', according to which our universe is but one out of a vast ensemble of physically real universes out there.

Some cases are relatively straightforward. Consider a simple theory that says that there are one hundred universes, and that ninety of these are lifeless and ten contain observers. What does such a theory predict that we should observe? Obviously not that we should observe a lifeless universe. Because lifeless universes contain no observers, an observation selection effect precludes them from being observed. So although the theory says that the majority of universes are lifeless, it nevertheless predicts that we should observe one of the atypical ones that contain observers.

Now let's take on a slightly more complicated case. Suppose a theory says that there are one hundred universes of the following description:

90 type-A universes; they are lifeless

9 type-B universes; they contain one million observers each

1 type-C universe; it contains one billion observers

What does this theory predict that we should observe? (We need to know that in order to determine whether it is confirmed or disconfirmed by our observations.) As before, an obvious observation selection effect precludes type-A universes from being observed, so the theory does not predict that we should observe one of those. But what about type-B and type-C universes? It is logically compatible with the theory that we should be observing a universe of either of these kinds. However, probabilistically, it is more likely, conditional on the theory, that we should observe the type-C universe, because that's what the theory says that ninety-nine percent of all observers observe.

Couldn't we hold instead that the theory predicts that we should observe a type-B universe? After all, it says that type-B universes are much more common than those of type-C. There are various arguments that show that this line of reasoning is untenable. We lack the space to review them all here, but we can hint at one of the underlying intuitions by considering an analogy. Suppose you wake up after having been sedated and find yourself blindfolded and with earplugs. Let's say for some reason you come to consider two rival hypotheses about your location: that you are somewhere on the landmass of Earth, or that you at sea. You have no evidence in particular to suggest that you should be at sea, but you are aware that there are more square meters of sea than of land. Clearly, this does not give you grounds for thinking you are at sea. For you know that the vast majority of observers are on land, and in the absence of more specific relevant evidence to the contrary, you should think that you probably are where the overwhelming majority of people like you are.

In a similar vein, the cosmological theory that says that almost all people are in type-C universes predicts that you should find yourself in such a universe. Finding yourself in a type-C universe would in many cases tend to confirm such a theory, to at least some degree, compared to other theories that imply that most observers live in type-A or type-B universes.

3

Let us now look a little more systematically at the reasoning alluded to in the foregoing paragraphs. Consider the following thought experiment:

> *Dungeon.* The world consists of a dungeon that has one hundred cells. In each cell there is one prisoner. Ninety of the cells are painted blue on the outside and the other ten are painted red. Each prisoner is asked to guess whether he is in a blue or a red cell. (And everybody knows all this.) You find yourself in one of these cells. What color should you think it is? —*Answer*: Blue, with ninety percent probability.

Since ninety percent of all observers are in blue cells, and you don't have any other relevant information, it seems that you should set your credence (that is, your subjective probability, or your degree of belief) of being in a blue cell to ninety percent. Most people seem to agree that this is the correct answer. Since the example does not depend on the exact numbers involved, we have the more general principle that in cases like this, your credence of having property P should be equal to the fraction of observers who have P. You reason *as if* you were a randomly selected observer. This principle is known as the *Self-Sampling Assumption*:[1]

> *(SSA)* One should reason as if one were a random sample from the set of all observers in one's reference class.

For the time being, we can assume that the reference class consists of all intelligent observers, although this is an assumption that needs to be revised, as we shall see later.

While many accept without further argument that SSA is applicable to *Dungeon*, let's briefly consider how one might seek to defend this view if challenged to do so. One argument one can adduce is the following. Suppose that everyone accepts SSA and everyone has to bet on whether they are in a blue or a red cell. Then ninety percent of the prisoners will win their bets; only ten percent will lose. If, on the other hand, SSA is rejected and the prisoners think that one is no more likely to be in a blue cell than in a red cell, and they bet, for example, by flipping a coin, then on average merely fifty percent of them will win and fifty percent will lose. It seems better that SSA be accepted.

What allows the people in *Dungeon* to do better than chance is that they have a relevant piece of empirical information regarding the distribution of observers over the two types of cells; they have been informed that ninety percent are in blue cells. It would be irrational not to take this information into account. We can imagine a series of thought experiments where an increasingly large fraction of observers are in blue cells—91 percent, 92 percent, . . . , 99 percent. As the situation gradually degenerates into the limiting hundred-percent-case where they are simply told, "You are all in blue cells," from which each prisoner can deductively infer that he is in a blue cell, it is plausible to require that the strength of prisoners' beliefs about being in a blue cell should gradually approach probability one. SSA has this property.

These considerations support the initial intuition about *Dungeon*: that it is a situation in which one should reason in accordance with SSA.

One thing worth noting about *Dungeon* is that we didn't specify how the prisoners arrived in their cells. The prisoners' history is irrelevant so long as they don't know anything about it that gives them clues about the color of their cells. For example, they may have been allocated to their respective cells by some objectively random process such as by drawing balls from an urn (while blindfolded so they couldn't see where they ended up). Or they may have been allowed to choose cells for themselves, a fortune wheel subsequently being spun to determine which cells should be painted blue and which red. But the thought experiment doesn't depend on there being a well-defined randomization mechanism. One may just as well imagine that prisoners have been in their cells since the time of their birth, or indeed since the beginning of the universe. If there is a possible world in which the laws of nature determine, without any appeal to initial conditions, which individuals are to appear in which cells and how each cell is painted, then the inmates would still be rational to follow SSA, provided only that they did not have knowledge of the laws or were incapable of deducing what the laws implied about their own situation. Objective chance, therefore, is not an essential ingredient of the thought experiment; it runs on low-octane subjective uncertainty.

4

So far, so good. In *Dungeon*, the number of observers featuring in the experiment was fixed. Now let us consider a variation where the total number of observers depends on which hypothesis is true. This is where the waters begin to get treacherous.

> *Incubator.* Stage *(a)*: The world consists of a dungeon with one hundred cells. The cells are numbered on the outside consecutively from 1 to 100. The numbers cannot be seen from inside the cells. There is also a mechanism called 'the incubator'. The incubator first creates one observer in cell #1. It then flips a coin. If the coin lands tails, the incubator does nothing more. If the coin lands heads, the incubator creates one observer in each of the remaining ninety-nine cells as well. It is now a time well after the coin was tossed, and everyone knows all the above.

Stage *(b)*: A little later, you are allowed to see the number on your cell door, and you find that you are in cell #1.

Question: What credence should you give to tails at stages (a) *and* (b)*?* We shall consider three different models for how to reason, each giving a different answer. These three models may *appear* to exhaust the range of plausible solutions, although we shall later outline a fourth model which is the one that in fact I think points to the way forward.

Model 1. At stage *(a)* you should set your credence of tails equal to fifty percent, since you know that the coin toss was fair. Now consider the *conditional* credence you should assign at stage *(a)* to being in a certain cell given a certain outcome of the coin toss. For example, the conditional probability of being in cell #1 given tails is 1, since that is the only cell you can be in if that happened. And by applying SSA to this situation, we get that the conditional probability of being in cell #1 given heads is 1/100. Plugging these values into the well-known mathematical result known as Bayes's theorem, we get

Pr *(tails)* | *I am in cell #1)*

$$= \frac{Pr\,(I\ am\ in\ cell\ \#1\ |\ tails)\ Pr\,(tails)}{Pr\,(I\ am\ in\ cell\ \#1\ |\ tails)\ Pr\,(tails) + Pr\,(I\ am\ in\ cell\ \#1\ |\ heads)\ Pr\,(heads)}$$

$$= \frac{1 \times 1/2}{1 \times 1/2 + 1/100\ \text{x}\ 1/2} = 100\,/\,101$$

Therefore, upon learning that you are in cell #1, you should become almost certain (Pr = 100/101) that the coin fell tails. *Answer: At stage* (a) *your credence of tails should be 1/2 and at stage* (b) *it should be 100/101.*

Now consider a second model that sort of reasons in the opposite direction:

Model 2. Since you know the coin toss to have been fair, and you haven't got any other relevant information, your credence of tails at stage *(b)* should be 1/2. Since we know the conditional credences (same as in model 1) we can infer, via Bayes's theorem, what your credence of tails should be at stage (a), and the result is that your prior credence of tails must equal 1/101. *Answer: At stage* (a) *your credence of tails should be 1/101 and at stage* (b) *it should be 1/2.*

Finally, we can consider a model that denies that you gain any relevant information from finding that you are in cell #1:

Model 3. Neither at stage *(a)* nor at stage *(b)* do you have any relevant information as to how the coin fell. Thus in both instances, your credence of tails should be 1/2. *Answer: At stage* (a) *your credence of tails should be 1/2 and at stage* (b) *it should be 1/2.*

5

Let us take a critical look at these three models. We shall be egalitarian and present one problem for each of them.

We begin with model 3. The challenge for this model is that it seems to suffer from incoherence. For it is easy to see (simply by inspecting Bayes's theorem) that if we want to end up with the posterior probability of tails being 1/2, and both heads and tails have a fifty percent prior probability, then the conditional probability of being in cell #1 must be the same on tails as it is on heads. But at stage *(a)* you know with certainty that if the coin fell heads then you are in cell #1; so this conditional probability must equal 1. In order for model 3 to be coherent, you would therefore have to set your conditional probability of being in cell #1 given heads equal to 1 as well. That means you would already know with certainty at stage *(a)* that you are in cell #1. Which is simply not the case! Hence we must reject model 3.

Readers who are familiar with David Lewis's *Principal Principle*[2] may wonder if it is not the case that model 3 is firmly based on this principle, so that rejecting model 3 would mean rejecting the Principal Principle as well. That is not so. While this is not the place to delve into the details of the debates about the connection between objective chance and rational credence, suffice it to say that the Principal Principle does not state that you should always set your credence equal to the corresponding objective chance if you know it. Instead, it says that you should do this *unless* you have other relevant information that needs to be taken into account.[3] There is some controversy about how to specify which sorts of such additional information will modify reasonable credence when the objective chance is known, and which sorts of additional information leaves the identity intact. But there is wide agreement that the proviso is needed. Now, in *Incubator* you do have such extra relevant information that you need to take into account, and model 3 fails to do that. The extra information is that, at stage *(b)*, you have discovered that you were in cell #1. This information is relevant because it bears probabilistically on whether the coin fell heads or tails; or so, at least, the above argument seems to show.

6

Model 1 and model 2 are both all right as far as probabilistic coherence goes. Choosing between them would therefore be a matter of selecting the most plausible or intuitively appealing prior credence function.

Model 2 says that at stage *(a)* you should assign a credence of 1/101 to the coin having landed tails. That is, just knowing about the setup but having no direct evidence about the outcome of the toss, you should be virtually certain that the coin fell in such a way as to create ninety-nine additional observers. This amounts to having an a priori bias towards the world containing many observers. Modifying the thought experiment by using different numbers, it can be shown that in order for the probabilities always to work out the way model 2 requires, you would have to subscribe to the principle that, other things being equal, a hypothesis that implies that there are 2N observers should be assigned twice the credence of a hypothesis that implies that there are only N observers. This principle is known as the *Self-Indication Assumption* (SIA).[4] My view is that it is untenable. To see why, consider the following example (which seems to be closely analogous to *Incubator*):

> *The Presumptuous Philosopher.* It is the year 2100 and physicists have narrowed down the search for a theory of everything to only two remaining plausible candidate theories: T_1 and T_2 (using considerations from super-duper symmetry). According to T_1 the world is very, very big but finite and there are a total of a trillion trillion observers in the cosmos. According to T_2, the world is very, very, *very* big but finite and there are a trillion trillion trillion observers. The super-duper symmetry considerations are indifferent between these two theories. Physicists are preparing a simple experiment that will falsify one of the theories. Enter the presumptuous philosopher: "Hey guys, it is completely unnecessary for you to do the experiment, because I can already show you that T_2 is about a trillion times more likely to be true than T_1!" (whereupon the philosopher explains model 2 and appeals to SIA).

Somehow one suspects that the Nobel Prize committee would be reluctant to award the philosopher the big one for this contribution. Yet it is hard to see what the relevant difference is between this case and *Incubator*. If there is no relevant difference, and we are not prepared to accept the argument of the presumptuous philosopher, then we are not justified in using model 2 in *Incubator* either.

7

What about model 1, then? In this model, after finding that you are in cell #1, you should set your credence of tails equal to 100/101. In other words, you should be almost certain that the world does not contain the extra ninety-nine observers. This might seem like the least unacceptable of the alternatives and therefore the one we ought to go for. However, before we uncork the bottle of champagne, ponder what this option entails.

> *Serpent's Advice.* Eve and Adam, the first two humans, knew that if they gratified their flesh, Eve might bear a child, and that if she did, they would both be

expelled from Eden and go on to spawn billions of progeny that would fill the Earth with misery. One day a serpent approached them and spoke thus: "Pssst! If you hold each other, then either Eve will have a child or she won't. If she has a child, you will have been among the first two out of billions of people. Your conditional probability of having such early positions in the human species given this hypothesis is extremely small. If, on the other hand, Eve does *not* become pregnant then the conditional probability, given this, of you being among the first two humans is equal to one. By Bayes's theorem, the risk that she shall bear a child is less than one in a billion. Therefore, my dear friends, indulge your desires and worry not about the consequences!"

Given the assumption that the same method of reasoning should be applied as in *Incubator*, and using some plausible prior probability of pregnancy given carnal embrace (say, 1/100), it is easy to verify that there is nothing wrong with the serpent's mathematics. The question, of course, is whether the assumption should be granted.

Let us review some of the differences between *Incubator* and *Serpent's Advice* to see if any of them are relevant in the sense of providing a rational ground for treating the two cases differently.

- *In the* Incubator *experiment there was a point in time, stage* (a), *when the subject was actually ignorant about her position among the observers. By contrast, Eve presumably knew all along that she was the first woman.*

But it is not clear why that should matter. We can imagine that Eve and Adam were created on a remote island, and that they didn't know whether there are other people on Earth, until one day they were informed that they are thus far the only ones. It is still counterintuitive to say that the couple needn't worry about the possibility of Eve getting pregnant.

- *When the subject is making the inference in* Dungeon, *the coin has already been tossed. In the case of Eve, the relevant chance event has not yet taken place.*

This difference does not seem crucial either. We can modify *Serpent's Advice* by supposing that the deciding chance event has already taken place. Let's say the couple has just sinned and they are now brooding over the ram- ifications. Should the serpent's argument completely reassure them that noth- ing bad will happen? It seems not. So the worry remains.

- *At stage* (b) *in* Dungeon, *any observers resulting from the toss have already been created, whereas Eve's potential progeny do not yet exist at the time when she is assessing the odds.*

We can consider a variant of *Dungeon* where each cell exists in a different century. That is, let us suppose that cell #1, along with its observer, are created in the first century, and destroyed after, say, thirty years. In each of the subsequent ninety-nine centuries, a new cell is built, allowed to exist for thirty years, and is then destroyed. At some point in the first century a coin is tossed and, depending on how it lands, these subsequent cells will or will not contain observers. Stage *(a)* can now be defined to take place in the first century after the first prisoner has been created but before the coin has been tossed and before the prisoner has been allowed to come out of his cell to observe its number. At this stage (stage *(a)*) it seems that he should assign the same credence to tails and the same conditional credences of tails given that he is in a particular cell as he did in the original version—for precisely the same reasons. But then it follows, just as before, that his posterior credence of tails, after finding that he is in cell #1, should be much greater than the prior credence of tails. This version of *Dungeon* is analogous to *Serpent's Advice* with respect to the non-existence of the later humans at the time when the odds are being assessed.

- *In* Dungeon, *the two hypotheses under consideration (heads and tails) have well-defined known prior probabilities (fifty percent), whereas Eve and Adam must rely on vague subjective considerations to assess the risk of pregnancy.*

True, but would we want to say that if Eve's getting pregnant were determined by some distinct microbiological process with a well-defined objective chance which Eve and Adam knew about, then they ought to accept the serpent's advice? If anything, the knowledge of such an objective chance would make the consequence even weirder.

8

The mystery that we are facing here is that it seems clear that both the serpent and the presumptuous philosopher are wrong, yet it seems as if the only model that yields this double result (model 1) is incoherent. One may be tempted to blame the strength of SSA for these troubles and think that we should reject it. But that, it appears, would transfix us on another horn of the dilemma, for we would then have to reject the cogent argument about the *Dungeon* thought experiment presented above, and, perhaps even more seriously, we would have failed to account for a number of very well-founded scientific applications in cosmology and elsewhere (which I lack the space to fully explore in this article).

There are a number of possible moves and objections that one can try at this point. But most of these maneuvers and objections rest on simple misunderstandings, or else they fail to provide a workable alternative to how to reason about the range of problems that need to be addressed. It is easy enough to come up with a method of reasoning that works in one particular case, but when one then tests it against other cases—philosophical thought experiments and legitimate scientific inferences—one usually soon discovers that it yields paradoxes or otherwise unacceptable results. Yet by seriously confronting this central conundrum of self-locating belief, we can glean important clues about what a general theory of observation selection effects must look like.

9

So where do we go from here? The full answer is complicated and difficult and cannot be fully explored in a relatively short paper like this one. But by helping myself to a fair amount of hand-waving, I can at least try to indicate the direction in which I think the solution is to be found.

One key to the solution is to realize that the problem with SSA is not that it is too strong but that it isn't strong enough. SSA tells you to take into account a certain kind of indexical information—information about which observer you are. But you have more indexical information than that about who you are; you also know *when* you are. That is, you know which temporal segment—which 'observer-moment'—of an observer that you are at the current time. We can formulate a 'Strong Self-Sampling Assumption' that takes this information into account:

> *(SSSA)* Each observer-moment should reason as if it were randomly sampled from its reference class.

Arguments can be given for SSSA along lines parallel to those of the arguments for SSA provided above. For example, one can consider cases in which a person is unaware of what time it is and has to assign credence to different temporal possibilities.

A second key to the solution is to see how the added analytical power of SSSA enables us to relativize the reference class. What this means is that different observer-moments of the same observer may use different reference classes without that observer being incoherent over time. To illustrate, let us again consider the *Incubator* thought experiment. Before, we rejected model 3 because it seemed to imply that the reasoner should be incoherent. But we can now construct a new model, model 4, which agrees with the answers that model 3 gave, that is, a credence of 1/2 of heads at both stage *(a)* *and* stage *(b)*, but which modifies the reasoning that led to these answers in a such a way as to avoid incoherency.

Suppose that just as before and for the same reasons, we assign, at stage *(a)*, the credences:

$$\text{Pr}(tails) = \tfrac{1}{2}$$

$$\text{Pr}(I'm\ in\ cell\ \#1 \mid tails) = 1$$

$$\text{Pr}(I'm\ in\ cell\ \#1 \mid heads) = 1/100$$

Now, if the *only* epistemic difference between stage *(a)* and stage *(b)* is that at the latter stage you have the additional piece of information that you are in cell #1, then Bayesian conditionalization of the above conditional credences entails (as in model 1) that your posterior credence must be:

$$\text{Pr}_{\text{posterior}}(tails) = \text{Pr}(tails \mid I'm\ in\ cell\ \#1) = 100/101.$$

However, when we take SSSA into account, we see that there are other epistemic differences between stages *(a)* and *(b)*. In addition to gaining the information that you are in cell #1, you also *lose* information when you enter stage *(b)*. At stage *(a)*, you knew that you were currently an observer-moment who is ignorant about which cell you are in and who is pondering different possibilities. At stage *(b)*, you no longer know this piece of indexical information, because it is no longer true of you that you currently are such an observer-moment. You do know that you are an observer who *previously* was at stage *(a)*, but this is an indexically different piece of knowledge from knowing that you are currently at stage *(a)*. Since your total information at stage *(b)* is not equal to the information you had at stage *(a)* conjoined with the proposition that you are in cell #1, there is therefore no requirement that your beliefs at stage *(b)* be obtained by conditionalizing your stage *(a)* credence function on the proposition that you are in cell #1.

Normally, this kind of subtle change in indexical information makes no difference to our inferences, so they can therefore usually be ignored. In special cases, however, including the thought experiments considered in this paper, which rely precisely on the peculiar evidential properties of indexical information, such changes can be highly relevant.

This does not yet show that your beliefs at stage *(b)* about the outcome of the coin toss should differ from those obtained by conditionalizing $\text{Pr}(tails|I'm\ in\ cell\ \#1)$. But it defeats the Bayesian argument for why they should be the same. If you regard these associated epistemic changes that occur in addition to your obtaining the information that "I'm in cell #1" when you move from stage *(a)* to stage *(b)* as relevant, then you can coherently assign a 1/2 posterior credence to tails.

Let *á* be one of your observer-moments that exist before you discover which cell you are in. Let *â* be one of your observer-moments that exist after you have discovered that you are in cell #1 (but before you have learned about the outcome of the coin toss). What probabilities *á* and *â* assign to various hypotheses depends on reference classes in which they place themselves. For example, can pick a reference class consisting of the observer-moments who are ignorant about which cell they are in, while *â* can pick the reference class consisting of all observer-moments who know they are in cell #1. *á*'s conditional credences are then the same as before:

$$\Pr_{\alpha}(\text{á is in cell \#1} \mid \text{tails}) = 1$$
$$\Pr_{\alpha}(\text{á is in cell \#1} \mid \text{heads}) = 1/100.$$

But *â*'s conditional probability of being in cell #1 given heads is now identical to that given tails:

$$\Pr_{\hat{a}}(\text{â is in cell \#1} \mid \text{tails}) = 1$$
$$\Pr_{\hat{a}}(\text{â is in cell \#1} \mid \text{heads}) = 1.$$

From this, it follows that *â*'s posterior credence of tails after conditionalizing on being in cell #1 is the same as its posterior credence of heads, namely 1/2.

SSSA does not by itself *imply* that this should be *â*'s posterior credence of tails. It just shows that it is a coherent position to take. The actual credence assignment depends on which reference classes are chosen. In the case of *Incubator*, it may not be obvious which choice of reference class is best. But in the *Serpent's Advice*, it is clear that Eve should select a reference class that puts her observer-moments existing at the time when she is pondering the possible consequences of the sinful act in a different reference class from those later observer-moments that may come to exist as a result of her transgression. For her to do otherwise would not be incoherent, but it would yield the strongly counterintuitive consequence discussed above. By selecting the more limited reference class, she can reject this consequence.

The question arises whether it is possible to find some general principle that determines what reference class an observer-moment should use. We may note that the early Eve's choice of a reference class that contains only her own early observer-moments and excludes the observer-moments of all the billions of progeny that may come to exist later is not completely arbitrary. After all, the epistemic situation that the early Eve is in is very different from the epistemic situation of these later observer-moments. Eve doesn't know whether she will get pregnant and whether all these other people will come to exist; her progeny, by contrast, would have no doubts about these issues. Eve is confronted with a very different epistemic problem than her possible children would be. It is thus quite natural to place Eve in a different reference class from these later people, even apart from the fact that this maneuver would explain why the serpent's recommendation should be eschewed.

Constraints on what could be legitimate choices of reference class can be established, but it is an open question whether these will always suffice to single out a uniquely correct reference class for every observer-moment. My suspicion is that there might remain a subjective element in the choice of reference class in some applications. Furthermore, I suspect that the degree to which various applications of anthropic reasoning are sensitive to that subjective element is inversely related to how scientifically robust those applications are. The most rigorous uses of anthropic reasoning have the property that they give the same result for almost any choice of reference class (satisfying only some very weak constraints).

In passing, we may note one interesting constraint on the choice of reference class. It turns out (for reasons that we do not have the space to elaborate on here) that a reference class definition according to which only *subjectively indistinguishable* observer-moments are placed in the same reference class is too narrow. (Two observer-moments are subjectively indistinguishable if they don't have any information that enables them to tell which one is which.) In other words, there are cases in which you should reason as if your current observer-moment were randomly selected from a class of observer-moments that includes ones of which you know that they are not your own current observer-moment. This fact makes anthropic reasoning a less simple affair than would otherwise have been the case.

The use of SSSA and the relativization of the reference class that SSSA enables thus seem to make it possible to coherently reject both the presumptuous philosopher's and the serpent's arguments, while at the same time one can show how to get plausible results in *Dungeon* and several other thought experiments as well as in various scientific applications, some of them novel. The theory can be condensed into one general formula: the Observation Equation, which specifies the probabilistic bearing on hypotheses of evidence that contains an indexical component.[5] Along with various constrains on permissible choices of reference classes, this forms the core of a theory of observation selection effects.

10

As a final example, let us consider an easy application of observation selection theory to a puzzle that many drivers on the motorway may have wondered about (and cursed). Why is it that the cars in the other lane seem to be getting ahead faster than you?

One might be inclined to account for phenomenon by invoking Murphy's Law ("If anything can go wrong, it will," discovered by Edward A. Murphy Jr. in 1949). However, a paper in *Nature* by Redelmeier and Tibshirani, published a couple of years ago,[6] seeks a deeper explanation. They present some evidence that drivers on Canadian roadways (where faster cars are not expected to move into more central lanes) think that the next lane is typically faster. They seek to explain the drivers' perceptions by appealing to a variety of psychological factors. For example:

- "A driver is more likely to glance at the next lane for comparison when he is relatively idle while moving slowly;"

- "Differential surveillance can occur because drivers look forwards rather than backwards, so vehicles that are overtaken become invisible very quickly, whereas vehicles that overtake the index driver remain conspicuous for much longer;" and

- "Human psychology may make being overtaken (losing) seem more salient than the corresponding gains."

The authors recommend that drivers should be educated about these effects in order to reduce the temptation to switch lanes repeatedly. This would reduce the risk of accidents, which are often caused by poor lane changes.

While all these psychological illusions might indeed occur, there is a more straightforward explanation for the drivers' persistent suspicion that cars in the next lane are moving faster. Namely, that cars in the next lane actually do go faster!

One frequent cause of why a lane (or a segment of a lane) is slow is that there are too many cars in it. Even if the ultimate cause is something else (for example, road work) there is nonetheless typically a negative correlation between the speed of a lane and how densely packed the vehicles driving in it are. This implies that a disproportionate fraction of the average driver's time is spent in slow lanes. If you think of your present observation, when you are driving on the motorway, as a random sample from all observations made by drivers, then chances are that your observation will be made from the viewpoint that most such observer-moments have, which is the viewpoint of the slow-moving lane. In other words, appearances are faithful: more often than not, for most observer-moments, the "next" lane *is* faster.

Even when two lanes have the same average speed, it can be advantageous to switch lanes. For what is relevant to a driver who wants to reach her destination as quickly as possible is not the average speed of the lane as a whole, but rather the speed of some segment extending maybe a couple of miles forward from the driver's current position. More often than not, the next lane has a higher average speed at this scale than does the driver's present lane. On average, there is therefore a benefit to switching lanes (which of course has to be balanced against the costs of increased levels of effort and risk).

Adopting a thermodynamics perspective, it is also easy to see that (at least in the ideal case) increasing the "diffusion rate" (that is, the probability of lane-switching) will speed the approach to "equilibrium" (where there are equal velocities in both lanes), thereby increasing the road's throughput and the number of vehicles that reach their destinations per unit time.

To summarize, in understanding this problem we must not ignore its inherent observation selection effect. This resides in the fact that if we randomly select an observer-moment of a driver and ask her whether she thinks the next lane is faster, more often than not we have selected an observer-moment of a driver who is in a lane which is in fact slower. When we realize this, we see that no case has been made for recommending that drivers change lanes less frequently.[7]

11

Observation selection theory (also known as anthropic reasoning), which aims to help us detect, diagnose, and cure the biases of observation selection effects, is a philosophical goldmine. Few branches of philosophy are so rich in empirical implications, touch on so many important scientific questions, pose such intricate paradoxes, and contain such generous quantities of conceptual and methodological confusion that need to be sorted out. Working in this area is a lot of intellectual fun.

The mathematics used in this field, such as conditional probabilities and Bayes's theorem, are covered by elementary arithmetic and probability theory. The topic of observation selection effects *is* extremely complex, yet the difficulty lies not in the math, but in grasping and analyzing the underlying principles.

REFERENCES

Bartha, P., and C. Hitchcock. 1999. No One Knows the Date or the Hour: An Unorthodox Application of Rev. Bayes's Theorem. *Philosophy of Science (Proceedings)* 66, pp. S329–S53.

———. 2000. The Shooting-Room Paradox and Conditionalizing on Measurably Challenged Sets. *Synthese* 108:3, pp. 403–437.

Bostrom, N. 1997. Investigations into the Doomsday argument. *Preprint.* <http://www.anthropic-principles.com/preprints/inv/investigations.html>

———. 2001. The Doomsday Argument, Adam and Eve, UN++, and Quantum Joe. *Synthese* 127:3, pp. 359–387.

———. 2002a. *Anthropic Bias: Observation Selection Effects in Science and Philosophy* (New York: Routledge).

———. 2002b. Self-Locating Belief in Big Worlds: Cosmology's Missing Link toObservation. *Journal of Philosophy* 99:12.

Dieks, D. 1992. Doomsday—Or: the Dangers of Statistics. *Philosophical Quarterly* 42:166, pp. 78–84.

Hall, N. 1994. Correcting the Guide to Objective Chance. *Mind* 103:412, pp. 505–517.

Leslie, J. 1996. *The End of the World: The Science and Ethics of Human Extinction* (London: Routledge).

Lewis, D. 1986. *Philosophical Papers* (New York: Oxford University Press).

———. 1994. Humean Supervenience Debugged. *Mind* 103:412, pp. 473–490.

Oliver, J., and K. Korb. 1997. *A Bayesian Analysis of the Doomsday Argument.* Department of Computer Science, Monash University.

Olum, K. 2002. The Doomsday Argument and the Number of Possible Observers. *Philosophical Quarterly* 52:207, pp. 164–184.

Redelmeier, D.A., and R.J. Tibshirani. 1999. Why Cars in the Other Lane Seem to Go Faster. *Nature* 401, p. 35.

Smith, Q. 1994. Anthropic Explanations in Cosmology. *Australasian Journal of Philosophy* 72:3, pp. 371–82.

Thau, M. 1994. Undermining and Admissibility. *Mind* 103:412), pp. 491–503.

12

Structuralism and the Independence of Mathematics

MICHAEL D. RESNIK

Michael D. Resnik is University Distinguished Professor at the University of North Carolina at Chapel Hill. His research interests include the philosophy of mathematics, philosophy of science, logic, and the theory of rationality. His books include Choices: An Introduction to Decision Theory, Frege and the Philosophy of Mathematics, *and, most recently,* Mathematics as a Science of Patterns.

Considered relative to our surface irritations, which exhaust our clues to an external world of physical objects, the molecules and their extraordinary ilk are thus much on a par with the most ordinary physical objects. The positing of these extraordinary things is just a vivid analogue of the positing or acknowledging of ordinary things: vivid in that the physicist audibly posits them for recognized reasons, whereas the hypothesis of ordinary things is shrouded in prehistory. . . . To call a posit a posit is not to patronize it. . . . Everything to which we concede existence is a posit from the standpoint of a description of the theory-building process, and simultaneously real from the standpoint of the theory that is being built. (W.V. Quine, *Word and Object*)

Mathematical objects, if they exist at all, exist independently of our proofs, constructions and stipulations. For example, whether inaccessible cardinals exist or not, the very act of our proving or postulating that they do doesn't make it so. This independence thesis is a central claim of mathematical realism. It is also one that many anti-realists acknowledge too. For they agree that we cannot create mathematical truths or objects, though, to be sure, they deny that mathematical objects exist at all. I have defended a mathematical realism of sorts. I interpret the objects of mathematics as positions in patterns (or structures, if you will), and maintain that they exist independently of us, and our stipulations, proofs, and the like.

By taking mathematical objects to be positions in patterns I see all mathematical objects as being like geometrical points in having no identifying features save those arising through the relations they bear to other mathematical objects in the structures to which they belong. Mathematicians talk of numbers, functions, sets and spaces in order to depict structures. Thus they might describe the natural number sequence (0, 1, 2, and so on) as the smallest number structure that has that has exactly one number (position) immediately following each of its numbers (positions) as well as an initial number (position), call it '0', which is preceded by no other numbers (position) in the structure. One of the important features of patterns is that they may occur or be embedded in other patterns. Take for example, simple songs. The pattern of notes exhibited in their initial verses usually recurs in subsequent verses. Furthermore, if we transpose the song into different keys, then the pattern of musical intervals occurs again and again in each new key, with each transposition being a different pattern of notes. I see mathematicians as making observations similar to these, as well as abstracting patterns from practical experience, finding occurrences of patterns in each other and 'combining' patterns to arrive at new ones.

Structuralist views of mathematical objects, of which mine is just one, have a reputable history among mathematicians that dates to at least the 1870s.[1] Dedekind expounded a version of structuralism, and we can find kindred themes in Hilbert too. But the recent spate of structuralist writings in the philosophy of mathematics has been in response to two influential papers by Paul Benacerraf, "What Numbers Could Not Be" (1965) and "Mathematical Truth" (1973).[2] In the first paper Benacerraf reflected on the variety of ways mathematicians have found for defining the natural numbers as sets.[3] Noting that these definitions are equally good from a mathematical point of view, he concluded that there is no fact as to which sets the numbers are, and consequently, that numbers are not sets at all. This was contrary to the teachings of Frege and Russell and many subsequent analytic philosophers, but Benacerraf continued with a more radical thought. Claiming that number theory is just the theory of a certain structure and that numbers have no identifying features except structural ones, he inferred that numbers are not objects at all, or as he put it, "if the truth be known, there are no such things as numbers; which is not to say that there are not at least two prime numbers between 15 and 20".[4]

I found myself unwilling to follow Benacerraf in his last step. His argument that number theory is the science of a certain structure was convincing, but unless something exhibits that structure number theory is vacuous. Moreover, Benacerraf's observations applied to all of mathematics. For throughout mathematics we find alternative (and incompatible) definitions of important mathematical objects. Real numbers may be defined as sets or as infinite sequences or as the sums of infinite series, functions may be defined in terms of sets or sets in terms of functions, and so on. Mathematics may well be the science of structure, but lest it be vacuous, the ontological buck most stop somewhere—things exhibiting the various mathematical structures must exist.[5]

Benacerraf's "Mathematical Truth" emphasized a different but much older problem. In the history of the philosophy of mathematics we find views that present a plausible account of mathematical truth by positing a mathematical ontology of abstract entities and views that present a plausible account of mathematical knowledge by emphasizing the role that symbol manipulation and proof play in mathematical practice. Yet nowhere can we find a plausible account of both mathematical truth and mathematical knowledge. If mathematics is about abstract entities that exist timelessly outside of space and time, then it's an utter mystery as to how we can access them and acquire mathematical knowledge. (This is the 'Access Problem'.) On the other hand, if we solve the Access Problem by taking the subject matter of mathematics to be symbols and proofs, we cannot account for the truth of mathematical sentences that purport to make claims about numbers, functions, sets and the like; for we know, thanks to logicians like Frege and Quine, that it is just a confusion to think that these are just symbols. So we are left with a dilemma: we can have a reasonable account of mathematical truth or a reasonable account of mathematical knowledge but not both.

But if we think of mathematical objects as like positions in patterns, then we may be able to solve both of Benacerraf's problems. For just as geometrical points have no identifying features—they all "look alike"—except the ones they have by virtue of their relationships to other geometrical objects, positions in patterns have no identifying features save those which they have in virtue of their relationships to other positions. This would explain why mathematicians don't care whether they define the numbers one way or another so long as the structure of the numbers is preserved, and it would explain why there is no fact of the matter as to whether the numbers are sets. That's just the way positions are. There is a lot more to my interpretation of mathematical objects as positions in patterns than I have presented here, but I want to leave it to discuss my approach to Benacerraf's other problem.[6]

Now one might think that we can access positions through accessing the structures or patterns containing them, and one might also think that something like pattern recognition would be a reliable means for so doing. Some of my earlier papers suggest such an approach, and I know through correspondence and conversation that the idea has found a number of friends. But recently I have not held such a view, and I am not sure that I ever have. Put loosely, I admit patterns that are not concretely instantiated. Now, perhaps, we come to know things about patterns by initially learning things about concretely instantiated ones. But even if this is true, I don't think it will be of much help in accounting for our knowledge of mathematical objects themselves. For mathematical objects, that is, the positions in patterns themselves are very abstract objects, and it is unclear how they could be presented to us by means of the more concrete things occupying them. At least it is unclear how they could be presented to us via an undoubtedly natural process. This is just a structuralist version of the Access Problem.

I don't see how you can avoid foundering on this problem if you face it directly. We have no causal access to mathematical objects or anything that could be taken to be their traces, since they have no traces. For the same reason we don't even have such access to structures though their instances or to types through their tokens. Of course, we often take instances of patterns and tokens of types to reflect features of the patterns and types themselves. For example, speaking of a letter qua type, we might say, "the letter 'A' looks like this," and then inscribe a token 'A'. But letter types are abstract entities, and as such they don't reflect light; so we "see" them only in an extended sense, and can never directly test hypotheses concerning their relation to their tokens.

In my book, *Mathematics as Science of Patterns*, I approached the Access Problem by applying a postulational epistemology to mathematics. My account had two parts. The first addressed the question of how the first mathematicians could have acquired mathematical beliefs without encountering mathematical objects. This question had puzzled many people influenced by the Access Problem. In answering it I hypothesized that developing, manipulating and studying notations for representing systems of concrete objects eventually led ancient mathematicians to posit mathematical objects qua abstract positions in structures. The second part of my account explained how these beliefs, though initially acquired in way that need not generate knowledge, could indeed, count as knowledge, and why standard contemporary mathematics is a body of knowledge too.

The second part of my epistemology is a pragmatic version of confirmational holism—the idea, originating in Duhem and extended by Quine, that hypotheses are confirmed or refuted in bundles rather than individually. The version I favor distinguishes between global (or holistic) conceptions of evidence and pragmatically grounded local conceptions of evidence. The basic idea is that from a logical point of view data will typically bear directly only globally upon relatively large systems of hypotheses, yet we can be pragmatically justified in taking certain data to bear upon a specific hypothesis. Biologists, for example, will be pragmatically justified in appealing to a conception of evidence local to biology to conclude, say, that a certain study refutes a certain biological hypothesis. They need not concern themselves with the fact that from the logical point of view the study also bears upon broader biological, chemical and physical hypotheses and the statistical methods they used. In applying these ideas to mathematics, I take its numerous applications to provide global evidence for mathematics, but I countenance local evidence for mathematical theories too. Indeed, as I see it, a hierarchy of (local) evidence for mathematics parallels the evidential hierarchy of the other sciences. Just as bits of elementary chemistry can support sub-atomic physics, some of the results of arithmetic and geometry can be tested against computations and measurements, analysis can be supported via its arithmetic and geometric consequences, more abstract theories confirmed via their consequences for analysis, and so on. Furthermore, I doubt that the local conception of evidence frees mathematicians from worries about whether the objects they posit exist. The history of the controversies over the negative, imaginary, and infinite numbers, infinitesimals, impredicative sets, and choice functions show that they frequently do concern themselves with the status of newly introduced mathematical entities, and try to find considerations favoring their existence.

I coupled this epistemology with notions of truth and reference that are immanent and disquotational. This means that they apply only to our own language, and serve primarily to permit inferences such as the following:

1) Everything Tess said is true, and she said, "Jones was at home;" so Jones was at home.

2) The term 'the Big Apple' is used to refer to New York City; thus if the Big Apple is hectic, so is New York City.

Even this modest conception of truth and reference allows one to formulate theses committing one to an independent mathematical reality. (One such thesis is that classical mathematical analysis is true whether or not we have proven it to be so.) Moreover, it avoids worries about how our mathematical terms 'hook onto' mathematical objects, and explains how initiating mathematical talk can enable us to refer to and describe objects to which we have no causal connection.

Further details of my account need not concern us now. But it is important for me to emphasize that two parts of my account are not tightly connected. It is true that after we have posited positions arranged in various patterns we can refer to them in order to interpret and make better sense of the experiences that led us to posit them. Moreover, I see these experiences as data that give some confirmation to the hypotheses postulating the positions. However, on my view, nothing in the course of positing, including having the experiences that motivated the positing, establishes the existence of the entities posited or the truth of the postulates concerning them. Exactly this feature of my epistemology has been the source of an important objection to it.

The problem is that in an important sense I turned my back on the Access Problem instead of solving it. I did show how we might have arrived at our mathematical beliefs through reasonable means and how they are part of a systematic whole that experience supports. But while this may show that our system of mathematical and scientific theories is internally coherent and squares with experience, it still does not show how mathematics connects to an independent reality.

Here is how Jody Azzouni has expressed his reservation:

> Some philosophers of mathematics marry an ontologically independent mathematical realm to a stipulationist epistemology. The result is unstable if only because such a union still craves explanation for why the stipulations in question correspond to properties of the ontologically independent items they are stipulations about.[7]

Azzouni is confident that I cannot meet his demand for an explanation of how mathematics is tied to an independent reality, because the practice of science and mathematics "offers no epistemic role for mathematical objects, and so does not respond to the worry that there are no mathematical objects for its theorems to be true of."[8]

Here Azzouni has in mind his 'Epistemic Role Puzzle', that is, the puzzling fact that whether or not mathematical objects exist, they seem to play no role in the things mathematicians do to obtain mathematical knowledge. This is a cousin of the Access Problem; for if mathematical objects are abstract entities, then it's unclear how they could play any role in mathematical practice. Unlike the objects that usually concern science, we cannot interact with them or physically manipulate them.

Now there are two ways one might to respond to the Epistemic Role Puzzle. First, one might explain why mathematical objects, by their very nature, could not and should not have an epistemic role; and then go on to argue that this still does not prevent us from having knowledge that is about them. This is what I tried to do in my book by interpreting mathematical objects as positions in patterns. Since it is the essence of a position that it has no function except to mark a place relative to other places in the pattern containing it, there is no basis for supposing that it has any properties that would allow us to detect it or manipulate it or otherwise involve it in our usual epistemic processes. Mathematics describes structures by telling how objects in them, that is, positions, are related. This is the only reason that it needs objects, and it requires no more of them than that they be related to each other in various ways. Thus in so far as mathematics concerns itself with structure and only structure; it is virtually pointless for its objects to have physically detectable features. Furthermore, if mathematics acknowledged any physical objects as its own proper objects, then it would be obliged to study their physical properties and would sacrifice its focus on structure. Thus, given the goals of mathematics, it makes sense for mathematics to ignore questions of the physical nature of its objects. And because mathematics does so ignore the physical nature of its objects, it is impossible for them to have any epistemic role in Azzouni's sense.

The second response would be to argue that in an indirect sense mathematical objects do indeed have an epistemic role. This is the sort of response that formalists who hold that mathematics is about formulas could make. Moreover, in a kind of convoluted way, it is open to me too. For, on my view, some mathematical notations mirror the structures they represent. For example, a finite sequence of inscribed unary numerals instantiates an initial segment of an omega sequence; a paper and pencil Turing Machine computation instantiates its abstract counterpart as does a formal derivation or a triangle on a blackboard. So one might argue that here at least structures and their positions do have a role in obtaining mathematical knowledge. I can think of two objections to this response: a) the response appeals to the relationship between types and their tokens, and the former are clearly concrete, so it is they, and not the types which have an epistemic role; b) the response goes through only if we posit structural similarities between the types and tokens in question, and we have no independent way of confirming that these similarities exist.

Later I shall argue that we don't directly access physical objects either but rather only through connections that we posit linking them to sense experience. If this is correct, then neither objection *(a)* nor objection *(b)* is compelling.

Let us assume for now that that I can respond successfully to the Epistemic Role Puzzle. I still don't think this sets to rest the general worry about my view. Ultimately, we may have a conflict between what Azzouni calls "coherentist epistemic positions"[9] and more foundational approaches. On the coherentist approach, if our current overall theory of the world is empirically adequate and meets other epistemic virtues, such as simplicity, generality, fecundity and consistency, then we have good reason to believe in the objects that it posits—all of them with no distinction being made between physical and mathematical objects. But according to Azzouni, this is not a true view of science: scientists expect their posits to have an "epistemic role of their own." This may be seen by "noticing how the actual objects under study play an official role in the evidence that epistemic processes are reliable or dependable; in light of this role, scientists are willing to describe such processes as leading to knowledge."[10] For example, suppose that physicists posit a new subatomic particle in order to make a certain group theoretic model apply to their data. Even if their theory very satisfactorily explains their data, typically they will refrain from affirming the existence of the posited particle until they have experimentally detected it. They will require observational evidence that they take to be a reliable indicator of the particle in question. Moreover, in explaining why the evidence reliably indicates the presence of the particle they will ascribe a role to the particle itself in the interactions producing the evidence. It seems then that the holist account of science, at least as expounded by Quine, is inaccurate. And if this is so, then it is reasonable to doubt its application to mathematical knowledge.

Now I think that Azzouni is right that the account of science that he attributes to Quine is not accurate. It is not clear whether this really is Quine's account, since in some of his latter writings Quine retreats from the strong holist theses he advocated in his earlier papers. In any case, if we modify holism, as I have, by distinguishing between local and global conceptions of evidence, then positing in the empirical sciences poses no problems. Empirical scientists are operating with a local conception of evidence which requires them to detect their posits; mathematicians are not.[11]

"Yes," one might object, "but it is exactly because mathematicians are not obligated to detect their posits that mathematical objects are not independent of us." To assess this claim, let us distinguish *ontological independence* from *epistemic independence*.[12] An entity is ontologically independent of us if it is not something that we make up, create or construct, etc.; that is, if it could or would exist even if we did not. From physics itself we know that subatomic particles and other unobservable objects are ontologically independent of us, since physics tells us that they (and the universe they inhabit) existed before we did and would have existed even if we had not. However, mathematics proper, being silent about the nature of its objects, simply does not address the question of their ontological independence. Rather it is philosophers, such as myself, who argue for their ontological independence by arguing that only an ontology of abstract entities can verify the existential claims of mathematics. Those offering the objection opening this paragraph think that unless we can show these abstract entities are epistemically independent of us, we should not accept this philosophical argument for the ontological independence of mathematical objects.

Now a major problem with this objection is that it is very difficult to characterize epistemic independence in a reasonably precise way that doesn't beg the question at issue or classify physical objects as epistemically *dependent* upon us. To illustrate this, I shall examine the following proposal by Azzouni:

> A requirement of our taking an object O to be [epistemically] independent of us is that, given any property attributed to O, we take ourselves as required to explain how we confirm that attribution in a way that non-trivially satisfies (*). Trivial satisfaction (*), or the irrelevance of (*) altogether from knowledge-gathering practices about O indicates that O is [epistemically] dependent on us.[13]

The condition (*) to which Azzouni refers is the following:

> (*) The process by which I come to believe claims about x's is *dependable* with respect to x's if and only if given that the process has led me to believe S(x) is true, then (under a broad range of circumstances) S(x) must be true, and/or given that the process has led me to believe S(x) is false, then (under a broad range of circumstances) S(x) must be false.[14]

In other words, on this proposal, an object is epistemically independent of us only if: 1) given any property that we attribute to it, we should ordinarily be able to determine by dependable methods whether the property in question applies to that object, and 2) there is a 'non-trivial' explanation of why our methods are dependable.[15]

In expounding (*) Azzouni writes that in the empirical sciences "processes which are taken to yield knowledge are seen as doing so precisely because they *do* (causally) connect us *to* objects in such a way that what the process gives as an answer covaries with the properties that the objects have."[16] Later he remarks, "Empirical scientific practice routinely worries about when measurements, observations, and instrumental interventions (with objects) can be trusted and when not; when artifacts of our epistemic means of access arise (and how we can recognize them)."[17] Here he is talking the dependability of quite specific scientific procedures or instruments. Their analogs in mathematics are algorithms, rules of thumb, estimation methods and approximation procedures; mathematicians *do* worry about the dependability of these things. Of course, they address their worries by taking some body of mathematics for granted and use that to demonstrate that the method in question is sound or sound for a significant number of examples. Accepted mathematics serves both as the source of data by which the methods are assessed and the background theory used to account for their virtues and foibles.

In both the mathematical and empirical cases one probes or checks or justifies a method, instrument, or datum by reference to a supposedly independent standard. Without such a standard it would be pointless to wonder about the reliability of the items in question. Thus we can calibrate a spring scale by weighing objects of known weights, and we can explain how it registers in response to the forces the objects placed upon it generate. But in order to do this we must assume that we have an independent and accurate method for determining the weights of the known objects, and that our theory of the scale is correct. Even when we give an object an epistemic role, doing so is relative to taking some parts of some theory of objects of that type for granted. When we use a telescope to confirm the existence of a planet originally posited to explain perturbations in the orbit of another planet, we presuppose a theory that permits us to conclude that what we are seeing through the telescope is a planet with sufficient mass to do the work. Thus it seems that both mathematicians and empirical scientists are concerned with issues of dependability and use similar means for addressing them.

What happens when we don't have an appropriately independent theory of the objects in question? According to Azzouni, if we *simply* say, for example, that our theory of the objects states that our methods for investigating them are dependable, then they are not epistemically independent of us—at least not yet—and we are not justified in asserting their ontological independence.[18] This threatens to undercut the epistemic independence of mathematical objects. We can explain the dependability of, say, our algorithms for calculating sums and products of numbers written in decimal notation by appealing to the recursive equations for addition and multiplication and definitions relating decimal numerals to unary numerals. We might explain the dependability of the former by defining numbers in terms of sets, but obviously the process has to end with assumptions that we cannot independently verify. Affirming that these assumptions are simply stipulated to be true will play right into Azzouni's hands, since the only explanation we will have at this point will be the 'trivial' one that the methods are dependable simply because they are (according to our theory of them).

Notice that Azzouni writes that it is a "requirement of our taking an object O to be [epistemically] independent of us is that, given *any property* attributed to O, we take ourselves as required to explain how we confirm that attribution in a way that non-trivially satisfies (*)."[19] The same requirement would hold for those who are realists about sub-atomic particles. But this seems to be too much to ask even when we consider relatively familiar objects like electrons, whose epistemic role certainly Azzouni acknowledges. The problem is that we sometimes use purely theoretical considerations to attribute properties to electrons that, as a matter of principle, we can't confirm experimentally. For example, electrons have the property of never being in a state in which they have an exact position and an exact momentum. My limited reading in the philosophy of quantum mechanics tells me that a number of theoretical considerations are needed to conclude that this is an objective feature of electrons and not just a limitation of our measuring devices. If so, then it would seem that in principle we cannot confirm this property of electrons by means of a process that satisfies (*). It may well be the case then that the only way we can confirm it, if at all, is by appealing to some well-confirmed scientific theory. Another example that comes to mind is the continuity of space-time, which seems experimentally indistinguishable from its density.[20]

Now if I am right about these examples, the process scientists have used here seems to be this: To confirm claims about physical objects, which cannot be tested directly by experiments, find a well-confirmed theory (in the usual sense) that implies the claim in question. Demanding that we explain why this process is dependable seems to be demanding too much: it is to demand that we explain why a well-confirmed empirical theory asserts the truth. Suppose that in the light of this, we conclude then that sometimes we are not obliged to explain how we can we confirm a property of certain physical objects "in a way that *nontrivially* satisfies (*)". Isn't this to conclude that (*) is irrelevant in these cases? Now we cannot conclude from this that Azzouni is forced to hold that these objects aren't ontologically or epistemically independent of us. For he only says that "the irrelevance of (*) *altogether* from our knowledge-gathering practices about O indicates that O is [epistemically] dependent on us . . ."[21] But it looks like this amounts to his acknowledging that when as a matter of principle (*) is irrelevant, we don't have to try to explain why our practices satisfy it. At most we need only explain why they fail to satisfy it.

This does not seem so different from the case of mathematics. Sometimes we raise issues of reliability and address them by citing accepted mathematical theories. Sometimes we don't raise considerations of reliability and simply depend upon the theory itself eventually being "confirmed." Moreover, in these cases, we are typically in a position to explain why we cannot apply Azzouni's criterion (*). The difference between mathematics and physics seems to be more a matter of degree than of kind with independent confirmation of our physical posits being more readily found and more frequently sought.

The difficulties we have found with Azzouni's proposal generalize to the type of position it reflects. This is the type of position that presupposes that we can access reality independently of our conceptual system. The problem is that our only access to any independent reality is through our sensations. Anything else that we access through them is mediated by hypotheses connecting the two. Walking through the woods during the fall I often smell an odor familiar from my medicine cabinet and infer that there must be some witch hazel nearby. My inference is based upon hypotheses linking the smell and the shrub, which I have conjectured but have never independently confirmed. Of course, with enough effort and care, I could test my hypotheses, but only through taking similar hypotheses for granted. Thus one of the first things I would try is to locate a specimen and smell it, but to do that I would need to know what witch hazel looks like (assume that I do). Most everyday physical objects are capable of affecting each of our five senses, and this provides us multiple ways of independently accessing them. And even when something affects only one or two senses—like the sun—we can often access it from multiple locations and at different times. All this confirms our belief that some enduring object is responsible for the sensations we have on these occasions. But each confirmation is relative to taking for granted myriad hypotheses connecting the object we posit and our sensations. Yet even in mathematics we can find independent links to the various structures it studies. Thus, we use numbers to count sheep, measure the length of a field, register the place of competitors in a race, and determine the iterations of an operation. These different empirical routes to the natural numbers give rise to different mathematical models (for example, set theoretic versus. geometric models) of the natural number sequence; and they lend credence to the idea that we are dealing with an independent reality. Again the difference between mathematics and empirical science seems to be a matter of degree.

To quote Quine, "everything to which we concede existence is a posit from the standpoint of a description of the theory-building process." We should add that anything we succeed in accessing we do so only by positing links between them and things whose accessibility we take for granted. Once we realize this, the idea that we can come to know things about patterns through their instances or about types through their tokens becomes much more palatable. As I noted earlier, on the sort of view of mathematical objects I advocate, this does give some mathematical objects an epistemic role.

Clearly, the things we (saints aside) believe in the most are the ones most intimately connected to our senses. We find it harder to doubt that we are standing on firm ground than that the prime numbers go on without end. This may be behind the philosophical intuition that mathematical objects don't exist. Rather than concede to the intuition, I acknowledge that our evidence for mathematical objects is less compelling than it is for every day material bodies, but I deny that we don't have sufficient evidence for the former. I also deny that we have stronger evidence for any physical object to which we have forged some observational connection than we have for any mathematical object. We have 'detected' quarks, but I find it a stretch to say that our justification for believing in them is stronger than our justification for believing in numbers.

Where does this leave us? Some philosophers worry that holding that we posit mathematical objects is incompatible with realism. To them mathematical posits smack more of fiction than of empirical science. Perhaps they came to this view through overlooking my claim that positing mathematical objects does not guarantee their existence and is only an initial step towards obtaining knowledge of the objects posited. In any case, they are likely to argue their point by emphasizing that mathematicians don't even try to detect their posits whereas empirical scientists normally do. Thus empirical scientists meet their obligations towards an independent reality while mathematicians don't. To this I have responded that the role of mathematical objects does not require them to be detectable; the local conception of mathematical evidence does not admit a place for detecting them. The real question is whether we can get 'independent' evidence for a set of axioms, and sometimes we can by modeling them in some previously accepted domain. This is something that mathematicians prize.

As Azzouni pointed out, we cannot explain the reliability of mathematical methods in terms of the mathematical objects themselves, whereas in empirical science we regularly account for the reliability of methods by assigning roles to the objects the methods concern. This is evidence of an independent domain. However, we should not overlook the effort mathematicians devote to establishing the soundness of their methods even if in so doing they don't give a role to individual mathematical objects. Moreover, through positing links between structures and their empirical instances, we can bring mathematical objects into the epistemic picture.

In concluding let me note that my defense of the combination of postulationalism and realism turned little upon structuralism or holism. Structuralism played a part in my response to the Epistemic Role Puzzle, but I think it would have been enough for me to say that mathematics concerns itself with only the structural features of its objects whether they are positions in structures or not. Holism occurred in my account of how we might confirm mathematical posits, but the important point that we can support them using the mathematician's (local) conception of evidence should be separable from my more global conception of evidence.

13

The Deep and Suggestive Principles of Leibnizian Philosophy

JULIAN BARBOUR

Julian Barbour is a theoretical physicist and author of The Discovery of Dynamics, *on the historical development of ideas about time and motion, and, more recently,* The End of Time: The Next Revolution in Physics. *He has been working on foundational issues in physics—in particular, the nature of time—and has mostly pursued his research independently.*

1. Introduction

The most obvious thing about the universe in which we find ourselves is its structure. Before the scientific revolution, the instinctive reaction of thinkers to the existence of perceived structure was to find a direct reason for that structure. This is reflected above all in the Pythagorean notion of the well-ordered cosmos: the cosmos has the structure it does because that is the best structure it could have. In fact, that is what the word *cosmos* really means—primarily *order*, but also *decoration, embellishment*, or *dress* (*cosmetic* has the same origin).

Kepler and Galileo were no less entranced by the beauty of the world than Pythagoras and they formulated their ideas in the overall conceptual framework of the well-ordered cosmos. However, both studied the world so intently that they actually identified aspects of motion (precise laws of planetary motion and simple laws of falling bodies and projectiles) that fairly soon led to the complete overthrow of such a notion of cosmos. The laws of the new physics were found to determine not the actual structure of the universe, but the way in which structure changes from instant to instant. Ultimately, no explanation is provided for the presently observed structure; it is simply attributed to an initial structure that was never *fashioned* by the laws of nature but merely continually *refashioned* thereafter. The initial and boundary conditions for our universe lie outside the purview of science. But all the structure we observe around us must ultimately be traced back to those mysterious initial and boundary conditions.

It is true that very often it does seem as if we possess law that directly determine structure. A first example is Darwinian evolution;[1] another is the dynamical self-organization of structure;[2] and a third is the way structure emerges from the inflationary scenario in modern cosmology.[3] However, the decisive common feature in all these cases is a very special initial condition, which is highly ordered and far from thermal equilibrium; this point is well brought out by Albrecht. Penrose has graphically illustrated the incredible improbability of such a highly ordered state arising by chance by depicting the creative divinity with a pin trying to locate the correct initial point in the space of initial states of the universe.[4] One cannot help wondering if modern science does not lack a key idea. Could there be some direct *structure-creating principle* that has hitherto escaped us?

A further reason for entertaining this idea seriously comes from the so-called 'problem of time' in modern attempts to create a quantum theory of gravity. Such a theory of gravity would simultaneously be a quantum theory of the entire universe. However, the highly flexible and relational manner in which time is treated in Einstein's theory of gravity is extremely difficult to reconcile with the role that time plays in quantum mechanics, since in the latter, time is essentially the external, absolute time that Newton introduced. In fact, some researchers in the field doubt whether time has any role at all to play in quantum cosmology, arguing that time is an emergent phenomenon. I find the arguments for this view strong, if not yet decisive, and some years ago published a book, *The End of Time*, suggesting that the next revolution in physics could well be the complete disappearance of time as an essential part of the structure of the universe.[5] Recent research in which I have been involved strengthens me in this belief.[6] This question mark over the very existence of time makes it even more pertinent to seek a structure-creating first principle, since one clearly cannot attribute structure observed in the here and now to 'initial' conditions if there is no sense at all in which one can speak about past and future but only 'elsewhere'.

I would like to suggest that, in this connection, it could be helpful to take a deeper look at the implications of Leibniz's philosophy. In fact, Leibnizian ideas crop up both explicitly and implicitly in many discussions of the conceptual problems of quantum gravity. For the most part they center on the notion of Leibnizian equivalence,[7] which amounts to the proposition that two seemingly distinct situations that are observationally indistinguishable are to be treated as identical. This is Leibniz's principle of the identity of indiscernibles. This and his principle of sufficient reason form the twin pillars of his philosophy—his two "great principles," as he called them. They appeared prominently in his famous controversy with Clarke in 1715–1716 about the foundations of natural philosophy, in which Leibniz critiqued Newton's concepts of absolute space and time.[8] (Clarke was 'tutored' in his responses by Newton.) To counter Newton's notion of a pre-existing absolute space in which all points are exactly identical, Leibniz claimed that such a situation would have presented God with an impossible decision—where precisely to place the contents of the universe. Why here rather than there? Leibniz argued that even God must have a sufficient reason for all His acts, and the impossibility of finding any such reason for any particular placement demonstrated that the notion of an absolute place could not be correct. Absolute space could not exist, and position must be relative. Space, argued Leibniz, is nothing more than the order of coexisting things, which are 'placed' solely by their positions relative to each other.

Unfortunately, Leibniz's intuitions regarding the needs of a dynamical theory were not as acute as Newton's. He failed to come to grips with Newton's dynamical arguments for absolute space. I have argued elsewhere[9] that it is possible to take on Newton's arguments effectively at the level of dynamics, but this is not what I should like to write about here. The point is that Leibniz's two great principles do not really give one an idea of quite how radical his philosophy is; potentially, his philosophy can have implications stretching far beyond his two normative principles. I believe that it does contain the seeds of a structure-creating first principle—and much more. This is what I want to explain. However, I do not in any way want to diminish the value of the two great principles. If you read through Einstein's papers in which he battled his way to the creation of his general theory of relativity, you will see that the spur that kept him going was, in fact, the principle of sufficient reason. Indeed, he carried on directly from where Leibniz was forced by his untimely death to leave the issue. As Einstein never ceased to point out, Newton's use of absolute space was tantamount, in modern terms, to the introduction of distinguished frames of reference (for the formulation of the laws of nature) under conditions in which it was completely impossible to find any reason why they should be distinguished. Einstein found this to be an affront to the principle of sufficient reason, and was therefore led to say that no such distinguished frames of reference can exist, or, rather, that all conceivable frames must be equally good for the formulation of the laws of nature. This was his principle of general relativity—and what a harvest it eventually yielded.

That, I think, is enough justification for taking Leibniz seriously. In the next section, I give a brief summary of what I take to be the most exciting and radical elements of Leibniz's philosophy. Then I present a model in which nontrivial structure is created as a first principle. In the final section, I comment on the Leibnizian aspects of such a model.

2. Variety Opposed to Uniformity

Leibniz developed what to many is a quite fantastical philosophy. To me, however, his philosophy is the one radical alternative to Cartesian-Newtonian materialism ever put forward that possesses enough definiteness to be cast in mathematical form—and hence to serve as a potential framework for natural science. To a large degree, he developed it in response to Descartes,[10] who had sought to account for the phenomenal world with the absolute minimum of concepts. If these were crystal clear, then surely we must intuit them directly by a capacity given to us by God, who would not deceive us in such fundamental matters. Ruminating along these lines, Descartes concluded that the material world consisted of just one single solitary substance with just one distinguishing attribute: extension. He argued further that this extended substance, matter, was divided into pieces that constantly moved relative to each other. Out of this higgledy-piggledy jostling, all the phenomena of nature must arise. This idea was a powerful stimulus to the mechanical model of the universe that was developed in the seventeenth century, according to which the material world consists of infinitely many essentially identical indivisible atoms in constant motion. This is reductionism in its classic form.

In his youth, Leibniz was 'infected' by this idea, as he often remarked later, yet he found what seems to be a serious flaw in Descartes's windswept ontology. If matter has but one distinguishing attribute, extension, how do we come to see *anything*? There are no attributes to distinguish one piece of matter from another. There is nothing in this scheme to explain the *variety of the world*. At the very least, Descartes would have needed to postulate a second attribute, probably more. It is interesting that, broadly, this is the route that was taken by physics, though founded on a much more secure empirical basis than Descartes had deemed necessary. Through much of the last century, one of the main goals of physics was to find the fundamental particles of nature. Even at the time when quantum mechanics was discovered, in 1925–1926, physicists believed that all matter was composed of only two fundamental particles—the electron and the proton. This picture does indeed look like a minimal extension of Cartesian reductionism. But during the course of the century, the number of so-called fundamental particles grew in a somewhat disconcerting manner, though our understanding of the way in which they interacted also progressed impressively. Now, if the superstring enthusiasts are correct, we are almost back to Descartes—all the phenomena of nature are to be understood as manifestations of sub-microscopic strings that wiggle in an eleven-dimensional space-time.

Leibniz, in contrast to Descartes, struck out in a very different direction. Like Descartes, he accepted that the universe consisted of infinitely many entities. However, these entities, which he called 'monads', were quite unlike atoms, which were always assumed to have identical properties. There might be several different kinds of atoms, but within each class all atoms were assumed to be identical. The only difference between them would be their positions and speeds in space and time. But Leibniz denied the independent existence of space and time. They were nothing but relations between things. Position in space and time could not be used as attributes to distinguish otherwise indistinguishable objects. I find this position very persuasive. The core of Leibniz's philosophy is the insistence on a proper *principle of individuation*. He argued that any contingently existing thing must be described by its attributes.[11] He then noted that one could never adequately distinguish a given thing by a finite set of attributes, since two different objects could well share those attributes but differ in other respects. It would be like trying to define a real number uniquely by a finite number of the digits in its decimal expansion. Leibniz argued that, once one starts on the true identification of an actual thing, one must always end by giving a description of the entire universe. His bold conclusion was that, in reality, actual things are simply descriptions of the universe from different perspectives, like all the different views of a city.

I am not going to attempt to explain how Leibniz, starting from such an idea, arrived at his full theory of monads—his *Monadology*.[12] That would take a book. Instead, I will simply try to summarize the key ideas as best I can. This is how I understand his scheme.

Leibniz held that the entire world consists of nothing but distinct individuals, and that the sole essence of these individuals is to have perceptions (not all of which they are distinctly aware of). This position is superficially similar to Berkeley's idealism,[13] according to which nothing exists except perceiving souls and ideas—perceptions—that God causes to appear to them. But there the similarity ends. The most radical element in the *Monadology*, postulated rather than explained or made directly plausible, is the claim that the perceptions of any one monad—its defining attributes—are nothing more and nothing less than the *relations* it bears to all the other monads.

The monads exist by virtue of self-mirroring of each other; they all define each other. A monadological world is a perfectly bootstrapped world. It tugs itself into existence out of the mire of nothingness somewhat after the manner that Baron Münchhausen got himself out of the bog.

Now how on earth could one begin to give substance to such a scheme? And why would one want to try? I would give three main justifications. First, the view that the world is relational is deeply persuasive and has been given strong support by the successes of general relativity and quantum mechanics. Thus any model that develops relational ideas in a radical way is likely to have some value. Second, such a model must, if it is to have any interest, have a nontrivial structure. Leibniz gives us a valuable hint for how structure can be generated as a first principle. I shall come to this in the next section, but the introduction explained why such a principle may well be needed by modern physics. Third, there is simply the intrinsic interest of the attempt. Leibniz was, after all, one of the greatest and most original thinkers of all time. The *Monadology* is a marvelous dream, far more inspiring than Cartesian materialism. Can we show that the dream is reality?

3. Maximal Variety

Leibniz is widely held to have argued that we live in the best of all possible worlds. Voltaire made great fun of this idea in *Candide*, depicting him as the ever-optimistic Pangloss. However, if one reads the *Monadology* carefully, one finds that the principle Leibniz took to be the one that brings the experienced world into existence (rather than some other possible world) is not so much a maximization of goodness, but is much more closely related to the principle of individuation that is the foundation of his philosophy. According to this principle, individuals are distinguished by variety. The very essence of being is variety. What one means by 'good' is notoriously difficult to define. How can one maximize something one cannot define? In contrast, something that *can* be defined and maximized is variety. Moreover, it is clear to me that this is the deeper meaning of Leibniz's scheme, for in paragraphs 57 and 58 of the *Monadology* we read:

> And just as the same town, when looked at from different sides, appears quite different and is, as it were, multiplied *in perspective*, so also it happens that because of the infinite number of simple substances [monads], it is as if there were as many different universes, which are however but different perspectives of a single universe in accordance with the different points of view of the monads. And this is the means of obtaining as much variety as possible, but with the greatest order possible; that is to say, it is the means of obtaining as much perfection as possible.

This passage prompted Lee Smolin and me, some years ago, to try to cast Leibniz's ideas into a concrete mathematical form. We published a few papers on the subject.[14] So far as we know, our models are the first such attempts of their kind. At the time, we harbored some hope that they might have direct application in physics. I am presently inclined to think that too optimistic and that the models have suggestive rather than prescriptive value. So, in the hope that one of my readers will take the original idea of maximal variety further, here is a description of the models. The first is more pure, the second more readily visualized.

First Model. A mathematical graph consists of *vertices* and *lines*. The vertices are going to model monads, the lines will represent the existence of relations between them. For convenience, we postulate that the number N of vertices is fixed. In the model, there is only one relation that can hold between two different vertices—either they are joined by a single line or they are not. More complicated models are possible but are not needed to get the concept across. Two examples are shown in Figure 1. It is important that the position of the vertices and the lengths of the lines joining them in the pictorial representation have no significance. All that counts is whether or not any two vertices are connected. It is assumed that each vertex is joined to at least one other vertex—the graph to which they belong is *connected*.

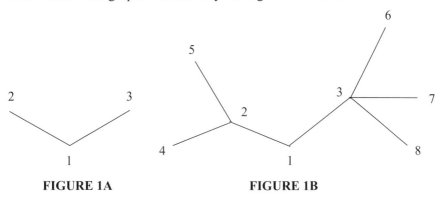

FIGURE 1A   **FIGURE 1B**

In many applications, graphs represent salient relations within structures. Inessentials have been abstracted away. In Euler's famous first use of graphs, the vertices represented places in Königsberg and the lines bridges over rivers between them. Euler's only interest was whether all the places could be reached in a continuous walk that did not cross any bridge more than once. In such problems, the lines and vertices can be defined and identified by attributes that are not represented in the graph. Some vertices may have no connections to any other vertices, but one can still say they exist. They are identified by *extrinsic* denominations.

To model the *Monadology*, I shall insist that all denominations are *intrinsic*. I am not allowed to point and say: "That is vertex 1." Only graph-theoretical elements can be used. For example, in Figure 1a, vertex 1 is unambiguously distinguished from the other two by saying that it is joined to *two* other vertices. Note than in such terms the two other vertices are indistinguishable. I shall call such a graph *non-Leibnizian*, since the two vertices seem to violate the principle of the identity of indiscernibles. Graphs in which all vertices are intrinsically distinguished are *Leibnizian*. For graphs with few vertices, it is difficult to find any that are Leibnizian. With increasing number N of vertices, the relative proportion of non-Leibnizian graphs among all those with N vertices falls rapidly.

The *r-step view* of any given vertex v in such a graph G is the sub-graph of G obtained by starting at the given vertex and keeping all the vertices and lines that can be reached in not more than r steps from v. The 1-step view of vertex 1 in Figure 1b is the complete graph in Figure 1a. The 2-step view of vertex 1 in Figure 1b is already the complete graph, but for vertex 8 the complete graph is only recovered with the 4-step view.

The concept of r-step views can be used to distinguish vertices. Two vertices with the same r-step views are r-step indistinguishable, or *r-indifferent*. On the other hand, if the views are intrinsically different, they are *r-distinct*. The *indifference* of vertex v in graph G is the minimal value of r at which v becomes distinct from *every* other vertex in the graph. If G has N vertices and is Leibnizian, then G has N indifferences, one for each vertex. Call the sum I of the values of these N indifferences the *graph indifference*. If G is non-Leibnizian, let I be infinite.

Consider all graphs with N vertices. They are finite in number. Each has a graph indifference I. Since I is positive, some graphs, or perhaps only one, will have I smaller than all the other graphs of N vertices. For simplicity, suppose there is only one such graph. Call it the *maximal-variety graph*. Its vertices are more varied, more readily distinguished, than in any other graph of N vertices. Maximal variety selects—calls into being if you like—a world whose individuals 'strive' to be as individualistic as possible. If, following Leibnizian epistemology, existence is identified as the possession of distinguishing attributes—the possession of positive variety—then a world in which this is well done is surely preferable to one in which distinction is botched. In this sense, a maximal-variety graph is the best of all possible worlds.

Second Model. Graphs are mathematically tractable but not readily visualized. The second model adds a bare minimum of spatial structure so that there is 'something to see'. Think of a wheel with N slots on its rim. Each slot must be filled with either a white ball or a black one. Suppose this done in some particular way. We are going to play essentially the same game but with a symmetry like the one inherent in the existence of matter and anti-matter. (Given a particle with some charge and handedness, then its antipar-ticle has the opposite charge and handedness.) Two slots, a and b, have a relative indifference $I(a, b)$ if they can be distinguished by the difference of their neighborhoods in a manner that does not say if neighboring balls are black or white or to the left or right. We can only say colors are the same *(S)* or different *(D)* and give the sequence. For example, the seven-member neigh-borhood with a at its centre might be characterized by *SSDaDDS*, which we regard as the same as its reflection *SDDaDSS*. Using such sequences to com-pare the neighborhoods of a and b, we establish how many steps away from them one must go before the neighborhoods become different. The number of the step at which they become distinct is the relative indifference. The rel-ative indifferences can be calculated for all pairs of the N particles. Summed, they give the total indifference I of the configuration. Once again, the con-figuration(s) with the lowest indifference have the maximal variety.

About ten years ago I did some computer calculations to find such con-figurations with the Macintosh computer I then possessed. I was able to do exhaustive calculations up to $N = 27$, which took the Macintosh about three days. Because the number of combinations that must be checked out grows exponentially with N, even with a modern supercomputer I doubt that calcu-lations much beyond $N = 50$ would be feasible. However, I think the results I obtained then may already characterize the insights that can come from max-imal variety. Let me first present them and then comment.

One can readily check that for $N < 7$, there are no Leibnizian configura-tions. They all contain at least two indistinguishable sites according to the above rules. For $N = 7$, there exists the solitary Leibnizian configuration.

(1)   xxoxooo,

which must be imagined bent into a ring with the first x (black) next to the last o (white). Since the model is color-symmetric, to say that a given site is black or white is purely nominal. The sequence ooxoxxx is counted as iden-tical to *(1)*. But if we are to see anything, we must make a choice. I choose to call the color with fewer sites black.

The configuration *(1)* is the simplest solution of our optimization program for structure generation. It anticipates all the maximal-variety configurations that exist up to my limit of $N = 27$. With few exceptions, the maximal-vari-ety configuration for a given N is not unique, though the number of such con-figurations is not large. For example, for $N = 14$ there are nine, for $N = 15$ three, for $N = 22$ four, and for $N = 27$ I found over twenty. I do not know if this indicates a qualitative change to significantly more maximal-variety configurations for each N. I found no evidence that the nature of the configurations themselves changes.

The following table gives all the maximal-variety configurations for $N = $ 21 to $N = 25$, which happen to be conveniently few in number:

N	Configuration
21	xxxooxoxoxoooxooooooo
22	xxoxoxoxxxxoooxoooooooo
	xxoxoooxooxoxoxooooooo
	xxxoxxxxooxoxoxooooooo
	xxoxoxoxxxoxxoxooooooo
23	xxxooxooxoxoxoooxooooooo
24	xxxooxooxoxoxoooxoooooooo
25	xxoxxoxoxoxxxoooxooooooo
	xxxoxxxxooxooxoxoxooooooo

Without exception, all the maximal-variety configurations possess certain very characteristic features. First, about one third of the configuration consists of a uniform run of sites of all the same color. As represented here, these are the zeros on the right. I shall call this uniform run *the space*. In all cases, the space is bounded at one end by a single site of the opposite color followed by another site of the same color as the space. At the other end of the space, there are always two or three sites of the opposite color. After that, the two types of site alternate, in a region that I shall call *the body*, in a manner that is impossible to predict without doing the calculations. However, the body is always asymmetric, having two different ends. That is predictable.

As a very simple model of the world and its evolution in time, one could suppose that the passage of time corresponds to the *creation of possibilities*, represented by an increase in the number N of slots that can be filled in such a model. Then the first instant of time corresponds to $N = 1$, the second to $N = 2$, and so forth. At each instant, the world is required to fall into a minimal-indifference configuration for that slot number—it is condemned to be creative forever and always to seek the maximal-variety configuration. The table shows us the evolution of such a world. We see a space and a body that evolve and grow in what seems to be a deterministic manner as far as the gross structure is concerned but in a probabilistic manner as regards the fine detail in the interior of the body.

Now, this is the kind of behavior that we observe in the actual world, in which the gross structure evolves in accordance with the deterministic laws of classical physics, while the microscopic structure obeys probabilistic quantum laws. At the time Lee Smolin and I developed such models, this outcome encouraged us to think that some form of theory based directly on the ideas of maximal variety could provide a realistic model of the universe. I still do not rule that out, but my thinking, influenced strongly by the belief that structure and variety hold the key to the laws of nature, has since developed in the somewhat different direction outlined in *The End of Time* and "Relativity without relativity" (notes 5 and 6).

There are several reasons why I have felt it worth returning to the idea of maximal variety. In the final section, I shall say something about its possible value for the light it casts on the kind of philosophical scheme Leibniz was trying to create. It might be a modest contribution to Leibnizian scholarship. To conclude this section, I want to say a few words about its possible value for certain basic issues in science and philosophy.

Let me start with holism versus reductionism and the related question of the whole and the part. It is the idea of an independently existing container space that makes the notion of atoms possible. When you look at the graphs in Figure 1, there is a temptation to think that the lines and vertices exist in themselves. This can be said of the actual lines and vertices on the paper, *but not of what they represent*. When you see a tree, that seeing is a primal fact. Just because you and the fact can be represented as a vertex and a line on paper does not give either you or the fact an independent existence. There's no paper in what you see. And you do not see yourself either. Properly understood, the graph is just one thing. Expanding the views from any one vertex, you always end up with the "universe" of the complete graph. There is a sense in which a vertex, identified with its fully extended view, is a part. But it is already the whole. The part is the whole, yet the whole is more than the part. Figure 1 does not look like much. But you comprehend it in a glance, and that comprehension is the perpetual miracle of simultaneous analysis and synthesis. You understand the connections in their totality but can also unravel them. Leibniz always said true unity is not achieved by mere aggregation like a heap of stones, but by a *principle of unity*. In its modest way, interpreted in pure graph-theoretical terms, a connected graph does express a principle of unity. It is a plurality within a unity, Leibniz's suggestive description of a monad. It is the principle of unity that makes the whole more than the part. If we can see the way to it, holism will trump reductionism.

When does information acquire semantic content? The well-known definition of information due to Shannon is extrinsic, not intrinsic.[15] Two agents agree to associate some meaning with a given set of symbols. The association is arbitrary. The same string of ones and zeros can represent a number or a declaration of war. Can such strings proclaim their own semantics? I believe they can, at least to some extent, if they possess an extremal property. The maximal-variety strings in the table do say what they are. They encode the law that brings them into being. In computer terminology, they are at once the algorithm, its outcome, and its meaning.

Somewhat related to this is the issue of defining order, disorder and complexity. Specialists give much thought to this. I am not going to claim that variety provides any definitive answers, but it does represent a specific and quantifiable measure of order. It may help us to understand the different kinds of order that are possible, for example in a crystal or in a living cell. Both are highly ordered but in very different ways. Random order is of a different kind and not like either. It is clear that a maximally varied configuration has an order more like that of a living cell than that of a crystal or random structure. In "Extremal Variety as the Foundation of a Cosmological Quantum Theory" (note 14), these thoughts are developed a bit further.

To conclude: Leibniz's ideas can help us to comprehend the ontology of a relational and holistic universe, and perhaps even to find its meaning.

4. Leibnizian Philosophy Interpreted though Maximal Variety

Although maximal variety was developed mainly with the (long-term) aim of creating new physical theories, it may have interest in its own right as a mathematical model of the *Monadology* that sheds new light on some of Leibniz's claims. There are, for a start, two intriguing aspects of the model.

First, if this model is ever transformed into some kind of fundamental description of the universe, physics will come to resemble biology: all of the entities in a maximal-variety configuration are created in a kind of ecological balance between competing individuals. Each is trying to be as individualistic as possible, but in a curious way this selfish behavior is necessary if anything is to exist at all (for to exist is to become differentiated and hence to emerge from the mist of nothingness). By making ourselves differentiated, we cannot help but make other beings differentiated at the same time. The lion and the gazelle make each other. Surely Leibniz would like this mathematical example of how seeming evil is needed to make even the best of all possible worlds. Long live Pangloss!

The second aspect warrants a lengthier discussion. Consciousness in a material world is so baffling that idealism has always seemed more cogent than materialism. But hitherto nothing significant in the way of mathematical support to rival the triumphs of physics based on the hypothesis of an external world has been forthcoming. It is all very well for Bishop Berkley to say that God implants ideas—perceptions—in our souls and that there is nothing more to it than that. But then why does God go to the trouble of ensuring that Einstein's general relativity correctly predicts the observed motion of the moon to millimeters? What weakens Berkeley's thesis is the incredible success of mathematicians and physicists in finding mathematical laws that presuppose an external world independent of consciousness. It is not good enough to say that God in his inscrutable wisdom has grounds to give us the impression that a world does exist out there. Scientists are not going to give up on the illumination that laws provide. To make idealism plausible, one needs laws that act directly and transparently on the raw stuff of consciousness: perceptions. Only then will the reductionist's atoms appear redundant. I want to suggest that Leibnizian principles might just enable the construction of a model of the world based directly on sense perceptions that does not lapse into solipsism or invoke a Berkeleian God who simply pops those perceptions into our souls. What I am going to propose now is, at the best, merely a demonstration of inherent possibility.

Suppose that a maximal-variety graph encodes the state of the world at a given instant. Take each view of the graph centered on a given vertex to represent the totality of the instantaneous perceptions of a sentient being—a monad. Each vertex 'generates' a different view, which is simultaneously a different monad. For a given vertex, the lines and remaining vertices of the graph stand for two things at once—the relations of that monad to the other monads at that instant and the perceptions of that monad at that instant. According to Leibniz, the two are one and the same thing. The bare mathematical structure can be given concrete meaning by saying that a line from vertex i to a vertex j that has no other connections means that vertex i has some definite experience, say being aware of the color white. If j is connected to one other vertex, that could mean i experiences the color blue. For each type of vertex to which connection is made, there could correspond a definite sensation. Given such a lexicon—the translation from the bare elements of the graph to actual experience—we could read off the experiences of each of the monads within the graph.

Note that although the property of being joined by a line is a reciprocal relation, so that if i has an awareness of j we must also assume that j has an awareness of i, what is actually experienced will, except in rare cases, be different. This is because the other connections from i and j are not the same, and, by hypothesis, it is these other connections that determine how each vertex is experienced. In addition, in a maximal-variety graph there is a premium on difference.

It is interesting to consider in this framework Leibniz's famous remark that monads have no windows through which attributes might enter or leave a monad (*Monadology*, Section 7). This is trivially true in the present model; for in the bare graph-theoretical terms the monad corresponding to a given vertex is nothing more that the listing of its connections to the other vertices. These connections are its attributes and it has no others. They could only be changed by considering a *different* (but similar) graph in which some of the connections have been changed. But, strictly, that is then a quite different world and consists of different monads. (Since we have assumed that the actually realized world is the one that exhibits the greatest possible variety, this modified world will possess less variety and hence fail to make it into existence—it will be one of Leibniz's 'possible worlds'.) Thus, each monad's attributes in the actually realized world are given once and for all. Each monad is, in fact, simply *the world as seen from its particular point of view*.

Seen in this light, I believe Leibniz was wrong to think that in a monadological world the mutual consistency of all the different monads—what he called the pre-established harmony—is a great miracle of God. In fact, it is a trivial consequence of the model. (The miracle is that *anything* is experienced.) In a graph, each vertex is willy-nilly a view of the whole from a given point of view. The graph defines all the views and enforces their mutual consistency. Moreover, as I have already said, it is inherent within the model that the whole consists of and defines its parts and that each part is simultaneously the whole.

In logical terms it may be true that the monads have no windows. But in another sense they are literally riddled with windows. What I as a particular monad experience is of necessity related to what the other monads experience. The experiences are not the same, but they are still related. Once I have achieved full self-awareness and understand in graph-theoretical terms why I have particular experiences, I will simultaneously know something about the experiences of the monad centered on the vertex responsible for my experiencing yellow. I can *peep* into the experiences of my fellow monads. Because of the way in which experiences are generated, we are all continually sharing experiences, though there is never identity of experiences.

In fact, the entire world is resolved into *pure shared experience*. This is an appropriate place to stop. If my conjecture is correct, this idea must resonate within you.[16]

This model is, of course, primitive, but it is always worth looking for different ways of conceiving the world. Let me leave the attempt at justification at that. However, I would like to make two comments about how my thinking has developed in the thirteen years since this model was first developed.

First, I have made no further attempt to develop mathematical realizations of idealism—not because I believe the venture is totally hopeless or worthless but because other goals, above all quantum gravity and advance in our understanding of time, seem to me more attainable. In fact, it was in the summer of 1991, while reading the proofs of my article "On the Origin of Structure in the Universe" in which I first presented this model, that I suddenly had the notion of a time capsule, which is now my preferred idea for overcoming the problem of time in quantum gravity, as explained in *The End of Time*. I cannot possibly go into details, but the key point is that a time capsule is a static highly ordered structure that contains what we interpret as records of a past that, strictly speaking, does not exist at all. If you have read my book, I am sure you will see how my earlier Leibnizian thinking helped me along the way to the idea.

Second, at the time that Lee Smolin and I developed these ideas, one of our aims was to try to construct a so-called 'hidden-variables' explanation of quantum phenomena. We wanted to explore the possibility that outcomes of quantum experiments that, in the laboratory, appear random but governed by probabilities are in fact uniquely determined by the overall properties of the universe. This is still a logical possibility, and Lee continues to take a lively interest in it. However, at the same time as I was working on the idea of maximal variety, I was also interacting with David Deutsch, who is one of the leading advocates of the many-worlds interpretation of quantum mechanics.[17] (He also contributed to this paper by proposing the precise definition of indifference in pure graph-theoretical terms.) Through David, I became convinced that the many-worlds interpretation needs to be taken seriously, and, in a somewhat modified form, it now plays a central role, along with Leibnizian ideas, in my current theory of time.

14

The Modern Neo-Positivist: A Tribute to W.V. Quine

WARREN GOLDFARB

Warren Goldfarb has been on the faculty of the Harvard Philosophy Department since 1975 and is the Walter Beverly Pearson Professor of Modern Mathematics and Mathematical Logic. His teaching and research interests include mathematical logic and the development of analytic philosophy, particularly Frege, Russell, Carnap, Quine, and Wittgenstein (both early and late).

I wrote these lyrics for Van Quine in May 1978, and presented them to him at the occasion honoring him upon his retirement from the Harvard faculty. Quine's liking for the Gilbert and Sullivan operas was well known.

I am the very model of a modern neo-posit'vist.
The only word I take is that of the atomic physicist
Who tells us what ontology, that is, the range of quantifiers
Meets up with our demand for truth (and more than truth we can't require).
'Tis theory-bound I know full well—it is the state that we are in.
There is no first philosophy, we can't be Archimedean
Thus my concerns are all within a framework that is naturalized
What's natural here is given us by what our science has surmised.

Good views are hence continuous with news from the laboratory
It's only mental myth that makes us think there is another story.

Upon a raft of Neurath's sort, in open sea we are adrift
And so I am the model of a modern neo-pragmatist.

On language, too, I've thought a bit—to most it was a bitter pill.
There are no grounds I said to talk of truths called 'analytical'.
To back this up I wrote some words on reference inscrutable
And on the different options that can make translations suitable.
This holds at home in what we do, not just in projects radical.
Homophony and charity are opposites that matter still,
Our manual is settled just by some amount of wantonness
And minds are shaped by practices likes bushes elephantinous.
With structure fixed we can research transparence and opacity;
The latter leads to total loss of reference-capacity,
But attitudes and modals here I'd like to excise from my list
And so I am the model of a modern neo-posit'vist.

I've put some work into those fields that are more purely logical.
Though ML fell, NF may do, despite its aspect magical
Ax Inf implied, full choice denied, and for the rest we'll wait and see
On whether there's a rel'tive proof that gives us its consistency.

More recently I've spent some time on quantifiers objectual
And whether substitution might be just as much effectual.
These logic matters mean a lot, they're at the center of our scheme
And so a neo-positivist had better look past what they seem.

My interests extend yet more, to things not philosophical.
I've toured throughout the world in places temperate and tropical
I know the roots of words and all the op'ras penned by G & S
And so I am the model of a modern neo-posit'vist.

Notes

1. Human Nature and the Character of Economic Science

1. For an example of more recent critical views of Mises's epistemological position, see Robert Nozick, "On Austrian Methodology," *Synthese* 36 (1977), pp. 353–392.

2. For an early statement of Mises's position, see his 1933 paper, "The Task and Scope of the Science of Human Action," *Epistemological Problems of Economics* (Princeton: Van Nostrand, 1960). Later and more detailed statements are his *Human Action* (New Haven: Yale University Press, 1949), *Theory and History* (New Haven: Yale University Press, 1957), and *The Ultimate Foundation of Economic Science*, revised edition (Kansas City: Sheed, Andrews, and McMeel, 1978).

3. This section draws, in part, upon the writer's *The Economic Point of View* (Princeton: Van Nostrand, 1960), pp. 51–57.

4. John Stuart Mill, "On the Definition of Political Economy," in *Essays on Some Unsettled Questions of Political Economy* (1844; reprint, London School of Economics and Political Science, 1948), p. 137.

5. As cited in Marion Bowley, *Nassau Senior and Classical Political Economy* (London, 1937), p. 61.

6. See Bowley, pp. 45–46.

7. For some account of these debates, see Mises, *Epistemological Problems*, pp. 18–22; Bowley, pp. 53–65.

8. See Mises, *Epistemological Problems*, for discussion of whether this observation might possibly be introspective.

9. This section draws, in part, upon the writer's *The Economic Point of View*, Chapter 6.

10. Although the book emphasizes its intellectual indebtedness to a number of Austrian economists (and in particular to Mises), we shall in what follows be contrasting certain aspects of Robbins's views with those of Mises.

11. Lionel Robbins, *An Essay on the Nature and Significance of Economic Science*, second edition (London: Macmillan, 1935), p. 16.

12. Robbins, pp. 16–17. For the extent to which Robbins was indebted to P.H. Wicksteed in this regard, see Robbins's introduction to P.H. Wicksteed, *The Common Sense of Political Economy* second edition (1934), p. xxii.

13. See Robbins, *Essay on the Nature and Significance*, Chapters IV, V.

14. Robbins, p. 105.

15. See Robbins, pp. 78–79, 115.

16. Robbins, pp. 116–17.

17. E. Streissler et al., eds., *Roads to Freedom: Essays in Honour of Friedrich A. von Hayek* (London: Routledge, 1969), p. 52.

18. Robbins, p. 105.

19. Buchanan, in Streissler et al., p. 52.

20. Robbins, p. 106.

21. For further development of ideas in this section, see the author's *Economic Point of View*, Chapter 7.

22. See his 1933 article noted above, n.2.

23. On this see V.C. Walsh, *Introduction to Contemporary Microeconomics* (New York: McGraw-Hill, 1970), pp. 17ff.

24. For an exposition of the differences separating neoclassical economics from the Misesian (modern Austrian) approach to economics, see the writer's "Entrepreneurial Discovery and the Competitive Market Process: An Austrian Approach," *Journal of Economic Literature* 35 (March 1997), pp. 60–85.

25. Mises, *Human Action*, revised edition (Chicago: Contemporary Books, 1966), p. 252.

26. On this see W.J. Baumol, "Entrepreneurship in Economic Theory," *American Economic Review* 58 (May 1968), p. 72.

27. Israel M. Kirzner, *Perception, Opportunity, and Profit* (Chicago: University of Chicago Press, 1979), Chapter 2.

2. The Hardest Logic Puzzle Ever

1. The extra twist of not knowing which are the gods' words for 'yes' and 'no' is due to the computer scientist John McCarthy.

2. A version of this article, translated by Massimo Piattelli-Palmarini, appeared in *La Repubblica* on 16th April 1992 under the title "L'indovinello più difficile del mondo" as well as in *Logic, Logic, and Logic* (Harvard University Press, 1998).

5. Frege's Theorem: An Introduction

1. Gottlob Frege, "Begriffsschrift: A Formula Language Modeled Upon That of Arithmetic, For Pure Thought," in J. van Heijenoort, ed. and tr., *From Frege to Gödel: A Sourcebook in Mathematical Logic* (Harvard University Press, 1967), pp. 5–82.

2. See Richard Dedekind, "The Nature and Meaning of Numbers," in *Essays on the Theory of Numbers*, translated by W.W. Beman (New York: Dover, 1963), pp. 44–115.

3. For discussion of Frege's axioms and his proof of this theorem, see my "Definition by Induction in Frege's Grundgesetze der Arithmetik," in W. Demopoulos, ed., *Frege's Philosophy of Mathematics* (Harvard University Press, 1995), pp. 295–333.

4. Interpretations can take a more complicated form, but we need not consider such matters here.

5. See Gottlob Frege, *Grundgesetze der Arithmetik* (Hildesheim: Georg Olms Verlagsbuchhandlung, 1966), Volume I, section 66.

6. For a detailed discussion of this proposal, see my "The Julius Caesar Objection," in R. Heck, ed., *Language, Thought, and Logic: Essays in Honour of Michael Dummett* (Oxford: Oxford University Press, 1997).

7. See Grundgesetze, Volume I, section 108.

8. See Crispin Wright, *Frege's Conception of Numbers as Objects* (Aberdeen: Aberdeen University Press, 1983), and Bob Hale, *Abstract Objects* (Oxford: Blackwell, 1988).

10. Frege is actually discussing the definition of directions here, but it is clear that it is meant to apply, mutatis mutandis, to the case of numbers and Hume's Principle.

11. In his *Mathematics in Philosophy* (Ithaca: Cornell University Press, 1983), pp. 150–175.

12. In his *Frege's Conception of Numbers as Objects*.

13. This observation was made, independently, by George Boolos, John Burgess, Allen Hazen, and Harold Hodes. For a proof, see the second Appendix to George Boolos and Richard G. Heck, Jr., "Die Grundlagen der Arithmetik §§82–3," in M. Schirn, ed., *Philosophy of Mathematics Today* (Oxford: Oxford University Press, 1997).

14. See my "The Development of Arithmetic in Frege's *Grundgesetze der Arithmetik,*" *Journal of Symbolic Logic* 58 (1993), pp. 579–601; reprinted, with a postscript, in Demopoulos, pp. 257–294.

15. See, for example, "Frege's Theory of Number."

16. See my "On the Consistency of Second-order Contextual Definitions," *Noûs* 26 (1992), pp. 491–94.

17. See Crispin Wright, "The Philosophical Significance of Frege's Theorem" and George Boolos, "Is Hume's Principle Analytic?" in Heck, op. cit.

6. What Is the Problem of Measurement?

1. W. Heisenberg, *Physics and Philosophy* (Allen and Unwin, 1959), p. 121.

2. The 'statistical interpretation', as advocated by Ballentine (*A Survey of Hidden-Variable Theories*, 1970), is an example of this sort of approach. Another example is the *S-Matrix* school in the early 1960s, which was explicitly opposed to the use of quantum field theory, and indeed of any dynamical theory in the usual sense, in hadron physics: the theory was to be formulated in terms of the S-matrix alone ('S' for scattering; a matrix compiling the input and output amplitudes among states of definite momentum.). See J. Cushing, *Theory Construction and Selection in Modern Physics: The S-Matrix*, Cambridge, 1990.

3. Einstein, famously, concluded that the state was incomplete. For an authoritative study of Einstein's views on this matter, see A. Fine, *The Shakey Game*, Chicago, 1986.

4. Correspondingly, Bohr later talked of "experimental conditions" rather than "observation." On the term 'phenomenon', we have from his biographer Abraham Pais: "he sharpened his own language, one might say, by defining the term 'phenomenon' to include both the object of study and the mode of observation" (*Niels Bohr's Times*, Oxford, 1991, p. 432). Compare the physicist J.A. Wheeler: "In today's words Bohr's point—and the central point of quantum theory—can be put into a single, simple sentence. 'No elementary phenomenon is a phenomenon until it is a registered (observed) phenomenon'." (in J.A. Wheeler and W. Zurek, eds., *Quantum Theory and Measurement*, Princeton, 1981). The quotations that follow are all taken from the Como lecture of 1927, in which Bohr first presented his interpretation of quantum mechanics (reprinted in N. Bohr, *Atomic Theory and the Description of Nature*, Cambridge, 1934).

5. The stability or otherwise of calculated probabilities under variation of the choice of cut is the business of decoherence theory to determine. See below.

6. J. von Neumann, F. London, and E. Wigner are the most important examples (see Wheeler and Zurek). Their latter-day followers include D. Albert, B. Loewer, M. Lockwood, and E. Squires; see for instance E. Squires, *Conscious Mind in the Physical World* (Adam Hilger, 1990).

7. See Heisenberg *op cit*, pp. 34–35. In other respects he took it to an extreme not contemplated by Bohr. Thus: ". . . the equation of motion for the probability function . . . now contain[s] the influence of the interaction with the measuring device. This influence introduces a new element of uncertainty, since the measuring device is necessarily described in the terms of classical physics; such a description contains all the uncertainties concerning the microscopic structure of the device which we know from thermodynamics. . . . It contains in fact the uncertainties of the microscopic structure of the whole world. . . . It is for this reason that the results of the measurement cannot be predicted with certainty." This is tantamount to explaining the quantum postulate itself—or at least indeterminacy—using classical concepts.

8. I am not suggesting that quantum indeterminacy and classical vagueness will be dealt with in the same way; on the contrary, there are precise quantum properties corresponding to any quantum mechanical state. The parallel is rather between classical concepts and quantum mechanical ones, on the one hand, and between ordinary language concepts and classical ones, on the other.

9. This is the one respect in which the GRW proposal, in its present form, may make definite predictions in conflict with the standard non-relativistic formalism.

10. This will be readily granted in the case of state-reduction theories, but in the case of the pilot-wave theory it is not so well recognized. See my "The 'Beables' of Relativistic Pilot-Wave Theory," in *From Physics to Philosophy*, J. Butterfield, and C. Pagonis, eds., Cambridge, 1999, for detailed arguments.

11. The relevance of split-brain scenarios, and particularly the work of Parfit, should be quite obvious (D. Parfit, *Reasons and Persons*, Oxford, 1984).

12. I would like to thank Burton Dreben for a careful reading and cogent criticism of an early draft of this paper.

7. Making Sense of Others: Donald Davidson on Interpretation

1. This chapter is the text of a talk presented to the Fellows Seminar of the University of Michigan Institute for the Humanities during the fall term of 1988. It was aimed at an audience of non-philosophically trained humanists from various disciplines. Its intention was primarily to bring (without too much distortion or technicality) a few of the more central strands of Davidson's program into enough focus to generate interest in and discussion of his views. By way of background, I recommended that the participating Fellows read Davidson's "Radical Interpretation," "Thought and Talk," "On the Very Idea of a Conceptual Scheme," and "Rational Animals." This paper, while not critical, was meant to be provocative.

8. Analyticity and Holism in Quine's Thought

1. W.V. Quine, "Two Dogmas of Empiricism," first published in 1951, reprinted with minor changes in *From a Logical Point of View* (Harvard University Press), pp. 20–46; "Carnap and Logical Truth," first published in 1960, reprinted with minor changes in *The Ways of Paradox* (Harvard University Press, 1966, 1976), pp. 107–132.

2. Paul Boghossian, "Analyticity Reconsidered," *Noûs* 30 (1996), pp. 360–391.

3. "Analyticity Reconsidered," p. 370.

4. Part of the answer may be that Quine's views were not fully developed at first, so that some of his work—perhaps especially "Two Dogmas of Empiricism," his most famous essay—

is misleading. Given the persistence of the misunderstanding, however, this can be only a small part of the answer.

5. Here I presuppose a rejection of the synthetic a priori. This is a point that Quine never questions.

6. "Epistemology Naturalized," in *Ontological Relativity and Other Essays* (Columbia University Press, 1969), pp. 69–90, 79

7. Whether, or to what extent, this is a correct diagnosis of the appeal of analyticity is, of course, a different question. In the case of Carnap, in particular, there is some reason to think that it does not take us very far. Carnap's technical conception of analyticity does not seem to be based on a notion of meaning, as antecedently understood. (Though he did think that a characterization such as "true in virtue of meaning" gives reason to think that there is an informal notion to which a technical conception more or less corresponds.) Our concern here, however, is with Quine, not with Carnap.

8. "Two Dogmas in Retrospect," *Canadian Journal of Philosophy* 21 (1991), pp. 265–274, p. 271.

9. In "Carnap and Logical Truth," Quine speaks of "palpable surface differences between the deductive sciences of logic and mathematics, on the one hand, and the empirical sciences ordinarily so-called on the other" (pp. 107–08).

10. This is not to say that the making of assertions is the only form of behavior that is relevant to meaning. In a closely related context (that of the indeterminacy of translation), Quine says, "The relevant evidence even goes beyond speech. It includes blushing, stammering, running away. It includes native customs and rites, and indeed any observable behavior that one can exploit in trying to get a clue as to how to translate the language" ("Comment on Hintikka," in Robert Barrett and Roger Gibson, eds., *Perspectives on Quine*, Blackwell, 1990, p. 176.)

11. "Truth by Convention," originally published in 1936, reprinted in *Ways of Paradox* (Harvard University Press, 1966, 1976), pp. 77–106, p. 89.

12. "Carnap and Logical Truth," pp. 113–14.

13. See W.V. Quine, *Word and Object* (MIT Press, 1960), pp. 10–11.

14. It might be thought that we need no reason, but make a wholly arbitrary choice. This is the position that Quine approvingly attributes to Carnap in his 1934 lectures. (These lectures were first given at Harvard in November 1934; they were reprinted for the first time in Creath, ed., *Dear Carnap, Dear Van*, pp. 47–103.) For some discussion, see the present author's " 'The Defensible Province of Philosophy': Quine's 1934 Lectures on Carnap," in Juliet Floyd and Sanford Shieh, eds., *Futures Past* (Oxford University Press, 2001), pp. 257–275. Can an arbitrary choice of this sort really generate an epistemologically significant distinction? This question relates to the more general issue of the epistemological significance of analyticity, to which we shall get shortly.

15. See *Word and Object*, section 12; for the most explicit possible statement, see "Two Dogmas in Retrospect," p. 270.

16. *The Roots of Reference* (La Salle: Open Court, 1974), p. 79.

17. See the series of videotapes entitled "In Conversation: W.V. Quine," Boolos panel. In the accompanying booklet, the relevant passage is on p. 18. The idea is suggested by Martin Davies. While Quine expresses some sympathy with it, he also says that it takes us further from observable criteria than his own definition.

18. Hilary Putnam, "The Analytic and the Synthetic," Minnesota Studies in the Philosophy of Science, III, eds. Herbert Feigl and Grover Maxwell (Minneapolis: University of Minnesota Press, 1962); reprinted in Putnam, *Mind, Language, and Reality* (Cambridge University Press, 1975), pp. 33–69.

19. Hilary Putnam, "The Analytic and the Synthetic," p. 68; emphasis in the original.

20. See section 12 of *Word and Object*, especially note 8, in which Quine approvingly cites Putnam and says explicitly: "My account fits with his. . . ."

21. "Two Dogmas in Retrospect," p. 270.

22. This point goes as far back in Quine's work as "Carnap and Logical Truth;" see especially section II of that essay.

23. "Reply to Hellman," in *The Philosophy of W.V. Quine*, p. 207; emphasis in the original.

24. Carnap, "Reply to Quine," in *The Philosophy of Rudold Carnap*, p. 921. He goes on to add, immediately, "not even the statements of logic and of mathematics."

25. I inject this note of qualification here because I do not think that Carnap is in fact trying to argue for there being an epistemological difference, at least not of the sort that Quine requires. But, again, the focus of our interest here is Quine, not Carnap, and from Quine's point of view I think the crucial issue is the epistemological difference, if any, between the two sorts of change.

26. A recent—and largely sympathetic—commentator on Carnap puts the point this way: "On Carnap's view, a confirmation theory is given only subsequent to and relative to a linguistic framework. Given a linguistic framework, we can define a confirmation theory for it. But the specification of the linguistic framework, and, thus, of the analytic sentences must come first. . . ." Alan Richardson, *Carnap's Construction of the World* (Cambridge University Press, 1998), p. 224.

27. Carnap, "Empiricism, Semantics, and Ontology," first published in *Revue Internationale de Philosophie* 4 (1950), pp. 20–40; reprinted in *Meaning and Necessity*, second edition, pp. 205–221, 214.

28. This suggests the application of the Principle of Tolerance at a meta-level: not only to the choice of language, but also to the philosophical conception of which the Principle of Tolerance is itself a part. See *Meaning and Necessity*, p. 204.

29. "Two Dogmas," pp. 41–42.

30. "Two Dogmas," p. 46. Quine later commented as follows on his use of the word "pragmatism": "This passage had unforeseen consequences. I suspect that it is responsible for my being widely classified as a pragmatist. I don't object, except that I am not clear on what it takes to qualify as a pragmatist. I was merely taking the word from Carnap and handing it back: in whatever sense the framework for science is pragmatic, so is the rest of science" ("Two Dogmas in Retrospect," p. 272).

31. The issues raised in this paragraph and the preceding are discussed in somewhat more detail in the present author's "Analyticity and the Indeterminacy of Translation," *Synthese* (1982), pp. 167–184.

32. I have indicated that there is reason to doubt this reading of Carnap. It is also worth noting, however, that there are passages in Carnap's writings that support it. Discussing the importance of Wittgenstein's notion of tautology to the Vienna Circle, Carnap says: "What was important in this conception from our point of view was the fact that it became possible for the first time to combine the basic tenet of empiricism with a satisfactory explanation of the nature of logic and mathematics" ("Intellectual Autobiography," in *The Philosophy of Rudolf Carnap*, p. 45.) The idea that what is needed is an explanation of the nature of the truths of logic and mathematics is precisely the point that Quine insists on.

33. Almost all, but not all; John Stuart Mill is the most obvious case on the other side. See John Skorupski, *John Stuart Mill*, especially Chapter 4.

34. "Reply to Hellman," in *The Philosophy of W.V. Quine*, p. 207; emphasis added.

35. Immediately following a discussion of holism, Quine says: "We had been trying to make sense of the role of convention in a priori knowledge. Now the very distinction between a priori and empirical begins to waver and dissolve. . . ." ("Carnap and Logical Truth," p. 122).

36. *Philosophy of Logic* (Englewood Cliffs: Prentice-Hall, 1970), p. 100; emphasis added.

37. "Reply to Parsons" in *The Philosophy of W.V. Quine*, pp. 399–400.

38. I am grateful to Andrew Lugg for his comments on an earlier draft of this essay, which is based on a talk that I first gave at a conference in honor of the memory of my teacher, the late Burton Dreben, who taught at Harvard from 1956 to 1990. I dedicate it to his memory. Throughout our conversations, and in his teaching more generally, Burt always stressed the complexity of what is often called 'the analytic-synthetic debate'. In the last philosophical conversation that I had with him, he particularly emphasized the role that holism plays for Quine. This essay is based upon those two points. I attempt to give a sketch of Quine's complex views on analyticity, a sketch that will emphasize the central role that holism plays in those views. I should emphasize that my primary aim is to show how the matter appears from Quine's perspective. From other points of view, most notably Carnap's, it would no doubt seem rather different at crucial points; I note some of these points in passing, but do not discuss them.

9. On Wanting to Say, 'All We Need Is a Paradigm'

1. For example, in David Hollinger's "Free Enterprise and Free Inquiry: The Emergence of Laissez-faire Communitarianism in the Ideology of Science in the United States," *New Literary History* 21 (1990), pp. 897–919; and Steve Fuller's *Thomas Kuhn: A Philosophical History for Our Times* (University of Chicago Press, 2000). Fuller and Hollinger argue that Kuhn's emphasis on 'the scientific community' was founded on the identification of the natural sciences as perhaps-inimitable paradigms of science, and had the result that science was more, not less, isolated from social factors than before Kuhn wrote. Thus they suggest, in particular, that it is a huge irony (see Hollinger, p. 914) that Kuhn's *Structure of Scientific Revolutions* (University of Chicago Press, 1970 [1962]) has been used as a manifesto by those of his fans who have sought to have exactly the opposite effect.

2. Cf. Kuhn's 'reply' to Feyerabend, on p. 237 of his "Reflections on My Critics," in Lakatos and Musgrave's *Criticism and the Growth of Knowledge* (Cambridge University Press, 1970).

3. "Two Letters of Paul Feyerabend to Thomas S. Kuhn on Draft of SSR" (edited by Paul Hoyningen-Huene), *Stud. Hist. Phil. Sci.* 26:3 (1995), pp. 353–387, 354–55. Feyerabend's quasi-Popperian commitment to normative philosophy of science is explicit here; the contrast with his later views on the normative inefficacy of methodological reflections on science should be evident (not to say blatant)—see the notes below.

4. "Explanation, Reduction, and Empiricism," in Feigl and Maxwell, eds., *Scientific Explanation, Space and Time*, Minnesota Studies in the Philosophy of Science, Volume 3 (University of Minnesota Press, 1962), p. 60. (Of course, Feyerabend will later change his 'view' on this point—he will countenance an opposition to normative methodological precepts greater even than Kuhn's. See the early chapters of the third edition of Feyerabend's *Against Method* [London: Verso, 1993].)

5. *The Structure of Scientific Revolutions* (University of Chicago Press, 1962).

6. At least, such is *Kuhn's* account of the failure of astrology to be a science, even in the days of its intellectual respectability. See pp. 7–11 of his "Logic of Discovery or Psychology of Research?" in Lakatos and Musgrave.

7. *The Ethical Animal* (London: Routledge, 1994), p. 51, final italics mine. Midgley is quoting from Slavney and McHugh, *Psychiatric Polarities* (Baltimore: Johns Hopkins, 1987), p. 8 and p. 123.

8. Cf. on this also p. 222 and p. 229 of Kuhn's *The Essential Tension* (University of Chicago Press, 1977).

9. Though having said that, I should if space permitted detail also why I think this position, this misreading, was so easy and attractive to make, and how Kuhn's invocation of terms such as 'pre-paradigm' guarded quite insufficiently against it. I think that Kuhn himself acknowledged these points in his later work, and in the shifted terminology that was involved in that work.

10. Feyerabend, p. 355.

11. Feyerabend on this score goes further than Kuhn: cf. for instance his remarkable words on the Copernican Revolution in *Science in a Free Society* (Verso: London, 1978), p. 65: "In the beginning [Copernicus's] view was as unreasonable as the idea of the unmoved earth must have been in 1700. But it led to developments we now want to accept. Hence, it was reasonable to introduce it and try to keep it alive. Hence, it is always reasonable to introduce and try to keep alive unreasonable views."

12. Common terms of criticism from analytic philosophers of Kuhn; in this instance, Feyerabend is quoting the words of Larry Laudan, from whom he is defending Kuhn and others in the paper currently being quoted from.

13. Pp. 236–37, "More Clothes from the Emperor's Bargain Basement; A Review of Larry Laudan's 'Progress and its Problems'," in Feyerabend's *Problems of Empiricism* (Cambridge Univerdsity Press, 1981), pp. 230–245. Lower on p. 237, Feyerabend adds: "Kuhn makes the highly interesting and revolutionary suggestion that *physics is a historical tradition and therefore as much in need of Verstehen* [interpretive understanding] *as history proper.* Laudan does not notice this feature of Kuhn's theory *(sic.)*."

14. Pp. 24–25 of "Some Observations on the Decay of Philosophy of Science," from *Philosophical Papers Volume 2: Problems of Empiricism* (Cambridge University Press, 1981), pp. 1–33.

15. Notice that on the surface I appear on this aspect of the point to find Feyerabend directly contradicting himself; because this appears to let Kuhn off the hook of 'writing an ideological history where historical facts could be read as methodological rules without any difficulty'—the very hook on which Feyerabend hangs him in the quotes with which I began this paper. It would take us too far afield to resolve this here: points to be noted include that (i) Feyerabend is quite happy unlike most philosophers, to contradict himself, and (ii) Feyerabend would stress that a fair appraisal of Kuhn involves looking at his work in its totality, not looking only at those parts of it which suit one's immediate purposes, and that that is what his grosser appropriators are doing—they don't even take the time to notice that Kuhn's account of paradigms and of normal science as the working out of a paradigm is *deliberately* imprecise and ambiguous. (Much like, I would add, Wittgenstein's 'parent'-concepts of language-game, form of life, and family-resemblance, which are not true 'technical terms' either.)

16. *The Idea of a Social Science* (London: Routledge, 1990 [1958]), p. 87.

17. Winch, pp. 160–61 emphasis mine.

18. Furthermore, attempts by economics to scientifize itself, to jump ahead of its clock (as it were), have often had nefarious consequences. A nice example is examined by R. Cooter

and P. Rappoport in their paper, "Were the Ordinalists Wrong about Welfare Economics?" *Journal of Economic Literature* XXII (June 1984), pp. 507–530. Cf. the following quotations: "[T]he elements of the older framework . . . are now viewed through the distorting lens of the ordinalist framework" (p. 508). "The received view is that ordinalism represents scientific progress relative to the material welfare school, but one can talk unequivocally about the progress of a science only when it continues to address the same questions" (p. 528). Here we have, one might argue, the trappings of Kuhnian (natural) science methodology, but the fundamental suspicion of Cooter and Rappoport is that, in *this* case, there were useful things which the abandoned research tradition (old-style Welfare Economics) still had and perhaps has to offer which are ruled out by the 'paradigm' which won the day, to our political as well as economic detriment: "The aim of this paper is to demonstrate that the arguments developed some fifty years ago to criticize the material welfare school do not in fact address the claims of that school, whose scientific integrity remains intact. This suggests that it may be fruitful to draw on the material welfare perspective in the analysis of present-day welfare problems, and perhaps warrants a comparison of the older view with the achievements of modern welfare economics" (pp. 510–11). Arguably, economists still need to worry about fundamentals, in a way that detracts from any claim that Economics has a paradigm. The likes of Cooter and Rappoport are themselves implicitly suggesting that any such claim is quite premature.

19. Here is another link with Wittgenstein. I believe that Kuhn was quite largely a descriptive and indeed therapeutic philosopher—he wanted to cure people of the philosophy of science, unless by 'philosophy' one was ready to mean something quite non-standard. Though it would take us too far afield to investigate here, I think that there are instructive affinities not only between Winch and Kuhn, but more generally between Stanley Cavell, James Conant, and others collected in my and Crary's *The New Wittgenstein* (London: Routledge, 2000) on the one hand, and the kind of perspective on philosophy that we find for example in Kuhn's *The Road Since Structure* (eds. Conant and Haugeland, University of Chicago Press, 2000), especially in some of the remarks of Kuhn's in the interview which closes that book, on the other. (See also my review of that book, forthcoming in the *British Journal for the Philosphy of Science*, and my "Kuhn: A Wittgenstein of the sciences?" forthcoming in *UEA Papers in Philosophy*.

20. My overwhelming and ineffable debt in the writing of this paper is to Wes Sharrock, who has immensely enriched my understanding of both Kuhn and Winch; and with whom I have written a book (which gives a 'Wittgensteinian' reading of Kuhn), entitled Thomas Kuhn (Oxford: Polity, 2002), from which this paper is an adapted and enlarged excerpt.

11. The Mysteries of Self-locating Belief and Anthropic Reasoning

1. For further explorations of this and related principles, see Bostrom (1997), (2001), and (2002b).

2. Lewis (1986)

3. See, for example, Hall (1994), Lewis (1994), and Thau (1994).

4. See Bostrom (2002a). Principles or forms of inferences that are similar to SIA have also been discussed by Dieks (1992), Smith (1994), Leslie (1996), Oliver and Korb (1997), Bartha and Hitchcock (1999) and (2000), and Olum (2002).

5.
$$P_\alpha(h \mid e) = (1/\gamma) \sum_{\sigma\varepsilon\Omega_h\cap\Omega_e} \frac{P_\alpha(w_\alpha)}{|\Omega_\alpha\cap\Omega(w_\alpha)|}$$ (Observation Equation)

Here, α is the observer-moment whose subjective probability function is P_α. Ω_h is the class of all possible observer-moments about whom h is true; Ω_e is the class of all possible observer-moments about whom e is true; Ω_α is the class of all observer-moments that α places in the same reference class as herself; w_α is the possible world in which α is located; and γ is a normalization constant

$$\gamma = \sum_{\sigma\varepsilon\Omega_e} \frac{P_\alpha(w_o)}{|\Omega_o\cap\Omega(w_o)|}$$

OE can be generalized to allow for different observer-moments within the reference class having different "weights", an option that might be of relevance for instance in the context of the many-worlds version of quantum theory.

6. Redelmeier and Tibshirani (1999)

7. The above reasoning applies to a driver who is currently on the road wondering why she is in the slow lane. When considering the problem retrospectively, that is, when you are sitting at home thinking back on your experiences on the road, the situation is more complicated and requires also taking into account differential recall (psychological factor may make you more likely to remember and bring to mind certain kinds of experiences) and the fact that while the slow lane contains more *observer-moments*, it may nevertheless be true that more *drivers* have passed through the fast lane.

12. Structuralism and the Independence of Mathematics

1. For a fuller exposition of alternative versions of structuralism as well as a brief account of its history see Stewart Shapiro, *Philosophy of Mathematics: Structure and Ontology* (Oxford University Press, 1997).

2. Benacerraf's papers are reprinted in Paul Benacerraf and Hilary Putnam, eds., *Philosophy of Mathematics, Second Edition* (Cambridge University Press, 1993), pp. 272–294 and pp. 403–420.

3. From the mathematical point of view any infinite progression of sets will serve for defining the numbers. Thus Zermelo defined them as follows: $0 = \emptyset$ (the empty set) $1 = \{\emptyset\}$, $2 = \{\{\emptyset\}\}$, $3 = \{\{\{\emptyset\}\}\}$, and so on. Von Neumann defined them alternatively as follows: $0 = \emptyset$, $1 = \{\emptyset\}$, $2 = \{\emptyset, \{\emptyset\}\} = \{0, 1\}$, $3 = \{\emptyset, \{\emptyset\}, \{\emptyset, \{\emptyset\}\}\} = \{0, 1, 2\}$, and so on. Another famous definition due to Frege and used by Russell defines 0 as $\{\emptyset\}$, 1 as the class of all unit classes, two as the class of all pairs, and so on. There are infinitely many variations on each of these themes.

4. "What Numbers Could Not Be," in Benacerraf and Putnam, p. 294.

5. I believe the thinking I have outlined in this paragraph was quite common thirty years ago. Today ways of resisting it are on the market, but surveying them would take us too far afield.

6. For more on my structuralist view, see my *Mathematics as a Science of Patterns* (Oxford: Clarendon, 1997).

7. Jody Azzouni, "Stipulation, Logic, and Ontological Independence," in *Philosophia Mathematica*, Series III, Volume 8 (2000), pp. 225–243, p. 232. See also his *Deflating Exis-*

tential Consequence (Oxford University Press, 2004) and his "Review of Michael D. Resnik's *Mathematics as a Science of Patterns*," in *Journal of Symbolic Logic* 64 (1999), pp. 922–23.

8. "Stipulation, Logic, and Ontological Independence," p. 226.

9. *Deflating Existential Consequence*, p. 109.

10. "Stipulation, Logic, and Ontological Independence," p. 227.

11. For further discussion, see my *Mathematics as a Science of Patterns*, Chapter 7 and my "Quine and the Web of Belief," in Stewart Shapiro, ed., *The Oxford Handbook of Philosophy of Mathematics and Philosophy of Logic* (New York: Oxford University Press, 2004).

12. Azzouni does not draw this distinction. For him, epistemic independence is a necessary condition for ontological independence.

13. "Stipulation, Logic, and Ontological Independence," p. 230. Azzouni uses the term "ontological independence" instead of "epistemic independence" in this passage. See the previous note.

14. "Stipulation, Logic, and Ontological Independence," p. 227.

15. According to Azzouni, the trivial explanation is this: A process P is reliable with respect to x's because they have the property that P is reliable with respect to them. *Deflating Existential Consequence*, p. 100.

16. "Stipulation, Logic, and Ontological Independence," p. 228, his emphasis.

17. "Stipulation, Logic, and Ontological Independence," p. 229.

18. This is because we have given the trivial explanation.

19. "Stipulation, Logic, and Ontological Independence," p. 230, my emphasis.

20. Another exception to Azzouni's requirement may be properties of objects that are true of them 'by definition', such as an electron's property of having one unit of negative charge.

21. "Stipulation, Logic, and Ontological Independence," p. 230, my emphasis.

22. I am grateful to Kenneth Walden for comments and encouragement. This paper grew out of a paper of the same title that I delivered in December 1999 at a symposium on the philosophy of mathematics, with Jerrold Katz and Stewart Shapiro, at the annual meeting of the Eatern Division of the American Philosophical Association.

13. The Deep and Suggestive Principles of Leibnizian Philosophy

1. C. Darwin, *The Origin of Species by Natural Selection* (1859).

2. I. Prigogine, *From Being to Becoming* (San Francisco: Freeman, 1980).

3. A. Albrecht, "Cosmic Inflation and the Arrow of Time," in J.D. Barrow, P.C.W. Davies, and C.L. Harper, eds., *Science and Ultimate Reality: From Quantum to Cosmos*, (Cambridge University Press, 2003).

4. R. Penrose, *The Emperor's New Mind* (Oxford University Press, 1989).

5. J. Barbour, *The End of Time* (Oxford University Press, 2000).

6. J. Barbour, B. Foster, and N. Ó Murchadha, "Relativity Without Relativity," *Classical Quantum Gravity* 19, 3217 (2002) (<http://arXiv.org/abs/gr-qc/0012089>); J. Barbour, "Scale-Invariant Gravity: Particle Dynamics," <http://arXiv.org/abs/gr-qc/0211021>; E. Anderson, J. Barbour, B. Foster, N. Ó Murchadha, "Scale-Invariant Gravity: Geometrodynamics," http://arXiv.org/abs/gr-qc/0122022.

7. G. Belot and J. Earman, "Pre-Socratic Quantum Gravity," in C. Callender and N. Huggett, eds., *Physics Meets Philosophy at the Planck Scale* (Cambridge University Press, 2001), p. 228.

8. *The Leibniz-Clarke Correspondence*, ed. H.G. Alexander (New York: Barnes and Noble, 1956).

9. J. Barbour, "Relational Concepts of Space and Time," *British Journal of Philosophy of Science* 33 (1982), p. 251.

10. R. Descartes, *The Principles of Philosophy* (1644).

11. See especially the Correspondence with Arnauld reproduced in: L.L. Leroy, ed., *Philosophical Papers and Letters* (Dordrecht: Reidel, 1969) and G.H.R. Parkinson, ed., *Leibniz: Philosophical Writings* (Dent, 1973).

12. The *Monadology* is included in both books (note 11).

13. G. Berkeley, *Treatise Concerning the Principles of Human Knowledge* (1712).

14. L. Smolin, "Space and Time in the Quantum Universe," in A. Ashtekhar and J. Stachel, eds., *Conceptual Problems in Quantum Gravity. Proceedings of the 1988 Osgood Hill Conference, Einstein Studies*, Volume 2 (Boston: Birkhäuser, 1991); J. Barbour and L. Smolin, "Extremal Variety as the Foundation of a Cosmological Quantum Theory," <http://arXiv.org/abs/hep-th/9203041>; J. Barbour, "On the Origin of Structure in the Universe," in E. Rudolph and I.-O. Stamatescu, eds., *Philosophy, Mathematics, and Modern Physics* (Berlin: Springer-Verlag, 1994).

15. C.E. Shannon and W. Weaver, *The Mathematical Theory of Communication* (Urbana: University of Illinois Press, 1949).

16. This article is based to a large degree on J. Barbour, "On the Origin of Structure in the Universe" (note 14). I have left the final paragraphs almost unchanged since they seem to me to make a valid point. They still make me think and I hope they have the same effect on you.

17. D. Deutsch, *The Fabric of Reality* (London: Penguin, 1997).

About the Editor

PHIN UPHAM has a BA in Philosophy from Harvard University, where he was Editor-in-Chief of the *Harvard Review of Philosophy*. He has a PhD and MBA from the Wharton Business School at the University of Pennsylvania. Phin currently lives in New York City. In 2002 he edited a collection of interviews with great philosophers titled *Philosophers in Conversation* and in 2008 he edited a collection of essays in philosophy titled *The Space of Love and Garbage*.

Index

Access Problem, in mathematics, 179–180, 182

Albrecht, A., 192

analyticity, 100–01; questions of, 102

analytic-synthetic distinctions, 106–08; questions of, 100

anthropic reasoning, 174

Aristotle, 42, 132

arithmetic axioms, and pure logic, 44

arithmetic truth, epistemological question of, 41, 44

Azzouni, Jody, 182–87, 189

Barbour, Julian: *The End of Time*, 192, 201, 205

Barchielli, A., 78

Bayes's theorem, 164, 174

Bella, M., 79

Benacerraf, Paul, 178–79

Bloom, Harold, 38

Boghossian, Paul, 99, 100

Bohr, Niels, 64, 65, 67–70, 72–75, 78

Boole, George, 42, 43

Bostrom, Nick: *Anthropic Bias*, 160

Boulez, Pierre, 39

Bowley, Marion, 3

Buchanan, James, 6, 10

Cairns, John E., 3, 10

Caldera, A., 79

Carnap, Rudolf, 43, 102, 103, 109–111; analytic-synthetic distinction in, 106–08

Carnot, 132

causation, as nomological entailment relation, 140–41

ceteris paribus laws: and asymmetric causal overdetermination, 138, 141–42, 148–153; and causation, 135–37; failures of, 142–46; and 'no interference' clause, 137, 146–48, 154–55; problem of, 137; qualifications of, 143–46; standard conception of, 136–38; and vacuity, 137, 155; and untestability, 137, 156

Clarke, Samuel, 193

coherentist epistemic positions, 183

comprehension axioms, 46

Conant, James, 20, 21, 22, 24

confirmational holism, 180, 189

Convention T, 94–95, 97

Copenhagen interpretation, 68, 70

cosmos, 191

Cushing, J., 79

Daneri, A., 78

Davidson, Donald, 81; on belief, 85–91; on conceptual schemes, 92–96; on Convention T, 94–95, 97; on disagreement, 86–87; on interpretation, 82–84; and belief, 85–86; on language and truth, 96; "On the Very Idea of a Conceptual Scheme," 92–94; principle of charity, 88; "Rational Animals," 89, 90, 91, 97; "Thought and Talk," 88, 89; on triangulation, 90; on truth, 96

223